UNCHARTED

Your Guide to Investing in the Age of Uncertainty

UNCHARTED

Your Guide to Investing in the Age of Uncertainty

By Andrew Packer

Humanix Books

www.humanixbooks.com

For information, contact:
Humanix Books
PO Box 1608
Lake Worth, FL 33460 USA
Website: www.humanixbooks.com
Email: info@humanixbooks.com

Humanix Books is a division of Newsmax Media. Its trademark, consisting of the words "Humanix Books," is registered in the US Patent and Trademark Office and in other countries.

Printed in the United States of America

Disclaimer: The information in this book is intended solely for information purposes and is not to be construed, under any circumstances, by implication or otherwise, as an offer to sell or a solicitation to buy or sell or trade in any commodities, currencies, or securities herein named. Information is obtained from sources believed to be reliable, but is in no way guaranteed. No guarantee of any kind is implied or possible where projections of future conditions are attempted. Past results are no indication of future performance. All investments are subject to risk, which should be considered prior to making any investment decisions. Consult your personal investment advisers before making an investment decision. See full terms and conditions at http://www.moneynews.com/Terms.

Packer, Andrew.
Uncharted : your guide to investing in the age of uncertainty / by Andrew Packer. — 1st ed.
p. cm.

ISBN 978-0-89334-895-3 (pbk.) — ISBN 978-0-89334-897-7 (e-book)

1. Investment analysis. 2. Portfolio management. 3. Investments. I. Title.
HG4529.P33 2012
332.6—dc23
2012027217

TABLE OF CONTENTS

Why You Need this Guide
By Bob Wiedemer

THE GLOBAL ECONOMY is stalled in an unprecedented fiscal and monetary sea. Five years after the start of the financial crisis, which burst a housing bubble and nearly took down the financial system, no clear path to prosperity remains.

Some countries have tried austerity, which sacrifices necessary growth to pay down the excesses. Others have tried to stimulate the economy, but fickle and timid consumers haven't taken the bait. Meanwhile, the causes of the crisis haven't been addressed. The same problems that got us into this mess could still occur again — and soon.

Investors, meanwhile, must now read between the lines of every politician's promise and central bank statement. Any future government plan can have huge and immediate implications for the markets.

While we are truly in uncharted waters, the world continues to move on. Investors must rebuild decimated retirement portfolios.

But there's a problem.

Ask ten different investors what their method or "style" is, and you'll likely get at least ten responses, if not more.

There are many who claim to know the secrets to investment success. Some focus entirely on some small niche in the markets and patiently wait. Others take a more expansive and global view. Some focus entirely on what makes a successful company successful, and others look entirely at the numbers.

Whatever styles or combinations are used, all investors are looking to do one thing: achieve excellent results in investing relative to the risk they take on.

In *Uncharted*, Andrew Packer reveals the fragile and unique situation that pervades the globe right now.

He then ties together the main threads necessary to create a successful investment tapestry — rigorous analysis, a global macroeconomic view, and the psychological behavior of the people who make up the market — and combines these elements in a way that accentuates the best of each of these investment strategies while minimizing their downsides.

INTRODUCTION

Here Be Dragons

> "To map out a course of action and follow
> it to an end requires courage."
> — *Ralph Waldo Emerson*

I NVESTING IS BOTH an art and a science.

In a way, it reminds me of antique maps. They're fascinating, and since they weren't mass-produced and measurements were often inaccurate, they (literally) illustrate the best of art and the best of mankind's early attempt at accurately recording knowledge.

Think about it: The shapes of familiar countries and continents on an antique map aren't quite right. They're more jagged or out of proportion. Early maps left unexplored territory to future explorers. On some of them was the Latin phrase: *Hic sunt dracones . . . Here be dragons.*

While some may interpret this literally, it was (at least in later years) meant more symbolically. Dragons were the great unknown . . . ignorance . . . the *real* monster to be slain by brave explorers.

Today, we've mapped the heights of the Earth. We're mapping the depths of the ocean and using incredible telescopes to peer further and with greater detail beyond our solar system. There is little left on Earth to explore in terms of new land, new territory, and new cultures. Gone are the days of the great expedition where a group of men can embark on a journey to find what's beyond the last-known mountain peak or horizon.

But, still, we face the uncertainty of the future. Even with no new land to discover, mankind continues to make tremendous scientific and technological progress. We find ways to do more with less. That prospect alone has tremendous investment implications. A new development could render one of the darling stocks of Wall Street obsolete. Indeed, in the investment world, fraught with sudden fortunes and sudden reversals, the future is the great unknown.

For example, at the start of 2008, oil prices stood at over $90 per barrel. By midsummer they had surged to $147. By the end of the year, however, oil prices had plummeted to under $40. It was easy to see rising prices continue or to see prices fall once they had moved up in such a parabolic fashion. But listening to the talking heads on CNBC or reading the pages of the *Wall Street Journal* at the time, you might have thought it was completely unpredictable and that investors would just have to deal with these extreme changes by simply staying the course and ignoring these short-term "gyrations."

Wall Street is no different. That's partly by design — millions are employed on Wall Street to keep the average investor constantly putting money to work. In some years, investing — especially in stocks but more recently in commodities and real estate — is seen as the road to endless, and more importantly, *easy* prosperity.

In other years, it has been a recipe for ruin. But we had a good run before it ended, right? And either way, the "house" (i.e., your brokerage firm or bank) always wins, whether it's with your commission dollars or with trillion-dollar taxpayer-funded bailouts.

It's a bit of a contradiction. These extreme moves in the market are at odds with what Wall Street tells investors. We're told to be sensible and own investments for the long term, but we end up acting like tourists at a Las Vegas craps table. We *intend* to be investors, we really do! But we seem to go to extremes: either we play the game, or we stand around counting our chips.

Either way, we don't get ahead because we take on too much risk and lose it all *or* because we don't take enough risk and lose our investment capital to inflation and transaction costs.

It's clear the traditional approach to investing today is far from rational. We chase returns. We stick with the crowd. We assume we can't all be wrong; so it's rational to invest in the market at all times (but we'll diversify in case an individual investment has a specific problem). It's safe in nature, but in investing, herding is a tactic that gets investors slaughtered like cattle.

That's especially true for American investors. The rapid change from an invincible consumer economy, robust with an ever-rising housing market to the subsequent collapse and nonexistent economic growth of the years following the 2008 market crash have hurt each and every citizen.

Homes can no longer serve as ATMs. No longer can we go to the grocery store or gas pump without increasing concern about rising prices. No longer can we go to our jobs day-in and day-out without wondering if (or even *when*) the ax will fall.

Indeed, our overreliance on easy-money policies, buckets of debt, and the willingness to meddle in affairs around the globe have sapped America of our once great financial might.

Our recovery process will be long and arduous. We will have to learn at some point (perhaps even soon) that we will simply have to do without things like bloated government pension plans, a vast array of medical and retirement benefits, and a global military organization.

But we are not there yet. Rather, we are living in an uncomfortable transition period — and most Americans have *no* idea how to handle it. It's like being on a ship in the eye of a hurricane — the storm isn't over, even though things are eerily quiet. That's when you need to keep your head about you and keep your map handy. It may be needed sooner than you think.

Americans are pulling retirement account funds (if they saved them in the first place) to meet their living expenses today. After nearly two years of paying down debt, we're going back to credit cards. For some, it means funding necessities rather than luxuries. For others, it's just a way of pretending their way out of hardship.

In short, those who haven't saved properly and don't understand the fundamentals of investing simply have little left. They can't be optimistic about the future because they don't see a way out of their troubles today.

Many investors simply chase returns. They get burned when markets correct. They lack the perspective, focus, and emotional determination to profit from the markets consistently.

Make no mistake — markets are the great humbler of men, and there will be inevitable losses. It is how we handle them that counts.

The first section of this book looks at these problems in more detail. Problems include current investment strategies and theories driving investment selection and the psychological drive that leads to substantial overvaluation or undervaluation. By understanding the problems the markets face, you'll be able to better cope over the next few years as an investor.

From analyzing, in the second section of this book, what works in investing and what doesn't, we'll find a better way forward. This approach is based on a careful study of market behavior and simple valuation techniques. When used correctly, it can make the difference from following the herd to outperforming the market consistently, year after year, *no matter what happens.*

In the third section of this book, we'll explore specific opportunities for investors to profit today from the continued monetary mayhem wreaking havoc on markets.

By the end, you'll know how the investment herd works, a better way to consistently find profitable opportunities, and specific ways to profit in today's market while honing your investment skills. As with any skill, it must be learned, practiced, and used in a variety of situations to be truly mastered.

That's something I've been working on since my study of the markets began in my childhood, and I'm still finding blind spots. As you'll read later on, my successes outnumber my mistakes — but, because I've learned so much more from my mistakes, I don't mind the occasional "lesson." I'll teach you some of those lessons, both good and bad, in Appendix A of this book.

No investor is perfect, but true perfection in investing is learning to quickly recognize opportunities, navigate potential dangers, and minimize mistakes. As for the perfection of never making a mistake, dream on!

Many investment books describe methods for allegedly beating the market that often come up short. Some emphasize companies with high growth. Some emphasize a company's current value. Others emphasize stocks that are going up . . . for the simple reason that they're going up!

All these strategies are simple and easy to understand. But they lack the perspective to fully realize the tremendous transfer of wealth happening today due to short-sighted government and monetary policies around the globe.

Investors following any one of these approaches at a given time without looking at the bigger picture expose themselves to a tremendous risk of losing substantial amounts of money. Simply put, it's using an obsolete guide, an outdated map.

Investors need a rational approach to investing, today more than ever.

Of course, the age we're living in makes the long term seem like a crapshoot between a glorious paradise and a scene from *Mad Max* or any movie set in a dystopian future. That's okay, because the excitement about investing comes from trying to analyze and predict the future. It's the quality of those predictions that ultimately determines gains and losses.

The future is the great unknown. While I've tried to be thorough, with all the rapid financial developments and ways the market can be manipulated, events will change. *But that's fine, because investing is a journey, not a destination.* Many changes will be scary and unforeseeable. Many developments, however, will be similar to problems we've seen before. Some changes will even be for the better.

So it's time to take control of your financial future, to do it yourself, and to move beyond trusting someone who's paid a commission to make the decisions for you — to move beyond trusting the government when they say that a problem has been "contained" or that "this time it's different."

So read on and watch your step . . . here be dragons.

1

Modern-Day Alchemy
Turning Cash into Trash

"You are an alchemist; make gold of that."
— William Shakespeare, *The Life of Timon of Athens*

DURING THE MIDDLE AGES, a group of men called alchemists performed numerous experiments. For some, the goal was to find a chemical mix that would stop aging. For others, it was to find a way to turn lead and other base metals into gold.

This search for a magical *kimia* (the Persian word for "elixir," later morphed into the word "alchemy," to turn lead into gold) never panned out.

Not only is this process still scientifically impossible, but it's in the world's best interest that such a creation never occur.

After all, alchemists struggled to create *more* value from *less* value. Turning the world's supply of lead into gold would vastly increase the amount of gold in the world. It would go from being a *precious* metal into a *common* metal. Gold would lose its value as a monetary metal through the inflation of the supply of gold. Instead of one gram of gold, one might need five pounds of the stuff to buy a loaf of bread!

While alchemists toiled with rudimentary experiments to increase the world's amount of gold, monarchs and sovereigns around the world stumbled onto a much more efficient way to create something

1

out of nothing — through currency. By the year 1565, a new word had come into circulation: debasement. Meaning to decrease the value of coins by increasing the amount of base metal within them, debasement also carries decidedly negative connotations. The word debasement is still used in modern times to remove a high honor, such as a knighthood in Great Britain.

At a time before printing presses, money was mainly gold and silver coins. Rulers learned quickly they could decrease the value of those coins by "clipping" the coins' edges and thus reducing their size. Monarchs could keep the gold saved by this process and enrich themselves.

Of course, such processes don't work. When coins got lighter or smaller or made of less valuable metal, it simply took more of them to purchase the same number of goods.

In other words, debasement led to inflation. More of the lesser-value coins were needed to make purchases. Older coins with higher precious metal content disappeared from circulation.

Alchemists failed in their work. But sovereigns, empowered by the threat of force, managed to do what the alchemists couldn't — impose inflation and destroy the value of currency.

Today, sovereign nations, like their kingly predecessors, look for ways to increase their wealth without working for it. But instead of doing their own work, they've outsourced it to today's modern-day alchemists — central bankers.

Of course, it isn't completely outsourced. Central banks such as the Federal Reserve may claim independence, but their structure and oversight typically binds them to the government in power. Don't let the periodic spats between a central bank and its government fool you. Since they're largely one and the same, such arguments are nothing more than posturing.

Nevertheless, the irrational belief that central bankers can "manage" an economy and "smooth out the economic cycle" is very much akin to the beliefs of ancient alchemists that there was a secret to turning lead into gold.

The difference between the alchemists and today's central bankers is clear: The alchemists knew they hadn't found what they were looking for yet. Unfortunately, central bankers think they already know!

Ironically, today's modern banking system comes from the role of goldsmiths during the Renaissance. Given the value of the gold they worked with, they employed guards, had top-of-the-line safes, and safeguarded their metal in other ways.

Naturally, this safety presented another business opportunity — merchants could leave items under the protection of the goldsmith — for a small fee, of course. Later this extended back to the very gold they made. When the gold was dropped off, the goldsmith would issue a receipt. In time, with enough gold on hand with the goldsmith, receipts could circulate instead of the gold.

Some astute goldsmiths realized that only a fraction of the receipts outstanding would be redeemed at any one time. By creating receipts in excess of other people's gold, they could enhance their earning power, and none would be the wiser . . . unless they went too far.

Today, the process is similar. A new bank deposit is lent out, with only a fraction of the capital staying at the bank as a reserve.

There is, of course, one key difference. Instead of having gold in the vaults of banks around the country, we have dollars. What's the difference? The difference is between something and nothing.

According to the Federal Reserve's pamphlet **Modern Money Mechanics**: "In the United States, neither paper currency nor deposits have value as commodities. Intrinsically, a dollar bill is just a piece of paper, deposits merely book entries . . . What, then, makes these instruments — checks, paper money, and coins — acceptable as face value in payment of all debts and for other monetary uses? Mainly, it is the confidence people have that they will be able to exchange such money for other financial assets and for real goods and services whenever they choose to do so."[1]

Without the backing of gold, the Fed has no limitation on what they can print or how much of it. We are no longer held by the anchor of prices in gold terms.

The Fed's role in today's alchemistic process is simple: It sets reserve ratios and interest rates. If the Fed feels that banks are being too loose with their low reserve ratio, they may ask them to keep more cash on hand.

By changing interest rates, which has historically been one of the Fed's main tools (a current rate target of 0–0.25 percent interest makes for a poor tool right now), the Fed sets the market on the rate that money is lent out.

With lower rates, the Fed hopes to spur individuals to take on debt to buy homes, purchase cars, take out business loans, and so forth. By raising rates, the Fed hopes to curtail new lending.

Of course, the Fed can't do it alone. Again, according to **Modern Money Mechanics**, "The actual process of money creation takes place primarily in banks."[2]

The key word in that statement is *primarily*. The US Treasury, in conjunction with the Bureau of Engraving and Printing, creates our paper currency, measured in M1 money supply. What the banks do is create new money through new debt.

Simply put, we have gone from a monetary system based on a limited, hard-to-find but easy-to-store metal (gold) and replaced it with easy-to-print money, thus conjuring up debt. In order to create money today, we must create debt. Either a bank must make a loan and create a new account for that loan money to exist in, or the Fed must purchase Treasurys so the US Treasury can print dollars.

Take a dollar bill out of your wallet. We all know the text it says on the front: "This note is legal tender for all debts, public and private." Well, what's a note? In financial-speak, a note is nothing more than evidence of a debt. Whether more paper bills are printed or whether accounts are created electronically, money today comes into existence via debt.

As a side note, silver has also been a part of monetary systems throughout history. Today, it is primarily an industrial metal but is still considered a valuable component in a sound monetary system by an ardent few. If you collect old currency, as I do, you may find an old US bill imprinted "Silver Certificate." They look like dollar bills but assure the holder that the US Treasury has one ounce of silver in their vaults. Go ahead; see if the US Treasury will give you silver for it.

Today, this paper-based system remains on life support following a massive credit bubble from 2003–2007 that collapsed spectacularly

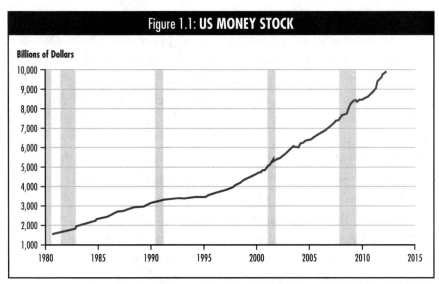

Figure 1.1: **US MONEY STOCK**

Source: Board of Governors of the Federal Reserve System | 2012 research.stlouisfed.org

Money stock has been constantly rising since the early 1980s, but the trend first accelerated in the late 1990s before rising at an even higher rate since the financial crisis struck in 2008.

in 2008–2009. Money creation, when measured in M1, is increasing. That's due to more physical currency in circulation.

But that's misleading about the overall money supply, since the primary driver of monetary growth has been the banking system and the creation of new loans. Consequently, a rise in M1 money supply isn't necessarily an indicator of higher inflation ahead.

When the full money supply, both M1 currencies and M2 bank loans are taken into account, we can see that the trend of an increasing supply of money has itself increased. In Figure 1.1, we can see that M2 has started rising rapidly since early 2009 when extraordinary measures were taken to bail out the banking system and keep the economy afloat.

These extraordinary measures go beyond the traditional role of setting interest rates. The Federal Reserve began buying up "toxic" mortgages, particularly subprime debts; made investments to stopgap financial companies (banks from giants like Citigroup and Bank of America all the way down to regional banks); and even loaned money to insurance companies like AIG and automakers under the Troubled Asset Relief Program (TARP).

The Fed has continued to make purchases of Treasurys under quantitative easing (QE) programs, during Operation Twist (when it sold short and medium-dated government bonds and bought long-term government bonds to keep interest rates low), and when other assets reach maturity. This has allowed the Federal government to run trillion-dollar deficits every year since 2008 without a massive explosion in interest rates.

It's a long process that still has a way to go, although it's likely that there will be periods where the trend slows down, such as during a credit crunch or because of fears of recession.

I'm basing that conclusion on the continual decline in the *velocity* of money. Velocity is a measure of how many times the same dollar can be used to purchase the same number of goods. Today's falling velocity rate, as seen in Figure 1.2, tells us that the rise of physical currency in M1 is not likely to have an inflationary effect.

The falling velocity of money means that banks and consumers are hoarding money. That's bad for a consumer-based economy because falling velocity indicates that more money is being saved rather than spent. Money supply can increase dramatically before inflation really ramps up.

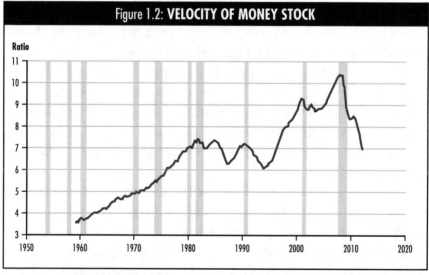

Figure 1.2: **VELOCITY OF MONEY STOCK**

Source: Board of Governors of the Federal Reserve System | 2012 research.stlouisfed.org

Since the start of the recession, the velocity of money has drastically fallen. Simply put, every dollar in circulation isn't being used in as many transactions as it used to be, offsetting the growth of the money supply.

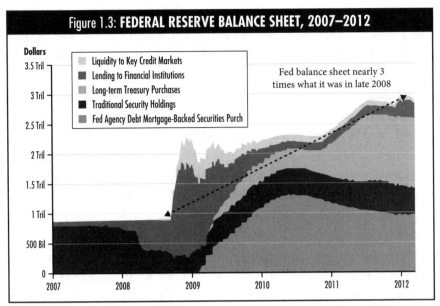

Figure 1.3: FEDERAL RESERVE BALANCE SHEET, 2007–2012

Source: www.mybudget360.com

At the height of the financial crisis, the Federal Reserve stepped in to purchase toxic assets. Since 2011, it has been gradually reducing these assets and investing the proceeds in Treasurys instead. In 2011, the Fed bought more than half of all new debt issued in the United States.

With inflation expectations rising, and actual inflation already here in rising food and energy prices, there is some risk of deflation without continual Fed asset purchases. If the Fed were to stop buying or reinvesting assets on its now expanded balance sheets, banks could again face the falling asset price and liquidity issues that they faced in 2008.

As you can see in Figure 1.3, prior to 2008, the Federal Reserve's balance sheet was comprised almost entirely of Treasury holdings. While the Fed is still actively purchasing Treasurys, new assets on the balance sheet, billed as "temporary" have become a permanent fixture. Not only that, by providing a clearinghouse for these assets above their true market value, the Fed has allowed banks to shift their bad debts off to taxpayers.

The first round of quantitative easing began in earnest in early 2009. The Fed started buying up so-called "toxic" mortgage-backed securities (MBS). It should be no surprise that once these toxic assets disappeared from the balance sheets of banks, much of the fear and uncertainty in the marketplace dissipated.

It's also no surprise that the start of the Fed's asset-buying program put a "floor" on financial markets. In the two years since, we've seen a stunning turnaround in markets, all thanks to the so-called "Bernanke put." This is simply an extension of the "Greenspan put" espoused by Bernanke's predecessor.

Basically, when markets appear jittery, the Fed chairman can issue a statement reminding everyone that the Fed stands willing to pump in money. This worked infamously well after the 1987 stock market crash. As credit-impaired companies like Bear Stearns were collapsing in 2007 and 2008, however, such statements alone had started to lose their value. More action was needed; hence the Fed bought up bad housing debt instead of its usual diet of Treasurys.

Nevertheless, the Bernanke put today has quite a premium: The Fed's balance sheet has grown by over $2 trillion (a 250 percent increase) since the start of the crisis. Many troubled assets have simply become the liabilities of the taxpayer, rather than the corporations that created them!

Indeed, by the time this book goes to print, the real size of the Federal Reserve's balance sheet won't matter. On September 13, 2012, the Fed announced their biggest initiative yet: QE3. This third round of quantitative easing, unlike its predecessors, isn't for a set amount of money. Rather, the central bank will begin buying $40 billion in assets each month in an attempt to bring down high unemployment.

In other words, the Fed hopes to help stimulate the economy and avoid the potential chaos of the economy slipping into another recession.

Yet this open-ended money printing brings to mind the kinds of rampant money creation that results in hyperinflation. But with the US economy still showing anemic growth at best, such a hyperinflationary act won't occur immediately — but the stakes are surely raised.

The Goal Is Stability, the Result Is Chaos

While the goal of alchemists was to create gold, the goal of the Fed was to "promote . . . stable prices."[3] Created as the belated result of the

Panic of 1907, it was thought that a central bank could bring an end to the periodic manias that swept through markets.

So, to determine if these modern-day alchemists have succeeded in their goal, we need simply look at how price levels have varied since the Federal Reserve came into being. Thankfully, we have a century of data for the Fed. There's also data going back as far as colonial times, but the further back we go the more unreliable it gets.

So, let's use the post–Civil War era (1870–1913) chart as a representative sample (see Figure 1.4).

It's plain to see that the Fed's initial efforts to promote price stability weren't successful; there were some pretty wild swings from extreme inflation to extreme deflation.

Following the end of the gold standard in 1933, periods of deflation, which worked to undo prior inflation and bring prices back in line, went the way of the 8-track player. For the baby boomer generation, inflation has been the normal investment climate, except for the recent credit crisis.

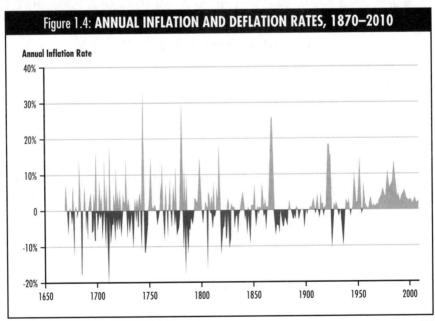

Figure 1.4: **ANNUAL INFLATION AND DEFLATION RATES, 1870–2010**

Source: CPI

Since the inception of the Federal Reserve, periods of deflation have become less frequent. Consistent, low levels of inflation have led to the dollar's 97 percent devaluation since 1913.

Without the wild swings of severe deflation, even a policy of mild, persistent inflation can be hugely damaging. Measured by the Consumer Price Index (CPI), prices in 2011 are roughly double of that in 1986. Not bad for a quarter century, right? Only if you exclude the cost of housing, energy, substitute steak for chicken, and make other adjustments.

In fact, thanks to the Bureau of Labor's "moving the goalposts" of the CPI, inflation has been substantially understated for twenty years. With the same weightings used in 1990, today's inflation rate is substantially closer to 10 percent — more than double the current CPI level!

Economists and investors tend to watch the CPI numbers closely to see if inflation is ramping up or cooling. But it should be clear to anyone that today's CPI simply does *not* tell the whole story, and in some cases may be completely disconnected from reality (see Figure 1.5).

By any measure, it's clear that the Fed is incapable of meeting its goal of producing price stability. With nearly a century of data behind

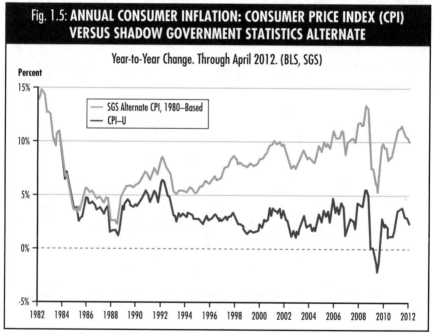

Fig. 1.5: ANNUAL CONSUMER INFLATION: CONSUMER PRICE INDEX (CPI) VERSUS SHADOW GOVERNMENT STATISTICS ALTERNATE

Year-to-Year Change. Through April 2012. (BLS, SGS)

— SGS Alternate CPI, 1980–Based
— CPI–U

Published: May 15, 2012 | Courtesy of ShadowStats.com

Using older methodologies for calculating inflation, today's ultralow rates of inflation actually appear to be closer to 10 percent per year.

us, we can say with certainty that the central bank has not maintained price stability.

If anything, our business cycles have gotten increasingly leveraged and extreme as a result the Fed providing liquidity "to stabilize the markets." All that means is that real value is destroyed to create the illusion that things aren't so bad.

The bottom line is this: persistent inflation gives debtors a windfall reduction in the value of the debt they owe.

Talk about alchemy! The dollar has turned from a gold-backed security into something backed by nothing more than perception. Perception wins in the short term. Economic reality wins in the long term.

In the long term, events cannot continue as they have. Eventually faith in the dollar will falter as it continues to get weaker. The government cannot infinitely run trillion-dollar deficits. The Federal Reserve must keep interest rates low to ensure the government can finance its debt — or else it will have to buy more and more, fueling inflation in the process.

One way or another, alchemy results in disaster, chaos, and squandered resources. If it were one lone alchemist in some medieval lab, the consequences would only be disastrous to one man. Alas, today's alchemy is global, reaching into the lives of billions.

The medieval alchemists created one benefit: By recording their experiments and the results, they may have laid the foundation for today's scientific method. Today's central bankers, however, have little to show other than how *not* to try and manage something as complex and intricate as the world's economy.

In a way, the world of the Middle Ages was the first age of currency debasement. In this first age, it was simple to hoard old coins with higher gold and silver content and use the newer ones of lesser value in trade.

For a brief period of human history, industrialization and the gold standard led to price stability *and* exceptional prosperity. As part of that prosperity, individuals can fractionally own entire companies in the form of stocks. They can own bonds and other financial assets that had previously been reserved only to an extremely wealthy few.

Along the way, the world has abandoned the stability of the gold standard. Our money system today is backed by nothing more than promises to repay. This is known as a *fiat* system.

Today, we find ourselves in a new age of currency debasement. Coupled with a more diverse series of assets, you will have to be more nimble and selective in your investment decisions ahead of the debt crises and currency crises that the unstable fiat money system breeds.

Investing passively in the market through a strategy of "buy and hold" has become more difficult (but not impossible). Why? Because the prospect of higher inflation in the future has the potential to eat away almost all positive returns.

The value of your money is beyond your control. It is set by central bankers, far removed from the daily problems of making ends meet at a time when gas prices are on the rise and food prices have surged. Simply saving money, already difficult for many financially strapped Americans, won't be enough. Over time, that money will lose its purchasing power, perhaps rapidly, perhaps gradually, but it *will* lose consistently.

But don't take my word for it. Most investors worth their salt are constantly looking for ways to find and invest in a way to take advantage of inflation, rather than subject themselves to the hidden tax it truly represents.

As Warren Buffett, a major worrier about the prospect of inflation, once pointed out, "The arithmetic makes it plain that inflation is a far more devastating tax than anything that has been enacted by our legislature. The inflation tax has a fantastic ability to simply consume capital. It makes no difference to a widow with her savings in a 5 percent passbook account whether she pays 100 percent income tax on her interest income during a period of zero inflation or pays no income taxes during years of 5 percent inflation. Either way, she is 'taxed' in a manner that leaves her no real income whatsoever."[4]

Alas, at times in the years ahead, we may *all* find ourselves in the awkward position of facing taxes in well in excess of 100 percent, once inflation is factored in. That's why every investor needs a plan to deal with inflation over the long haul. The recent bouts of deflation experienced since the start of the financial crisis will eventually become forgotten memories, as central bankers would rather tolerate modest inflation than deal with *any* deflation.

We know that the current fiat system will face more major crises. Factor in the coming tsunami of entitlement spending for the Baby Boomers, and it's clear that the foundations of America's economy today are unsustainable. We simply don't have the resources to handle an unexpected or unknown economic shift.

You need both the intellectual capacity to reason past these crises and the ability to make rational decisions to avoid the kind of emotional entrapment that destroys returns as well. Most of all, we must beware today's alchemists: central bankers in highly indebted countries are determined to turn their cash into trash.

WRAP-UP
Why Investors Face a Chaotic World and Why That Isn't New

- Mankind has long struggled to create value where there is none. In the Middle Ages, it was via alchemy. Today, it's done through the manipulation of fiat currencies.
- While this manipulation may create the illusion of prosperity in the short term, it creates long-term problems. The global economy is still suffering the "hangover" from too much liquidity over the past few decades.
- Ostensibly, such schemes are created under the guise of creating stability. Instead, things are more chaotic than they would have been had there been no interference in the first place.
- Modern-day alchemy generally risks higher inflation rates, which can be devastating. Liquidation of prior bad decisions, however, means that there's a tug-of-war at place right now between inflation and deflation.

2

Rational Statistics, Irrational Investment Implications

"Too large a proportion of recent 'mathematical' economics are mere concoctions, as imprecise as the initial assumptions they rest on, which allow the author to lose sight of the complexities and interdependence of the real world in a maze of pretentious and unhelpful symbols."

— *J.M. Keynes*[5]

L IFE KEEPS MOST PEOPLE TOO BUSY to actively deal with their portfolios. Instead, they invest their hard-earned dollars in index funds, mutual funds, exchange-traded funds (ETFs), and various investments in their 401(k)s. This is a better alternative than stuffing cash under the mattress.

By taking advantage of these choices, investors have a decent shot of seeing their investments beat inflation over the long term. They also, however, set themselves up for substantial risks that can destroy their wealth.

Unless you have a master's degree in statistics or a background in the instability of human nature, odds are that you (and your broker) are basing your investment policy on mistaken ideas. How? By putting into practice what's called *modern portfolio theory*.

That's right; you aren't operating under cold, hard facts set in stone when it comes to your investment money and your retirement nest egg. Rather, you're doing what physicists do in a lab — putting a *theory* into practice.

This isn't necessarily a good or a bad thing. In science, a theory is never true *per se*; it just hasn't been proven false yet!

Unfortunately, several tenets of modern portfolio theory, which work in most cases, seem to fall apart in extreme cases. (And we are living through one of those extreme cases now.) The problem is that this theory drives the investment decisions of banks, insurance firms, hedge funds, pension plans, and nearly all of the market's big movers.

Knowing the shortcomings of this theory explains why so many were blind to the housing bubble and market crash in 2008, why so many were blind to the huge opportunity to buy stocks at their most reasonable prices (relative to earnings) in over a decade in the spring of 2009.

We need to debunk this theory piece by piece. Doing so will show us why fund investments may be costing you hundreds of thousands of dollars in mistakes over time.

Note: it's going to get a little heavy on theory, so readers who are still relatively new to investing may want to skip to the chapter summary at the end and pick up the details after reading through the rest of the book.

Bell Curves Are Ringing in Investor's Ears

Most financial theories, such as modern portfolio theory and the Black-Scholes method of option pricing, are based on the premise that prices follow a bell curve.

We all know the basics from school. Most observations (99.7 percent) tend to fall within three standard deviations of the central mean (the peak point of the bell curve) shown in Figure 2.1.

What does that mean? It means from day to day, prices shouldn't go up or down too much. For the stock market as a whole, one standard deviation is around 1.15 percent based on the historical data. So if markets moved up or down 2 percent on a given day, it would be within two standard deviations, or two sigmas, named after the Greek letter (Σ) used to represent deviations in statistics).

In science, most data tends to sort itself into one of these curves over time. You'll see bell curves when looking at the average growth

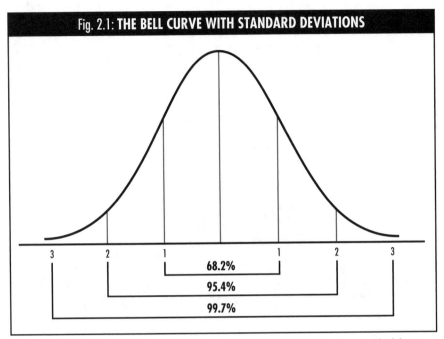

Fig. 2.1: **THE BELL CURVE WITH STANDARD DEVIATIONS**

| 3 | 2 | 1 | 1 | 2 | 3 |

68.2%

95.4%

99.7%

The standard bell-shaped curve: most events — 99.7 percent — will fall within three standard deviations of the mean.

patterns of trees, the outcome of two dice being thrown ten thousand times, and so on.

Since modern portfolio theory is a huge leap in bringing some of this rational scientific analysis to financial decisions, most analysts will tell you it's critical to understand the bell curve. That's all fine in theory. But as Yogi Berra said, "In theory there is no difference between theory and practice. But in practice, there is."

The most fitting distribution for stocks exhibits a very poor fit throughout the range of the data. While stocks have had more up years than down years, most observations occur within the 0–10 percent range. Note that's below the 10–11 percent most analysts spout as the "average return." There are some pretty fat tails on both sides — 1931 and 2008 for declines — and some big bounces over 40 percent from depressed prices on the right side (although half of those are from the 9th century) extremes.

It is evident that, although annual stock returns **resemble** a bell curve, there is a lot of chaos for the investor. Look at the column

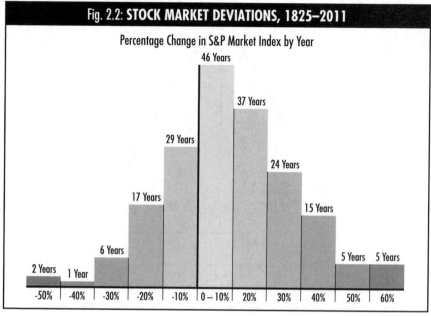

Source: Standard & Poor's, author

While market returns appear to roughly fall under a bell-shaped curve, the extreme tail ends suggest that, over a longer period, stock market returns may appear more volatile than a traditional curve.

leading losses in 2000, 2001, and 2002. Returns went from bad to worse before a major bounce in 2003. And 2008 ended up being the second worst year on record.

Do you still feel safe with a "buy-and-hold" strategy after the past decade? Had you bought a blue-chip stock like Coca Cola in 2000, your capital would have returned nothing. Shares were at $70 in 2000 and still at $70 in 2012. Dividends would have been a saving grace, but factor in inflation and you would have still lost money in real terms.

With less than two hundred years of data to work with, we really don't have enough to build a better model. It may take ten thousand years to get enough yearly returns to where the distribution truly resembles a bell curve or to know if a more accurate shape would better resemble market returns.

In other words, the market is young. And not just relatively young — we could look at some of the rapid changes over the past decade as the equivalent of the "Terrible Twos." In the past fifteen years, we've seen the rise of online trading, the decimalization of stocks, and the increase of trade in former emerging markets.

Neither you nor I will live long enough to see markets fully mature. We have to deal with the investment reality of the present.

Looking at bell-curve distributions overlooks stock returns based on the underlying facts that stocks are proportional ownership claims on the future earnings of companies. Wild changes can and do take place based on expectations of economic growth, perceived future interest rates, and corporate financial health.

Taking a more fundamental approach, where returns on stocks are based on expected corporate improvements, it would make more sense to invest in companies when it appears that a period of economic growth is expected.

Ironically, that's typically toward the end of a market contraction, when fear runs rampant! That's a plus for most investors though, because that's where the most compelling valuations are, and those who have the courage to buy then are rewarded with major rallies.

Unfortunately, there's more than just the fact that this "map" of market returns just doesn't fit the road we've already traveled.

Modern portfolio theory — still used by most of the major players from big banks to insurance companies to investment firms — has a whole slew of other things that just don't add up.

And, like a flawed mathematical equation, it's all in the assumptions.

Modern Portfolio Theory Assumptions

One of the most pervasive, wealth-destroying myths on Wall Street is the idea that markets are efficient.

Gallivanting under the name efficient market hypothesis (EMH) like a modern Don Quixote, this theory tilts at the windmill that markets accurately reflect all relevant pricing information at all times and investors stand no chance to outperform the market.

The conclusion of this dogma is that the optimal way to invest is to dollar-cost average new positions and buy and hold. But they're wrong. This type of investing is nothing but mental laziness. It's hardly a rational way to view the role of markets, which not only tend to move to extremes, but do so even as players have moved to computer-ized trading to "get rid of the emotion" in investing.

Ah, but were that true! Alas, a computer program is only as emo-tional as the programmer. There's an old programming saying about that: "Garbage in, garbage out."

And the efficient market theory is largely based on certain assump-tions that go into it. These assumptions are a cornerstone of efficient mar-ket theory, which in turn is a cornerstone of modern portfolio theory.

There are a lot of assumptions, both about investors and about the structure of markets. The assumptions start out sounding pretty ratio-nal, until you look at the math. From there, it's a slippery slope into chaotic investment returns. Here's a closer look at each of them and why they all have their shortcomings.

As you'll see, this theory is riddled with more holes than Bonnie and Clyde.

ASSUMPTION #1:
Asset returns are normally distributed random variables (bell curves).
We've already looked at the fact that stock returns don't quite get to that overall bell shape. But on a deeper level, what this assumption tells us is that returns should nearly all fall within three standard devi-ations (three sigmas).

As any investor of the past five years can attest, moves well beyond the typical three-standard deviation occur rather often. In the 2008 market crash alone, four of the twelve months were beyond the typical three standard deviations of markets as a whole.

As you can see from Figure 2.3, the last time such extreme events occurred was during the 1987 market crash. Then, you'd have to go back to the Depression era to find such volatility.

Specific days were even worse. Three days in October 2008 saw daily changes of more than six standard deviations from the mean (otherwise known as six-sigma events), with the one-day plunge in markets on October 13 a staggering nine standard deviations.

Modern portfolio theory relies on data being processed within the lens of up to three standard deviations, where one event per year is likely to occur outside that area.

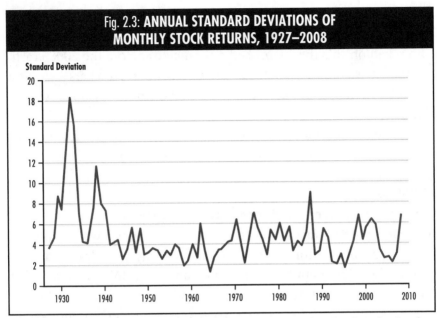

Fig. 2.3: **ANNUAL STANDARD DEVIATIONS OF MONTHLY STOCK RETURNS, 1927–2008**

If market returns fell under a normal bell-shaped distribution, there would be only a few isolated incidents where standard deviations rose above three. As you can see, this is not the case.

Statistics tells us that a six-sigma event should happen approximately once every 1.5 million years. Table 2.1 shows us how often other such rare events are likely to occur as well.

But a six-sigma event happened three times in stock indices during October 2008 alone!

Tab. 2.1: **STANDARD DEVIATION RANGE AND EXPECTED FREQUENCY OF EXTREME EVENTS**

Deviations	Percent in Range	Expected Frequency Outside Range	Approx. Frequency for Daily Event
1	68.26%	1 in 3	Twice a week
2	95.45%	1 in 22	Every three weeks
3	99.73%	1 in 370	Yearly
4	99.994%	1 in 15,787	Every 43 years (twice in a lifetime)
5	99.99994%	1 in 1,744,278	Every 5,000 years (once in history)
6	99.9999998%	1 in 506,842,372	Every 1.5 million years

Source: http://mathworld.wolfram.com/NormalDistribution.html

Remember: This is the core, fundamental premise upon which all other parts of modern portfolio theory are based. This is why many who relied on this theory missed out on clues before the 2008 crash, whether it was the news stories about strawberry pickers buying a $750,000 home or the inverted yield curve (more on both in later chapters).

One important note: These were major market index returns. Individual stocks were, and continue to be, *massively* more volatile.

ASSUMPTION #2:
Correlations between assets are fixed and constant.

In the novel *Atlas Shrugged*, Ayn Rand creates a world where political bureaucrats, in an effort to stabilize the economy, pass draconian legislation forbidding anyone from doing anything different than what they did the year before.

People must work the same job, earn the same money, and spend that money the same way. This act is justified in that it will curtail economic collapse. Rand shows that, in reality, when the world becomes a fixed and constant place, no progress can be made.

So it's incredibly offensive that this is one of the assumptions of modern portfolio theory.

There's another name given to this situation by economists of the Austrian school (a set of economic beliefs). They call it the "evenly rotating economy."[6]

As Austrian economist Ludwig von Mises describes it, "There is no choosing and the future is not uncertain as it does not differ from the present known state. Such a rigid system is not peopled with living men making choices and liable to error; it is a world of soulless unthinking automatons; it is not a human society, it is an ant hill."[7]

In other words, every single commodity company on the planet should sell exactly as much this year as it did last year. Prices would remain unchanged and quantities available in the same proportion. (In other words, we would have to live in a world where it would always cost the same to extract gold from a mine. In reality, of course, we know that rich veins are exhausted and finding new metals entails different costs per ounce extracted.)

Human beings would be automatons, incapable of change. There would be no technological breakthroughs. This is so clearly wrong that, frankly, it should be enough to shut up anyone talking up the benefits of modern portfolio theory.

That's what it would take to ensure that correlations between asset classes never change. So, no big deal, right? Just the end of society as we know it. Sure, gas prices wouldn't go up anymore, but we wouldn't have new car models or iPads either.

Of course, should this bizarre state of affairs break down and there were a market crash, all assets relative to cash would start correlating with each other nearly perfectly. That's what happened in 2008 as investors and funds scrambled to get out of risky assets and hold cash. Everything, even gold, sold off all at once.

Correlation changes with the facts. Steel gets cheaper than copper; some people use more steel and less copper. A new technology comes along and disrupts the status quo . . . creative destruction at its finest.

And when the next crash finally comes, all investments lead to ruin.

ASSUMPTION #3:
All investors aim to maximize economic utility (to make as much money as possible for a given level of risk).

This one sounds much more reasonable than the second assumption. Of course we all want to make as much money as possible! The problem is that risk isn't a set number — it's an ever-changing variable based on the activity of the market and our own financial situation and mood.

That's why some investors with millions of dollars will opt for a portfolio consisting entirely of municipal bonds, while another investor with a similarly sized portfolio may opt to invest in a basket of small-cap Chinese stocks.

In order for this assumption to be true, all investors would be chasing the most volatile stocks imaginable on a regular basis.

That means grandma is off to the races to bid on Apple, Chipotle, and other high-beta stocks that move far more than the market does on a given day (up *or* down). Never mind the periodic wipeouts. Never mind investing for dividends or for steady gains.

Of course, nobody wants to lose money . . . but some investors don't mind having a loss or two to sell off and "harvest" during tax season to keep their bill to Uncle Sam low.

ASSUMPTION #4:
All investors are risk averse.

This is a direct contradiction of the above assumption. Investors can't simultaneously strive for the most money possible and still want to avoid all risks.

Investors simply can't know or understand risk beyond the idea that they may permanently lose their capital in an investment (unless they're leveraged, in which case they may lose more).

Why? Because any measure of risk typically used by today's money managers is backwards looking, like volatility or moving averages. It doesn't tell investors a clue about what will happen in the future.

Collateralized debt obligations (CDOs), essentially bundles of mortgages, some with a pristine credit rating and some that would best be described as junk, during the housing bubble were rated as AAA, safe investments. Risk-averse mutual funds, insurance companies, and retirees clamored for them, as they gave off a higher yield than other AAA-rated instruments like US Treasurys.

Combine this fact with the last assumption, and suddenly a lot of bad behavior during the housing bubble makes sense.

ASSUMPTION #5:
All investors have access to the same information at the same time.

The *Journal of Financial and Quantitative Analysis* conducted a study that has shown that during the 1990s boom, corporate insiders beat the market by 6 percent per year. Obviously these insiders have data well before the general public.

But that's just half of the 12 percent market-beating return that members of the US Senate average every year.[8]

While these results make one wonder who the ultimate insiders are, it also makes it painfully aware that some investors simply have information well before the general public.

The only difference is that in the case of a company's key officers, such as the CEO or CFO, it's considered illegal to trade on such information. In the case of Congress, it's legal.

ASSUMPTION #6:
Investors have an accurate conception of possible returns.

For this assumption to hold, we wouldn't find market extremes. Bubbles wouldn't be able to form. In the case of housing during the bubble, for example, investors wouldn't have accepted the possibility that housing prices could rise by double-digit rates each year.

So we know that this assumption also doesn't hold water.

If anything, most investors are overconfident and arrogant in their abilities. They cling to a projected return (this hot stock will shoot up 50 percent in the next six weeks) and keep clinging to it long after they should have left (okay, once it rallies back to break even, I'll sell).

Sometimes, this may work out well. Undoubtedly some investors who bought Walmart or Microsoft during their initial public offerings (IPOs) weren't fully cognizant of how well these companies would perform against the overall market.

Either way, the future is riddled with uncertainty. Possible returns on any investment can and do change with any new data available. So having an accurate conception of returns is impossible for most.

ASSUMPTION #7:
There are no taxes or transaction costs.

No taxes? Now that's an assumption we'd all love to have in the real world!

Without transaction costs, however, I wonder who would play the role of broker? And why aren't they charging money for the service they provide?

As for taxes, lower rates have always been better for capital and job formation. But a big question presents itself: would inflation be considered a tax for the purpose of this assumption?

As I write, the true rate of inflation is about a 6 percent tax bite on any profits investors take, *whether the nominal dollar value of an investment moves up or down.* It may even be more or less depending on whose statistics you believe.

I imagine if tax rates on investment were to fall to zero, there would still be inflation to contend with. Speaking of inflation, despite its prevalence over the past century, portfolio theory dismisses its role altogether. It's never even mentioned. That's a pretty big omission!

ASSUMPTION #8:

All investors are price takers, which means their actions do not influence prices.

Not true at all. If you dump enough money onto the market, the price moves. Pure and simple.

Or sometimes there's just thin volume, and the price moves a bit as part of the market's daily give-and-take between buyers and sellers. If I offer to buy one hundred shares of McDonald's at a penny less than the most recent trade on the market, get filled on that order, and then the next trade is for the original price, I have moved the market, however briefly and for however much.

Now, say I want to buy one hundred shares of McDonald's two hours after the market closes because I've been listening to some talking head on TV list his reasons for owning the stock. With fewer sellers and the regular market closed, it may take more than a penny to move the share price. I'd face an initial loss as the price comes back down when regular trading resumes.

Clearly, whether you're buying after hours or when the market is open, the mere act of your purchase is a new signal to market participants to take into account.

ASSUMPTION #9:

Any investor can lend and borrow an unlimited amount at the risk free rate of interest.

While borrowing a few trillion dollars and buying up the entire market at today's low interest rates has its appeal, it would step on the above assumption about not being able to influence prices. In order to buy everyone out, I'd have to move prices.

If this assumption were true, other market participants would undoubtedly want to try and do this first. It would simply be a race to the bottom for mankind if any investor could borrow such large amounts at such a low rate.

ASSUMPTION #10:
All securities can be divided into parcels of any size.

Unless you're investing directly with a company and having the dividends reinvested, fractional shares can't exist. After some of the other assumptions, it's a bit odd that this one has a bit of truth to it.

If you're going to be a sensible investor, you must look at all these assumptions, and their shortcomings, when considering the utility of data produced under this theory.

In most cases, the facts point to "garbage in, garbage out." This theory told us that McDonald's was correctly priced at $15 in 2003, after the company had its first-ever quarterly loss and its glory days of growth were over, when shares, in fact, were depressingly low.

This theory also told us that stock in Crocs footwear (NASDAQ:CROX) at $80 could continue to grow its market share well after everyone who wanted a pair already had one and the price for the stock was, actually stratospherically high.

The Market's Forever Blowing Bubbles

Even though these assumptions range from somewhat sensible to ludicrous, many investors still use this approach, even though they're aware of its shortcomings.

To me, the biggest shortcoming is the idea that returns are evenly distributed. If this were true, there would be fewer speculative bubbles and fewer crashes.

Investors would realize that an economy built on tulip trading, land speculation, or tech stocks was absurd compared to the needs of the overall economy.

Indeed, the historical incidence of such events, even since modern portfolio theory came out, continues to stand as empirical evidence against man's scientific taming of the markets.

We would also see no need for speculation. But it's precisely because we're dealing with the future, with the unknown, that speculation comes into play. And speculation can often end up being a self-fulfilling prophecy, creating and exacerbating market bubbles in defiance of a rational portfolio theory.

A bubble is a market situation when investors are encouraged by higher prices, rather than discouraged by them. It's a complete break from the status quo. You don't go buying up steaks at the supermarket because the price has gone up in the past few weeks and you want to sell them to your neighbor at a higher price on Memorial Day weekend. You buy the chicken that's on sale instead.

At every other point in life, we tend to be on the lookout for bargains. We wait for sales at the mall. We take advantage of "going out of business" sales. (And isn't it odd that some companies seem to never quite make it to bankruptcy despite these signs?)

But a bubble is that little tug that says, "This time it's different." And, rather than be skeptical, we completely succumb to its siren song of fat profits. We stop being those rational agents that, according to theory, we must be at all times.

Bubbles are clearly based on emotion, namely, greed. The bubble grows by this psychological breakdown, akin to a virus. New investors are excited by the returns of prior investors and think that they will do the same — or better.

They completely ignore that original investors may have gotten in while the asset was unloved and that this depressed the price compared to its true value. Later investors might have gotten in at a fair price, but at that point there were so many buyers relative to sellers that prices just started to shoot up.

Fundamental analysis goes out the window. Cash flows? Who needs 'em! Or the dreaded "I know it will go up," said without any rational basis for doing so.

Markets move from extreme overvaluation to extreme undervaluation. We're all familiar with the 1929 top in markets, which popped with a spectacular crash and subsequent, brief rallies, to reach a low in 1932.

Adjusted for inflation, the 1968–1980 "sideways" market, where the nominal value of the Dow ended up near the same price, also marks a period of movement from extreme overvaluation to extreme undervaluation.

In the 1960s, lazy investors (now armed with modern portfolio theory) simply looked to top companies of the day. Because they assumed that the market always priced in all information fully, and that they couldn't move the market, buying shares of these companies at current prices always made sense.

Naturally, these high-flyers, called the Nifty Fifty, kept going up in price as investors moved the market up.

These are extreme examples, and they've been magnified by the shift from a gold-backed currency to a dollar that can simply be printed at will. When looking at the Dow priced in gold over the past two hundred years, as shown in Figure 2.4, we get a clearer picture on the relative value of stocks versus a more stable unit of measure.

We can see that the market is little more than a pinball, bouncing from one extreme to the other:

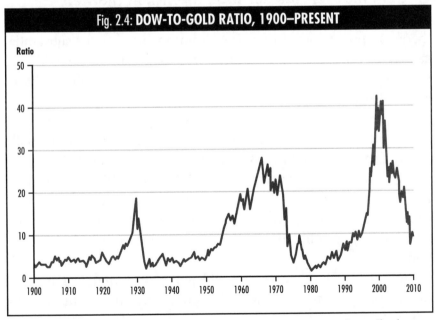

Source: Sharelynx.com

Priced in gold, stocks have tended to trade in a narrow range. As the restraints of the gold standard have been removed, this range has significantly increased.

In other words, the idea of an "average" is average at best. History shows us that markets don't stay near averages before getting caught in a mania or a depression. Rather, markets are usually making the journey from overvaluation to undervaluation, and it's only over time where "averages" seem to imply some kind of fair value for markets as a whole.

Markets are rarely at some average where they're "fairly valued." Ignoring modern portfolio theory, investors can see that there are times when they should reduce their stake in the stock market and times when they should, like a well-trained poker player with a winning hand and statistics on his side, go "all in."

The same is **even more true** of individual stocks, which is why you should be looking to individual companies that are undervalued and shun (or short) those that are overvalued (as I'll show you in later chapters).

Efficient Markets Riskier than Inefficient Markets

If you truly believe that markets are accurately pricing in formation, there's no point in investing. There's no opportunity for substantial gains. New data could send stocks down, just as much as it could send stocks up. Just put all your money in index funds and enjoy the life of existentialism.

In short, efficient markets sound inherently riskier than inefficient ones. With mispricing in inefficient markets, you can sell substantially overvalued assets and buy substantially undervalued ones.

For some, that's just what happened. Opportunities abounded in 2007 and 2008 to sell overpriced assets and sit in cash until more compelling valuations occurred. Opportunities abounded in early 2009 to pick up solid companies at a discount to the value of their underlying assets.

But if you believe markets are efficient, stocks were just as accurately priced in early 2009 as they were nearly 40 percent higher a year before.

Modern portfolio theory also claims that this is impossible to outperform the markets as a whole. If that were true, absolutely no investor in history could have beaten the market over a prolonged period of time without some kind of substantial inside information or foreknowledge of market events.

Okay, maybe a few. After all, if you have one hundred thousand people flipping coins, odds are that at least one of them will get heads fifty times in a row.

But there's way more than one. Some are household names. George Soros, Peter Lynch, Warren Buffett, John Paulson (who made billions by betting against, or "shorting the "fairly valued" housing market), and the list goes on.

Since mainstream financial education today still allows this lie to permeate, there's a bigger risk: not only are markets inefficient, governments help keep them that way.

There are arbitrary rules on short sales. There are protocols for shutting down exchanges in the event that the market falls by so many points in a day. There are changes in margin requirements for commodity and derivatives. An efficient market is a free market, not one where a sudden change of information is prevented from being reflected in a new price for an asset.

What lesson can we take away from this? It's that markets are much less efficient than most folks think — which is why risk is perpetually understated. But there's also the huge potential for opportunity as a result.

Use Intrinsic Value, not Market Prices, as Your Guide

If markets are truly bastions of inefficiency, you have two choices as an investor. Either you can ride markets like a roller coaster, or you can find a way to smooth out the dips and invest in a way that minimizes your downside.

How? By never forgetting that there are two keys to rational investing: ignoring the noise and focusing on the truth. **The way to do this is to determine a company's true, intrinsic value.**

Of course, even the idea of a "true" value is one of the most difficult mental exercises in investing. That's because this value will be *subjective* to the assumptions you make in your calculations.

You can't just go online and look it up the way you can find a company's earnings per share or dividend yield. What's even more challenging is that shares should be bought *below* this intrinsic value to reduce potential losses if your estimate is wrong.

Outsmarting emotions is the really tricky part: When stocks are collapsing, you'll have to ignore the instinct to cash out and run from the markets and instead start buying. Fortunately, there are several tools available to help you invest at the right time.

The first is to use "stink bids" by placing orders with your broker far below the current market price (and at a discount to your estimation of a company's intrinsic value).

This method was used by the late Sir John Templeton. During the Great Depression, Templeton bought up shares of every company trading for less than $1. Some companies were already filing for bankruptcy, but many good companies had sold off with the bad. Within a few years, Templeton was able to reap substantial profits from this unusual investment idea — and his wealth only grew from there. But the idea of determining a low price and letting the market come to him was a powerful idea that he used throughout his investment career.

Once Templeton calculated a potential investment's intrinsic value, he'd then place an open order with his broker to buy the stock at a price where there was a margin of safety to that value. Naturally, that price would be considered a "stink bid": it would typically be significantly lower than market expectations that it wouldn't get triggered for weeks or months.

But here's the key: If you were watching a stock fall and fall and fall, would you be willing to finally pick up shares when it reached a price where you absolutely *knew* you had a margin of safety?

Odds are, no. That's because by the time a company does reach that price, other events have conspired either around the specific company or markets as a whole that make everyone wary. They'd rather have cash.

While it's a simple rule of thumb to buy when everyone wants cash, when the time comes, odds are you're going to have to ignore your emotional inclination to go with the herd and be as fearful as they are.

You can emulate Templeton's discipline. Set buy prices for companies that are below your estimate of what they're truly worth. Then be patient. Go watch paint dry or do something else with your day while markets are open.

If you're cash heavy and are impatient, you can sell options. If the stock isn't that overpriced, and markets look like they'll trade sideways for a while, then you can buy the stock and sell call options against the position. This is known as *covered-call writing*.

If the stock's really overpriced, you can instead sell put options. It's a bit more unusual but can be a great way to buy a company at a great price — and get paid to wait. That's because, in addition to the small income from selling the put, you'll also get the right to buy the stock at a price that's acceptable. In today's world of low interest rates, it's not a bad way to set yourself up to buy shares of a great company at a great price — and get paid for doing so.

It's not a free lunch, but it's akin to a few appetizers. It can hold you over and generate some income until the buying feast begins.

Asset Allocation: Not as Simple as a Few Charts Would Have You Believe

Here's a fun experiment: call up your broker and ask him about diversification. Odds are they'll say something about owning a tech stock, a financial stock, a consumer goods stock, a health-care stock, and maybe a bond fund. If your broker is prudent enough, he'll recommend leaving some cash on the sidelines, if only to ostensibly move somewhere where a compelling value presents itself.

Unfortunately . . . that's probably it. Cash, stocks, and bonds. This is what usually passes for asset allocation, an essential component of investment returns.

Sure, maybe your assets will be broken down more specifically into international versus domestic stocks and corporate versus government bonds, but at the end of the day it's three asset classes — and it's likely all denominated in dollars.

Considering the myriad of asset classes out there, such a portfolio is really only diverse within the categories of stocks and bonds. It's overlooking a slew of commodities, real estate, currencies, and exceedingly esoteric assets such as art and rare coins.

The second component of asset allocation is usually determined by your appetite for risk — the more you seek, the more your portfolio is typically weighted by equities.

Typically, when opening up an account, it's up to you to sit down with your broker and determine what kind of risk you can tolerate. And once you've opened up your account, you probably haven't given that a second thought. But if you're taking long positions in automatically diversified portfolios, then those weightings won't change even if your appetite for risk has. Or, as Warren Buffett has said, "Wide diversification is only required when investors do not understand what they are doing."

Enter the Need for Tactical Allocation

Clearly, mainstream thought on asset allocation is inflexible and static. True asset allocation needs to be nimble and dynamic. This flexibility serves two purposes: to limit losses and to always rotate to the area with the most prospective gains.

One of the biggest problems investors face in determining asset allocation is whether to adopt a policy of strategic asset allocation or tactical asset allocation. Many simply fail to delineate between the two, opting for the combination of buy-and-hold and optimism. It's a poor strategic blunder, lacking in tactical mobility, and one that nearly guarantees that the war for gains in your portfolio will clearly be lost as chaos impacts asset values.

Strategic asset allocation seeks to capture gains over the long term. That means several quarters, if not several years. A strategic allocation decision may be made based on a compelling valuation or a long-term demographic or growth story. And if any of those things changes, the strategy needs to change — immediately.

Conversely, tactical asset allocation looks for quick gains — provided there's a sufficient margin of safety to justify it. Examples include trading the Forex (FX) market, buying a stock right before an upside earnings surprise, or shorting the stock of a company about to go bankrupt — in short, any situation where the potential for profit exists now but perhaps for only a few more quarters going forward.

You'll need to carefully balance between your strategic and your tactical trades. You don't want to go overboard on trading. No matter how much you try to outsmart the markets, you'll have some losers. Also, you'll have short-term capital gains taxes on the winners. The time constraints of researching such a position add strain as well.

On the other hand, a buy-and-hold approach is prone to tremendous wipeouts without a proper exit strategy in place. And most investors fail to take these strategies into consideration.

But there's no fixed or optimal percentage of where your assets should be invested. One, it's a deeply intimate thing. Two, it's subject to change at whim.

In principle, then, the ideal asset allocation mix is to employ tactical asset allocation to preserve against losses on the strategic level. Profits from tactical-level investments can be spread further between the strategic and tactical levels — wherever the best value lurks.

Continual rotation out of the overvalued and into the undervalued, whether strategic or tactical, will, over the long haul, create positive returns when adjusted for inflation.

Many investment advisors lump asset allocation into two broad assets: stocks and bonds. There are a few tools online to figure out the appropriate mix, but the traditional level was originally 60 percent stocks and 40 percent bonds. That's still touted today.

Another style involves taking the number 120, subtracting your age, and using the result as the percentage of your investment dollars in stocks, while investing the rest in bonds. The idea is to grab higher returns from stocks when younger, increasing bond exposure when older.

Of course, this simplistic measure doesn't take into account being long stocks during periods of overvaluation, nor the possibility of being heavily invested in bonds when the bubble bursts.

But any way you look at it, the concept of asset allocation as a totally solvable problem is a false one. It allocates 0 percent to a myriad of asset classes such as currencies, commodities, collectibles, real estate, "absolute return" products like managed futures, options, and shorting. It makes no difference between the short run and the long run.

For the average broker, though, this mix works well for many reasons:

First, it means you must periodically "rebalance" between stocks and bonds depending on how the portfolio has done, reevaluation of risk, and so on. This means commission dollars for the broker.

Within these two broad asset classes, a broker may advise breaking down further into other areas (value stocks vs. growth stocks, government bonds vs. corporate bonds, etc.). This provides even more opportunities for commission dollars!

Even with a low-cost brokerage, you still don't want to put the broker's children through college with fees, transactions, and so forth!

The best solution is twofold: follow Thoreau and simplify, simplify. The ten best investment ideas you identify will perform better than your thirty best investment ideas and still give you ample diversification.

Second, look for longer-term ideas that will play out over at least twelve to eighteen months so you're not tempted to do something crazy each month — and you'll get invested in the greatest asset of all.

When thinking about assets, we need to do two things: 1) gain real returns after taxes and inflation and 2) do so with a level of risk we're happy with. In investing, we can look at assets that can hold up well in inflation, like companies with a strong brand that can pass on all higher costs to consumers. The real trick is that neither future tax rates nor future inflation is known when making investment decisions. That's why the best asset class of all is *any* asset that maximizes *unrealized capital gains.*

It's where the world's three wealthiest individuals hold the bulk of their wealth — Carlos Slim in America Movil, Warren Buffett in Berkshire Hathaway, and Bill Gates in Microsoft. It's not the shares that they own, it's the gains they've had on them in the *decades* they've owned them that are so valuable!

That's also why your best bet is to maximize tax-deferred vehicles like 401(k)s and Roth IRAs (but don't forget to keep money elsewhere too). As long as shares are never cashed, the taxes are deferred *indefinitely.* Imagine doing that with income or property taxes!

Most importantly, the last thing you should do is be beholden to **someone else's idea of asset allocation and risk**. Only *you* know the best investment mix for your individual needs.

WRAP-UP

Lessons for Investors Embracing a More Rational Approach by Ignoring Finance Theory

- Traditional investment thinking starts, and in many cases ends, with the notion of a bell-curve distribution. Such thinking implies that about two-thirds of the time, the stock market should fluctuate around 1.5 percent every day.
- The data fits a bell curve poorly. Most years, the stock market returns 0–10 percent and exhibits a slightly upward bias. Why? Because markets are an amalgamation of businesses for sale, and changing information causes wild changes in the perception of the future value of those businesses.
- Many assumptions of modern portfolio theory do away with reality to make the theory "fit." Stocks are more volatile than statistics would have one believe. Correlations change constantly. We don't live in a world without taxes or transaction costs. Investors can influence asset prices.
- Efficient markets, should such a thing ever exist, would be riskier than an inefficient one. That's because inefficient markets generate opportunities to buy companies at a great discount to their true value.
- The market is your servant, not your master. By exercising patience, investors can buy when it's right for them. When is it right? When a stock is trading at a discount to its calculated intrinsic value.
- Asset allocation isn't as simple as the charts look. It's necessary to consider total expected return in both the short term and long term for a variety of asset classes, not just stocks, bonds, and cash.

3

Ain't Misbehavin'
Let the Herd Mentality Work for You

"But man is a free agent, and consequently fallible. He is subject to ignorance and to passion. His will, which is liable to err, enters as an element into the play of economic laws."

— *Frederic Bastiat*[9]

I F FINANCIAL THEORIES backed by mathematics don't perform as expected, it's because there's one wrench in the machinery of turning investing into a science. That wrench is human behavior.

Humans are impulsive, volatile, arrogant, and extreme. Unlike portfolio theory, it's difficult to sum up human behavior in a few different mathematical equations. Humans will bring chaos to order, and with it, increasing unpredictability. On its face, that sounds like a bad thing. It means more volatility, more extreme markets.

For rational investors, that's really an opportunity in disguise. Think about it: What, really, is a market? It's a sum of individual humans, each one bringing a different set of ideas, emotional sensitivity, and goals. That's what we're truly left with once we strip away the false assumptions of modern portfolio theory, and what a glorious thing it is!

So, really, as a rational investor, you should want markets to be irrational. It makes it easier for significant mispricing, which means more chances to sell overpriced assets, buy underpriced ones, and make substantial profits.

The concept of human will and emotion playing a role in the investing process is hardly a new one. Most successful investors at some point or another incorporate this kind of basic psychology, **whether they recognize it or not.**

- John Templeton often spoke of buying at the "point of maximum pessimism." Another version of this statement, attributed to a few different people, is "buy when there's blood in the streets."
- Peter Lynch proposed getting investment ideas from the mall, where a hot new store might make its stock a compelling buy.
- And, of course, Ben Graham asked readers to imagine a fictitious business partner, the bipolar Mr. Market. Some days, the depressed Mr. Market would sell you part of his stake in your business for far less than it was worth. Other days, he'd happily buy shares from you at exceptional premiums.

Human emotion plays a substantial role in investing, not only for the extreme optimism and pessimism of market prices, but, stepping back, fundamental miscalculations of individual stocks.

Psychologists have identified dozens of potential shortcomings in the human mind when it comes to decision making. Some are rooted deep in evolutionary past. Some are simply because we don't have the specialized knowledge to deal with them. The cause isn't relevant to us as investors, so instead let's dig a little deeper into the three most common psychological shortcomings that every rational investor should know of.

The Key Psychological Mistakes Everyone Makes

In the 1970s, psychologists Amos Tversky and Daniel Kahneman elaborated several heuristics (strategies developed based on prior, real-world experience, akin to a "rule of thumb") that individuals tend to use when making decisions using incomplete data.

Since investing involves both the certainty of prior events (such as historical earnings growth, dividend payouts, and the like) and the uncertainty of future events (effects of competition, a new product, or a marketing strategy), it's clear that you have to rely on some set of rules to predict future events.

Representativeness: Why We Underestimate Things

This "rule of thumb" means that we have the tendency to severely underestimate, not only the events themselves, but how they relate to other events.

When people are asked to calculate the odds that Event A belongs to Class B, probabilities are based by the degree to which A *resembles* B, not the overall picture. Tversky and Kahneman tested this concept with a simple problem:

> A cab was involved in an accident. Two cab companies, the Green and the Blue, operate in the city. Eighty-five percent of the cabs in the city are Green, and 15 percent are Blue.
>
> A witness identified the cab as Blue. The court tested the reliability of the witness under the same circumstances that existed on the night of the accident and concluded that the witness correctly identified each one of the two colors 80 percent of the time, but failed 20 percent of the time.
>
> What is the probability that the cab involved in the accident was Blue rather than Green knowing that this witness identified it as Blue?[10]

Go ahead and make your own guess. If only 15 percent of the cabs are Blue and the witness is right 80 percent of the time, then you might reason that the high probability of certainty combined with the low possibility of the occurrence makes this observation close to a "sure thing." But use some simple math and see what you can come up with.

You might multiply the 85 percent of cabs that aren't Blue by the 80 percent rate of the witness to reach 68 percent.

But surely that can't be right! The witness is 80 percent sure that it was a member of a very small class. Shouldn't it be *higher*?

Most who took the original study gave probabilities of over 50 percent that the cab involved was Blue. Some even gave probabilities over 80 percent (likely relying on the numbers of 85 percent and 80 percent in the original problem).

In reality, the odds that the cab identified as Blue really was Blue were only 41 percent.

Using a mathematical formula called Bayes' theorem, which takes into account the proper weighting of the variables, we can calculate the following:

- Eighty-five percent of the cabs are Green. The witness incorrectly identified the color 20 percent of the time. Eighty-five percent times 20 percent comes to 17 percent. That is the probability that the witness incorrectly identified a green cab as blue.
- Fifteen percent of cabs are blue. The witness identified the correct cab 80 percent of the time. Fifteen percent times 80 percent comes to 12 percent. That's the probability that the witness correctly identified the cab as Blue.
- Adding together the 12 percent and 17 percent, we get a 29 percent chance of the witness identifying the cab as Blue.
- Dividing the 12 percent chance of a correct identification into the 29 percent chance of correct identification, we arrive at our final answer. There's only a 41 percent chance that the cab identified by the witness as Blue is truly Blue.

Astounding, isn't it? What sounded like a sure thing — or something pretty close to a sure thing (the kind of opportunities that investors usually seem to face) turned out to be much less favorable than expected.

The implications go beyond making rational investment calculations. In the above case, let's assume a cab driver goes to trial for the hit-and-run.

Many studies show that jurors are *most* swayed by witness testimony, rather than subject-expert testimony or hard evidence. Jurors are hearing from a real person, oftentimes much like themselves. If the witness is believable, the jury can be swayed by the perception he gives off, rather than the precision of his statements.

As some of this occurs on the subconscious level, the same way people might judge someone they're meeting for the first time, jurors might never realize that they're allowing their emotions to compromise their judgment.

As any good lawyer will tell you (for a fat hourly fee), witness testimony is the most unreliable. Add in the ability of the average juror to perform math, and you've got a recipe for poor judgments . . . and even *worse* verdicts.

If you knew conclusively that the odds of someone being guilty were 41 percent, less than half, you'd have a shadow of a doubt and would vote to acquit. But what if the jurors did some rudimentary math and estimated an 80 percent chance? Would that really be enough to remove all doubt? After all, even with the 20 percent error rate in the courtroom, the witness was *sure* at the time.

(If you're interested in thinking these issues through, you might consider two Henry Fonda movies: *12 Angry Men*, the well-known classic about using simple logic to sway a jury, and Alfred Hitchcock's *The Wrong Man*, which is based on a true story and demonstrates the fallibility of eyewitnesses.)

Availability: Why Misleading Data Leads Us to Overestimate

The next rule of thumb is availability. This means when someone is asked to calculate the probability of an event, the "availability" of data that may or may not be relevant may skew the actual results.

For example, what animal is more dangerous: a shark, an alligator, or a deer?

If there's been news of a shark attacking a surfer in California or an alligator chasing after some retiree in Florida, most people quizzed by the local news would undoubtedly say that an alligator or a shark are the most dangerous. Deer don't make the news.

So which would you pick? If your inner contrarian went with deer, you're well on your way becoming a much better investor.

The odds of being killed by a shark or an alligator are appallingly low. Fewer than a hundred incidents from sharks and alligators are reported each year *combined*. But they're well-publicized. They make news headlines around the world.

Meanwhile, the National Highway Traffic Safety Administration estimates that deer kill 150 people each year. Beyond that, there are over 10,000 injuries and $1 billion in vehicle damage spread over 1.5 million car accidents. Most of these accidents, at best, make the local news.

Bottom line: Disney was wrong to make mankind the villain in the movie *Bambi*.

In short, while there may be data that's easy to find, we're more likely to remember and focus on something that instead appeals to our emotions. That's why a gruesome and deadly shark attack sticks in our mind as more dangerous than a frolicking deer in the woods.

Americans Made America Unsafe after 9/11

It's almost a cliché to say that most Americans *underestimated* the risks of a terrorist attack before 9/11. But, post-9/11, many Americans went too far in the other direction. Americans overestimated the risk of a terrorist attack, particularly on airlines. Even factoring in the 9/11 attacks themselves, air travel remains one of the safest modes of transportation yet devised.

Nevertheless, irrational behavior reigned. Air travel took a substantial hit, even as new safety features and security screening procedures came into practice to reduce the possibility of another 9/11-type attack on airlines.

With fewer travelers flying, more than one million Americans opted to hit the road instead in the 2001 holiday season. It should be no surprise that more motorists on the road offered more opportunities for horrific traffic accidents.

Michigan's Transportation Research Institute estimates that there were an additional 1,018 traffic fatalities nationwide as a result in the months immediately following the 9/11 attacks. Estimates range higher if you include the years it took for air travel to return to pre-9/11 levels, at perhaps 2,500–3,000 traffic fatalities.[11]

But, either way you look at it, almost as many Americans died from their changed behavior following 9/11 than the actual attacks themselves. This same type of behavior occurs in the markets every day, as investors significantly underestimate the risks they undertake.

Overestimating a Stock's Prospects: The Fast Path to Destitution

The investment world is riddled with the beaten-down stocks that were once high-flying "must-buy" Wall Street darlings. At some point, the huge growth rates just weren't sustainable, and the investors who made ridiculous assumptions about these stocks future prospects received the ridicule of a reduced share price.

It all starts out the same. A company with a hot product makes its IPO, the analysts are selling the moon, and the high valuation is backed by the company's prior growth numbers.

Of course, nothing grows to infinity. Most companies will never be the size of ExxonMobil or Walmart, especially if they operate in a narrow niche or only market to a small group.

This is especially true of stocks in "fad" products. Crocs (NASDAQ:CROX), maker of plastic footwear, saw its shares decline from over $66 to under $2. Specialty soda company Jones Soda

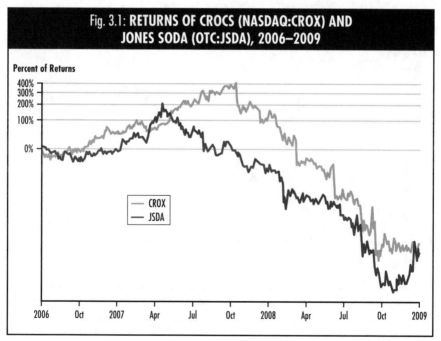

Fig. 3.1: **RETURNS OF CROCS (NASDAQ:CROX) AND JONES SODA (OTC:JSDA), 2006–2009**

Source: Standard and Poor's

Companies in a small niche will see their share prices obliterated when they hit the limits of their growth. Companies with a broader reach are apt to perform better.

(OTC:JSDA) suffered a similar fate around the same time, as we can see in Figure 3.1.

Availability isn't just limited to hubris and good news. Bad news can keep a lid on prices long enough for you to establish a big position and wait for the availability of bad news to eventually sweep away.

Declines Often Lead to Substantial Bounces

What are the odds of the market crashing after a sharp decline? In fact, not that good. When investors are shying away from stocks following a precipitous decline, cash balances increase. If asked, it's likely because of fears of further declines. That's the psychology of the market at work.

But the truth is: The bigger the decline, the better the chances of a substantial bounce. You just have to be ready for it.

Market professionals after the 1987 market crash stayed "cash heavy," despite the major correction. Mutual fund cash levels peaked

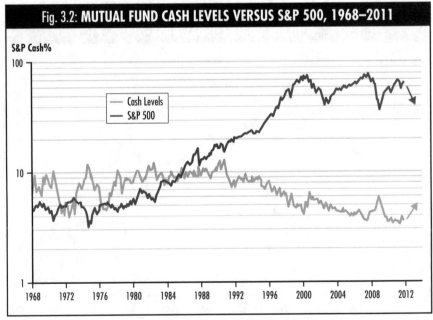

Fig. 3.2: MUTUAL FUND CASH LEVELS VERSUS S&P 500, 1968–2011

Source: Standard and Poor's

When mutual funds have a lot of cash lying around that can be put to work in the market, there is the potential for stocks to rally. When mutual funds are fully invested, there are few new potential buyers, so stocks have likely reached a short-term peak.

at over 11 percent, as they had before in 1981 and 1974 before that. That's a great indicator to look at the overall pricing of the market shown in Figure 3.2.

As you can see in Figure 3.2, when cash levels at mutual funds climb over 10 percent, it's a great time to get into the market. When mutual funds start putting cash to work, rallies begin.

When this process is starting out, however, there's a lot of bad news still scaring investors into cash. This high availability of bearish news doesn't take into account the historically high amounts of cash sitting around earning next to nothing. Eventually, that cash will have to be put to better use in the markets.

In the spring of 2009, even as the market bottomed, many were still predicting the end of the world. By the time phrases like "green shoots" got thrown around in midsummer, stocks were well into their bounce from oversold levels.

Of course, it goes the other way also. When there's a huge availability of good news in the markets, investors are willing to pay beyond any rational calculation of the underlying business, and chase high-flying stocks. When that happens, it's better for you to take the contrarian route and cash out.

Better opportunities will likely present themselves before too long. And if anything, most news in investing is typically just noise that serves to distract most investors from more important investment factors. Sometimes it's in short-term data like one company's specific earnings numbers. Other times, it's talking heads discussing why one asset that went up 5 percent today is in a bubble while another that went up 10 percent has plenty more "room to run."

It may be easier to remember the availability rule of thumb as akin to the "gambler's fallacy." When a gambler is tossing a coin and it comes up heads five times in a row, the gambler may think that this trend continues. Obviously, in a coin toss, each result has a 50 percent chance of coming up either heads or tails. Less obviously, each toss is a new event, *independent of prior results.*

In short, most available evidence and anecdotes amount to little more than rear-view mirror investing. You should be concerned with the future, not past performance.

In any prediction, where a seemingly relevant value exists (called the *anchor*), we make estimates based off this anchor when determining our answers. The anchor could either come from a preexisting assumption or could be formed in the question.

For example, you might ask someone, "Do you think the population of Canada is more or less than 25 million?" As a follow-up to this yes or no question, ask this person what they think the specific population is. Odds are, their answer is now "anchored" to whether it is more or less than twenty-five million. (For the record, it's around thirty-four million.)

In politics, anchoring is effectively used when it allows a participant to obtain more than what they wanted in the first place. If someone has a loaf of bread and you want two slices to make a sandwich, demand the whole loaf. When the counteroffer of half the loaf is made, you're up substantially from what you originally wanted. Best of all, the negotiator on the other side thinks a tremendous compromise has been reached.

In investing, where prices rapidly change, anchoring is unfortunately rampant. During the housing boom, inexperienced investors were constantly reassured that housing prices had consistently gone up over thirty years (coincidentally well-timed with the long-term decline in interest rates), that housing was less risky than investing in stocks, and that there had never been a nationwide recession in housing prices the past thirty years.

For anyone still not convinced, the worst-case scenario was that nobody would sell if prices weren't going up, so prices would simply stop rising for a bit while the market "caught up."

Anchoring also hinders investors clinging to a losing position. How often have you heard someone say, "Once that stock gets back to the price I bought it at, I'll sell. It's only a loss on paper until then."

Economics has a term for a prior decision that doesn't work out: a *sunk cost*. This is important for you to understand and heed this concept wisely, so you can review losing positions while hopefully keeping your emotions in check.

The real question you should ask in this position is: Would I buy this today? If not, it's time to sell and buy an investment that is worth owning at today's prices.

Where Human Emotion and the Rational Market Behavior Meet

Now that we've covered some of the big blind spots that irrationally influence most investor's decisions, we're ready to move past the decision and into the emotion once an actual trade is made.

The efficient market hypothesis assumes that *markets* are rational. There's no emotional involvement. Yet study after study shows that individual investors — who, in aggregate, *are* the market — have a very strong sense of loss aversion. They'll do anything to avoid feeling like they're losing money, from doubling down on bad bets to justifying a loss with other data somewhere else.

That's because people are "loss averse." Losing half your money in an investment makes most people feel *worse off* than the happiness they'd get from doubling their money in an investment.

Loss aversion is partly why so many investors underperform the market: When things get tough, they sell (at a loss). When things look good in the market (after a rally), they buy in. Loss aversion, ironically, leads to *greater* losses than investing with a bemused detachment to the short-term gyrations of the market.

It's a well-researched area, but it's difficult for anyone employing mathematical financial models to use. Why? Because this kind of valuation is subjective to each individual. One investor might feel the need to make a $5 gain to offset a $1 loss. Another might be fine losing $1 or $2 with equal possibility of gains. It's why some people are flashy high rollers, some people play the penny slot machines, and some people don't even gamble.

In other words, the utility of gains and losses is defined by the individual. In order to calculate it, we'd need to know how an individual would respond *in that very moment*. And we'd need to recognize that individual views on gains and losses can vary depending on what is being gained or lost.

Those without a substantial background in the history of markets and the mathematical likelihood of returns will likely be overconfident in their assessments (as will those who don't have that background but think they do). While this may remain undiscovered as long as prices keep going up, it can lead to huge problems when things don't work out.

This oscillation between fear and greed can also be thought of in terms of confidence. No matter the term that's used, however, it isn't just limited to investing.

Overconfidence in the Markets Costs Money, Overconfidence Elsewhere Costs Lives

Investing isn't rocket science, or at least it shouldn't be. But overconfidence has led to disastrous results in both.

Consider the tragic destruction of the space shuttle *Challenger* in 1987. Management at NASA predicted the probability of the launch failure at one in one hundred thousand (a 0.001 percent chance). If those odds were true, then there could have been a space shuttle launch *every day* for almost 274 *years* with only *one* explosion.[12]

By comparison, this made the space shuttle sound safer than *flying*. A compilation of Federal Aviation Administration (FAA) data at www.planecrashinfo.com suggests that someone making an average of one round-trip flight per year has lifetime odds of about one in sixty-six thousand of dying in a plane crash.[13]

That should have been a red flag to the members of the commission, but most didn't have the background to challenge the assumption. Most members of the congressional task force appointed to find out what went wrong were swayed by these statistics and reassurances that it was a freak event.

But physicist Richard Feynman disagreed. In the final report to Congress, Feynman's conclusions were relegated to a ten-page footnote labeled "Appendix F." That's unfortunate, because Feynman's conclusions noted the hubris that went into undertested technology.

NASA's top-down approach to building the space shuttles meant that minor problems throughout often went undiscovered for longer and multiplied due to the vast number of pieces that went into the construction of the shuttle. From Bayes' theorem, we know that the more working pieces there are that go into an estimate, the greater the chances that any estimate will end up being incorrect.

Feynman predicted that the true chances of failure were much higher, closer to one in one hundred or 1 percent. Even taking into account early rocket tests that failed to "get the kinks out" of this new technology, it was clear that management at NASA was substantially overstating the safety of the space shuttle program.

By interviewing NASA engineers, Feynman found from their estimates that the true odds of a *Challenger*-type disaster were closer to one hundred to one, as he himself had predicted. As Feynman concludes in his contribution to the commission:

> Official management . . . claims to believe the probability of failure is a thousand times less. One reason for this may be an attempt to assure the government of NASA perfection and success in order to ensure the supply of funds. The other may be that they sincerely believed it to be true, demonstrating an almost incredible lack of communication between themselves and their working engineers.
>
> Let us make recommendations to ensure that NASA officials deal in a world of reality in understanding technological weaknesses and imperfections well enough to be actively trying to eliminate them. They must live in reality in comparing the costs and utility of the Shuttle to other methods of entering space.[14]

Not all of the kinks in the shuttle program were worked out. Sadly, on February 1, 2003, the space shuttle *Columbia* suffered the same fate as the *Challenger*.

In investing, overconfidence acts as leverage to greed. That's lead to wealth-destroying mistakes. In other human endeavors, it costs lives, in markets, just your money. But if it's so difficult, does that mean we simply trust our money with experts? That's what the fund industry would have you believe.

But make no mistake: The so-called experts, even those in high places, are just as fallible. And when they mess up, it's even worse.

The Blind Leading the Blind: Even the "Experts" Running Things Get It Wrong

> When good news about the market hits the front page of The New York Times, sell.
> — *Bernard Baruch*

Even those who *do* have a substantial background in historical market performance and the mathematics behind returns can often get it wrong.

Commenting on the cooling housing market in 2006 at an event in Canada, Alan Greenspan said, "I suspect that we are coming to the end of this downtrend, as applications for new mortgages, the most important series, have flattened out . . . There is a good chance of coming out of this in good shape, but average housing prices are likely to be down this year relative to 2005. I don't know, but I think the worst of this may well be over."[15]

Greenspan was right . . . for about a year. Then the bubble in housing finally burst.

Now, we shouldn't blame someone just for sitting in the "hot seat" of Fed chairman. So instead, let's look at a 2005 CNBC interview with the then-chairman of the president's Council of Economic Advisors.

Don't worry; he's a household name too: Ben Bernanke.

> *CNBC:* Ben, there's been a lot of talk about a housing bubble, particularly, you know from all sorts of places. Can you give us your view as to whether or not there is a housing bubble out there?
>
> *BERNANKE:* Well, unquestionably, housing prices are up quite a bit; *I think it's important to note that fundamentals are also very strong.* We've got a growing economy, jobs, income. We've got very low mortgage rates. We've got demographics supporting housing growth. We've got restricted supply in some places. So it's certainly understandable that prices would go up some. I don't know whether prices are exactly where they should be, but I think it's fair to say that much of what's happened is supported by the strength of the economy.
>
> *CNBC:* Tell me, what is the worst-case scenario? We have so many economists coming on our air saying 'Oh, this is a bubble, and it's going to burst, and this is going to be a real issue for the economy.' Some say it could even cause a recession at some point. What is the worst-case scenario if in fact we were to see prices come down substantially across the country?

> *BERNANKE:* Well, I guess I don't buy your premise. It's a pretty unlikely possibility. ***We've never had a decline in housing prices on a nationwide basis.*** So, what I think what is more likely is that house prices will slow, maybe stabilize, might slow consumption spending a bit. I don't think it's gonna drive the economy too far from its full employment path, though.[16]

Here we see several of those psychological factors discussed earlier come into play. While noting that housing prices have been exceptionally strong, tying them to other economic fundamentals represents the folly of *representativeness*.

In retrospect, we might be able to give some kind of weighting to various factors that contributed to rising home prices in the past decade. We could then arrive at a very small percentage outcome that housing prices were fairly representative of all those factors.

Instead, we'd probably find housing prices were rising at such a clip that, to use those misleading bell curves, they were several standard deviations outside the norm and thus were highly susceptible to decline in value.

Secondly, when Bernanke states that there was never a nationwide decline in housing prices, he was *anchoring* himself to old data. Just like predicting the chances of a devastating terrorist attack in New York City on September 10, 2001. Such an event was well outside the mental zone of nearly everyone before it happened.

To paraphrase the concluding line of Feynman's report on the space shuttle and apply it to the need to incorporate behavioral finance when making investment decisions: "For a successful investment strategy, reality must take precedence over the public's opinion, for economic reality cannot long be fooled."

WRAP-UP
Understanding of the Herd Is the Beginning of Investment Wisdom

- Human behavior is the proverbial monkey wrench in the supposedly orderly system of financial markets.
- While that sounds like a bad thing, it's really a good thing for investors. It makes it easier to find incredible bargains to buy and overpriced stocks to sell.

- Representativeness overstates the chances of a favorable outcome. In terms of investing, it ensures that investors become overconfident more easily.
- Availability skews data based on information that's readily available. In today's information-saturated world, if you're willing to dig deeper and find more obscure data, you can get a better picture for what's really going on. Knowledgeable investors know that deer are more dangerous than sharks.
- Anchoring and adjustment ensure that stubborn human will compromise the returns of investors.
- Between emotion and the false sense of optimism driven by key heuristics, even the so-called experts get it wrong. As an investor, don't be afraid to go against the crowd.

4

NonEconomic Forces
Also Distort the Market

———

“And from personal experience, let me just say this:
Wage and price controls are bad for business, bad for
the working man, and bad for the consumer. Rationing,
black markets, regimentation — that is the wrong road for
America, and I will not take the Nation down that road.**”**
— *Richard Nixon, Oct. 17, 1969*[17]

I MAGINE YOU'RE PLAYING A GAME of football with some friends. Halfway through, some of your friends decide they want to play baseball
instead. Ten minutes later, they start incorporating rules from rugby.
When you do something that they don't like, they instantly disagree with
you and change the rules to turn your legal move into an illegal one.

That's how government policies continually affect the market.

In fact, arbitrary government "game changers" can be the biggest
source of chaos in the markets. That's because some benefit from government largesse, while others are hit with crippling legislation that
impedes their ability to compete globally.

We've already seen the role of central bankers and some of the political decisions that exacerbated the housing crisis, but there are a myriad
of other things the government can (and probably will) do to enhance,
rather than abate, uncertainty, thus bringing out chaos in the process.

The first thing the government does is commit psychological war-
fare against its citizens. It uses the tools and resources at its disposal to
advance its own agenda. I call this "perception management."

What do I mean? It's simple.

We all know the old saying "perception is reality." Government takes this as its mantra. Really, we all do, as we touched on in Chapter 3 with regard to our human psychological shortcomings that can taint our investment decisions.

But government takes it to an art form.

In 2011, we saw how rapidly perception — and reality — changed in markets on a daily basis. That's especially true of European markets, where Greece teetered on the brink of defaulting on its debts for the third time in eighteen months.

Politicians and bankers proudly called their solution to the Greek crisis a "haircut" in 2011. Sounds like a nice term, at least compared to what it really is — a default.

Language is precise, and substituting different words makes a vast difference to change perception. Government reports and interviews with the complacent media are full of such terms.

Greece's "haircut" was a staggering 50 percent. Imagine putting a substantial amount of your wealth in US bonds, only to wake up one morning and find the value knocked in half. You wouldn't call that a haircut, you'd call that an outrage. A travesty.

This is the third time Europe has had to deal with Greece. Even with a 50 percent haircut, it won't be the last. Despite the announcement of austerity measures, Greece still won't bring in enough revenues to make full payments on its debts.

This is just yet another so-called solution that partially involves extending and pretending. Beware Greeks bearing bonds.

And beware government pronouncements about the economy.

While the job market looks to be on its way to a healthy recovery in the early part of 2012, the unemployment rate hasn't come down because of a surge of new job creation in the private sector. Even government job growth has flattened out.

Rather, the unemployment rate has improved because the Bureau of Labor Statistics has removed millions of long-term unemployed from their official numbers. Sure, during a prolonged recession some employees are simply going to exhaust their benefits. But to assume that they're no longer looking? That somehow they can simply disappear from government statistics? How bizarre.

A piece of data called the "labor force participation rate" tells the true story about how American workers are disappearing from the job market — but you won't find that data anywhere near a market-moving headline talking about the latest drop in unemployment.

Everyone has an agenda, and with the largest resources, it's easy for government's perception to define reality.

At least, until things go wrong. What happens when things do go wrong? That's the next problem that governments impose on the market.

Perpetual Motion Machine: How Governments Expand Thanks to Crises of Their Own Creation

Throughout 2011, Fed chairman Ben Bernanke described rising rates of inflation as "transitory."

What a fun word.

Words like "temporary" and "transitory" are merely government-speak for *permanent*. Beyond the language, we run into a real problem. A temporary crisis often ends with permanent government regulation and oversight, allegedly to keep it from occurring again.

Consider this: In 1898, the naval cruiser *USS Maine* sank in Havana harbor. Whether the ship was destroyed due to a spontaneous combustion in its coal bunker or as the result of a passive mine, America went to war with Spain.

At the time, Congress was in a bind to raise money. These were the days after the Civil War era income tax had been declared unconstitutional, and raising tariffs would hurt economic growth (shocking as it seems today, we used to be an export-driven nation).

A new tax was needed to balance the budget resulting from the breakout of war with the Spanish Empire. So Congress started to tax telephones, a budding new technology that only the wealthiest in the United States could afford.

Thus the federal telephone excise tax, affectionately known as the Telephone Tax, was born.

This so-called "temporary" measure didn't die after the four-month conflict with Spain ended. It wasn't repealed until 1902. But it inevitably came back.

The tax first came back to help fund World War I and was reinstated later to combat deficit spending during the Depression. In fact, it was reinstated as part of the Revenue Bill of 1932. Then it was simply reauthorized twenty-nine times.

The telephone tax met a *partial* repeal in 2006.

But there's a bigger picture than what Congress should spend its time debating. In a perfect world, it'd be a part-time job, so they could spend some time as productive members of society.

The original tax was 1 cent for a 15-cent minimum telephone call. That's a tax rate of 7 percent. It decreased as the cost of the phone call rises. It's only a 1 percent tax when the call costs $1.00.

But, like any "temporary" government measure, the only thing that was temporary about it was the low starting rate.

Back when the tax was partially repealed in 2006 (mostly on long-distance calls), the burden had drastically increased. "This is a good first step in alleviating consumers' telephone tax burden, which currently accounts for more than 18 percent of the average bill," stated Verizon Vice President Tom Tauke at the time.[18]

In fact, the excise tax on local calls still stands. But it's not one cent; it's a 3-percent burden. Today, this form of the telephone tax brings in over $5 billion dollars. Some temporary measure! No wonder millions have ditched their phones for better technologies like email or Skype.

Don't even get me started about other "temporary" measures such as Social Security and food stamps. It reminds me of one of Ronald Reagan's better quips, "Government programs, once launched, never disappear. Actually, a government bureau is the nearest thing to eternal life we'll ever see on this earth!"

Governments sell temporary measures to fix a problem. Those measures rarely go away. Neither do the problems. It is a dangerous, slippery slope where new regulatory changes can adversely affect investors at any time.

Rational Self-Interest of Government Employees: The One Reason Why There Will Always Be Another Crisis

Here's a bit of career advice: Don't be a whistleblower. It's a thankless job, with few rewards.

Just ask Harry Markopolos, a financial analyst and forensic accountant. He spent nearly ten years providing documentation to the Securities and Exchange Commission (SEC) that Bernie Madoff was running a Ponzi scheme. What did he get for his troubles? A pat on the back, having to testify before Congress, and a book deal.

Why was the SEC so lax on Madoff? There were other indications, although none were as thorough as the ones prepared by Markopolos. Isn't the purpose of the SEC to protect investors and enforce the rule of law?

When government agencies fail in their duty to regulate an industry because of bureaucratic ineptitude or a cozy relationship, we get regulatory capture. In some cases, it gets so bad that government employees who try to do their job (or blow the whistle on those failing to do theirs) end up being fired and blacklisted.

That was the case of Gary Aguirre, who was wrongfully terminated for trying to investigate *possible* insider trading charges. It took four years of legal battles, but in the end Aguirre got a wrongful termination settlement of $755,000. It certainly didn't hurt that the allegations proved true.

Unfortunately, this problem isn't just limited to the financial industry.

The Mineral Management Service (MMS) allowed dozens of companies to drill in the Gulf of Mexico without first getting environmental impact statements as required by law. MMS reports on offshore drilling highlighted the benefits of offshore drilling and downplayed the rising number of spills. [19]Were it not for BP's *Deepwater Horizon* spill, we'd still be in the dark to some of MMS's practices.

In Japan, the Nuclear and Industrial Safety Agency approved extensions without significant review. In 2006, the agency relaxed standards that allowed plant operators to perform their own inspections. One month before an earthquake and tsunami ravaged the country in 2011, this agency approved a ten-year extension on the oldest reactors at the Fukushima plant.[20]

Whatever form the next crisis takes, regulatory capture will play a substantial role. So long as regulatory agencies can ignore the law in exchange for smooth relations and perks from the industry they're supposed to regulate, we're in a dangerous position.

Clearly, we don't need more laws and regulations. If we simply enforced existing laws, we'd probably find we could do away with a lot of regulation. Getting rid of excessive regulation and compromised regulators would do wonders to get America's economy back on track. Letting bad institutions fail instead of receiving bailouts would help reduce systemic risk. Reward individuals for having the moral courage to come forward, rather than penalize them.

Until we do, there will *always* be another crisis brewing. It won't always be financial, and it won't always be predictable. This means investors should always be on their toes and pay attention to what a regulator is saying about the companies they regulate. If they don't seem to care much at all, beware.

Government Policies Lessen the Effects of Demographic Destinies

Remember when Japan was buying everything in sight in the 1980s? Many thought that their economy would overtake America's by the end of the century. But those fears never materialized. Japan crashed, and the country is arguably starting a *third* "lost decade."

Why? Because of one nonfinancial trend that has a huge impact on long-term investments. I'm talking about demographics. Japan's reversion to slow growth can be attributed to an aged population.

According to the Central Intelligence Agency's (CIA) *World Factbook*, the median age in Japan is 44.6 years, while in the United States it's 36.8 years. The retired segment of Japan's population makes up a larger percentage than it does in the United States (at least for now). Only Mexico has an older median age.[21]

China and Japan have a lot of differences, but the demographics in the Middle Kingdom suggest that China's rapid growth must decline. Things may appear to be going full speed ahead, but China faces a tremendous crisis in the decades to come.

That crisis stems partially from China's infamous one-child policy. It's led from a fertility rate of 6.1 in 1955 to 1.8 in 2010. Essentially, the average female has gone from producing six children to around two on average. Ironically, as China becomes wealthier, more women there are viewing reproduction as an impediment to affluence.

Understanding a country's demographic trends adds other compelling criteria to look for in any investment. Following the baby boomers in the United States, for example, one might have invested in Kimberly Clark for diapers in the 1940s, Mattel and McDonald's in the 1950s, financial services in the 1980s, and health care and real estate investment trusts (REITs) today.

China continues to build the infrastructure of the first-world country that it aspires to. There are plenty of investment opportunities there that have nothing to do with demographics.

World population reached seven billion in 2011. Longer-term projections indicate that this growth is starting to lose its legs. Within a century, global population may actually end up lower than it is today.

Identifying demographic trends and changes to those trends can provide a simple way to screen for companies to own for long-term investment success. We'll touch on that point in later chapters.

A Modest Defense of Capitalism

Government interventions, in whatever form they take, contribute significantly to economic woes. So, then, if that's part of the problem, we should take the opposite tack and look for the solution.

It's none other than capitalism.

To me, there's nobody more admirable than a successful businessman. These are the people who have a vision and execute it. They create jobs, opportunity, and economic growth along the way. They risk their personal capital. They help give people, not only work, but purpose in their lives. In a way, the work they do is *more* important than charity, because it's *only* out of the excess of success that charity becomes possible.

It's not just charity, either. Without someone, somewhere, doing productive work and paying a part of their excess as taxes, you couldn't have generous government programs either.

But there's another, more important reason. It's because businesses are often labeled as evil, even though they've been one of the great bringers of peace on earth.

This is already demonstrated in the McDonald's Theory of Conflict Prevention. It's the simple observation that no two nations, once they each have a set of golden arches, have ever gone to war with each other. (Let's hope it continues.)

That's the power of capitalism. Buying the world a Coke won't bring peace on earth, but thinking up ways to better the lives of your fellow man while making a living in the process just might. When people focus on growing the economic pie, they're less focused on finding militant ways to grab the largest slice of a smaller pie.

But it doesn't stop there.

Businesses today succeed amidst the angry curses of various constituents who demand their heads (and annual bonuses) on a pike.

They do it in willful opposition to a government that condescendingly forced health-care regulations on them, not to mention other onerous regulations, fees, and taxes.

They do it in spite of a media that portrays businessmen as villains, even though Hollywood accounting practices make it possible for billion-dollar–grossing *Harry Potter* movies to be a *loss*.[22]

They do it in the face of laws of supply and demand and an ever-changing environment where there's no "sure thing."

Or, perhaps, they do it *because* of all these assaults on business and capitalism. Or they live for the challenge. Because they're on Earth to build something for themselves, for their community and for the future of mankind. It's that pioneering spirit that made America great. We need more of that today.

That's why the average businessman deserves your gratitude. After all, no matter where the economy goes, the simplest way to beat inflation over the long run is to invest alongside business by owning stocks.

Without the risk-takers of capitalism, you'd have to raise your own livestock and grow your own produce and sew your own clothes. And as for time with the family, there'd be plenty of time for that during a long day plowing fields and growing crops.

Business isn't the bad guy. Success simply breeds jealousy. Hatred of capitalism is just a red herring. Unfortunately, it's a popular scapegoat for the government when one of its plans goes awry.

WRAP-UP
Lessons of Government Intervention

- Government intervention can take many forms. Like a spoiled child, it can often change the "rules of the game" in the middle of play, much to the dismay of everyone else.
- Government has a powerful influence on the media, and the much vaunted "fourth estate" has given government a free ride to redefine words as it sees fit to shape and modify public opinion.
- Regulators, the creation of government legislation, have a far too cozy relationship with the industry they're supposed to be regulating. Until regulators and businesses start treating each other like the loyal opposition and there isn't a revolving door of jobs between the regulators and business, there won't be any credibility to the idea that government regulations are designed to protect the public.
- Policies enacted by government always have an economic impact. Some, like demographic changes resulting from China's one-child policy, will take generations to unfold and impact society.
- As an investor, there are ways to take advantage of these distorted markets in the years to come.

Government intervention is the chief source of uncertainty in the market. It makes the role of the businessman exponentially more difficult. But the capitalists are the true heroes of society. They create jobs, make wealth possible, and make the world a more peaceful place. This stands in stark contrast to government's record of wars, currency debasements, fear, uncertainty, and doubt. Government isn't your meal ticket; capitalists are . . . they'll just make you work for it.

5

The Forest
Thinking Globally

"In economics, the majority is always wrong."
— *John Kenneth Galbraith*

I T'S A CLASSIC JOKE: A man is driving on the freeway when his cell phone rings. He picks it up and his wife speaks frantically: "Honey, they just said on the news that there's a maniac driving the wrong way on the freeway!"

The man replies, "It's not just one car. It's all of 'em!"

The humor, of course, comes from the man's erroneous perspective. (If he were investing, we'd cheer him for going against the herd!)

As an investor, you need perspective on the overall global economic picture. Ideally, individual companies that can take advantage of these trends and are favorably priced should allow you to maximize profit potential while minimizing the risk of a permanent loss.

It wouldn't do much good to buy a cash-flowing piece of real estate before the crash sent prices lower. It wouldn't do much good to buy an undervalued stock while the market is sending signals of an imminent crash. If you did, you could open yourself up to potential losses outside your control. In terms of risk, it's like driving the wrong way on the freeway.

Combine this "big picture" perspective with undervalued individual investments, and you've got a recipe to step in when many investors are still in panic and rushing toward the exit. Sticking to one over another passes up opportunities.

There are hundreds of pieces of data that can fall in the category of macroeconomics, the study of the economy's overall "big picture." But a handful can easily and quickly provide compelling, proven clues for investors as to where they should allocate their investments.

Looking at the top ten indicators may be a bit much, so I've pared the list down to seven key areas that give you the best clues about the future of the global economy. It's not essential to memorize these. It's just important to get some clarity on what information moves markets.

Gross Domestic Product (GDP)

Gross domestic product is a snapshot of a country's economic size. That's great for seeing how countries measure up against each other

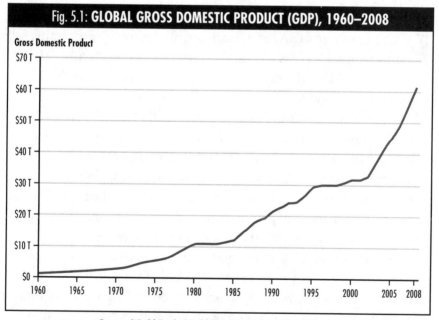

Fig. 5.1: GLOBAL GROSS DOMESTIC PRODUCT (GDP), 1960–2008

Source: World Bank, World Development Indicators | Last updated October 1, 2010

World growth has rapidly accelerated since the end of the Cold War and the triumph of capitalism over state-run economies.

globally, but the true value in tracking GDP is how it changes over time and in finding out which countries are growing the fastest.

GDP growth is the measure used to determine how well a country is performing economically. If growth is flat or falls for two consecutive quarters, that country's economy falls into a recession. That's why GDP numbers are scrutinized by Wall Street traders, even though it's such a broad, sweeping piece of data.

Figure 5.1 shows that global GDP has surged since the early 1990s, following the collapse of the Soviet Union and the promarket reforms undertaken in countries like India and China.

For many Americans, the rise of China and India is a mixed blessing. These countries offer substantially lower labor costs, driving down prices on manufactured goods. But it also means a transfer of

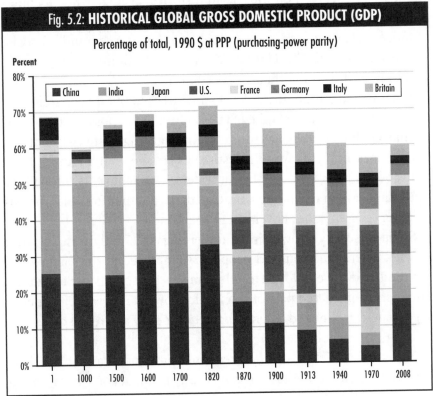

Fig. 5.2: **HISTORICAL GLOBAL GROSS DOMESTIC PRODUCT (GDP)**

Percentage of total, 1990 $ at PPP (purchasing-power parity)

Sources: Angus Maddison, University of Groningen; The Economist

Prior to the industrial revolution, India and China have dominated global GDP. Looking over the past two thousand years, Europe and the United States are the real emerging markets.

manufacturing and service jobs to countries with lower employee pay, health-care costs, and labor rights.

Ultimately, free trade is a blessing, despite short-term challenges. As countries like China and India take over call centers and computer manufacturing plants, American innovation is needed now more than ever.

That's because, historically, China and India have dominated global GDP. It's only as these countries abandoned free-market principles and rejected the opportunity for global trade that their economies stagnated while the rest of the world caught up and surpassed them.

Just take a look at Figure 5.2.

Based on this data, it's clear that investors will want to overweight India, and to a lesser extent, China over the next few *decades*. Both countries are below their long-term historical average when it comes to their share of global GDP.

Indeed, we may even want to look at the past few hundred years, where Europe and the United States came to dominate the global economy, as little more than an aberration!

What will the future look like? Estimates vary, but it's apparent that China will overtake the United States before India, possibly by 2050 if China's GDP continues to grow at high-single digit rates without any major snags along the way. The estimates are shown in Figure 5.3.

In today's turbulent investment waters, GDP comes with one *very* important caveat: It can be manipulated. Part of the "formula" for calculating GDP includes government spending.

So, if a country's government undertakes a $5 billion make-work project, where ten thousand people are employed to dig ditches and ten thousand are employed to fill them in, this activity, which zeroes out, is still considered part of economic growth! This wasteful spending is magically defined as a net benefit to society as a result of current calculation methods.

Nevertheless, GDP is still a "headline" piece of data that can drive short-term market moves. This can have a big impact on trades, investments, and the like. More importantly, longer-term trends in GDP will be one of the first areas professional investors look at to determine if the economy is growing, or if we're shifting into a recession.

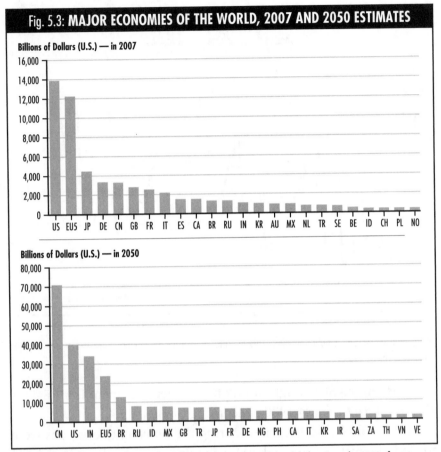

Fig. 5.3: MAJOR ECONOMIES OF THE WORLD, 2007 AND 2050 ESTIMATES

Billions of Dollars (U.S.) — in 2007

Billions of Dollars (U.S.) — in 2050

China and India will be vying with the United States for the top spot in the global economy by 2050, if not sooner.

Employment

Is the economy growing? Are we creating new jobs? Are workers who get laid off in an old industry finding productive employment in a new industry in a short amount of time?

The answers to these questions help define how healthy the economy is.

Employment growth is a sign of a healthy economy. Rising unemployment shows that our economy is in trouble. This is a lagging indicator, meaning that the data presented lags the general economy. The economy as a whole may start turning around before employment picks up. In the same way, the economy may start turning down before the pink slips start appearing on employees' desks.

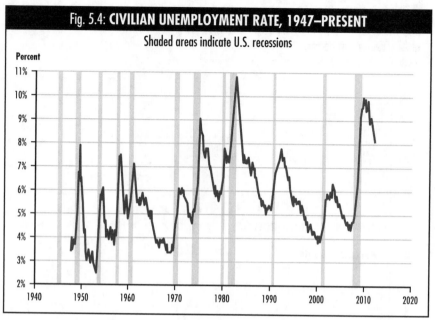

Fig. 5.4: CIVILIAN UNEMPLOYMENT RATE, 1947–PRESENT

Shaded areas indicate U.S. recessions

Source: U.S. Department of Labor: Bureau of Labor Statistics | 2012 research.stlouisfed.org

Unemployment remains stubbornly high. This indicates that economic opportunities are scarce and the economy is still fragile.

In the United States right now, official unemployment is as high as it's been since the early 1980s, according to Figure 5.4.

That should be no surprise. During the housing boom, jobs were created in construction, real estate, lending, and the like. Completed homes and buildings were occupied by renters and tenants, creating huge growth sprawls in the deserts of California and Arizona, as well as the coast of Florida.

But this graph is a bit misleading. That's because the calculations used to determine unemployment data have changed over the years. Using methods that were common only twenty-five years ago, unemployment in the United States today would be a shocking 20 percent!

How badly are the statistics manipulated? That's tough to tell, because you can't see exactly how these numbers have changed like in the Consumer Price Index (CPI) (see below).

But one key measure is the "birth/death" adjustment rate. This adjustment takes into account the unemployment rate when adjusted for changes in the population.

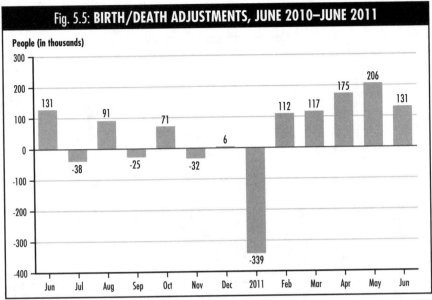

Fig. 5.5: BIRTH/DEATH ADJUSTMENTS, JUNE 2010–JUNE 2011

People (in thousands)

Source: BLS

Fifty-two percent of all jobs created between the middle of 2010 and 2011 weren't actual jobs—just adjustments to Bureau of Labor Statistics calculations. This means the job market is worse for a real person seeking employment.

Or at least it should. Between the middle of 2010 and the middle of 2011, this adjustment was responsible for listing 606,000 jobs that wouldn't have existed otherwise. That's 52 percent of all jobs created during this period.

And that's on top of so-called "seasonal adjustments" that are also made every year that seem to magically create jobs and keep a lid on the unemployment rate.

There's another way to use employment data to determine the health of the economy: the duration of unemployment. There will always be some jobless in any economy, but in an expanding economy, the duration of unemployment should decline as workers find new jobs more quickly.

Judging by the current duration of unemployment, it's clear that high unemployment rates are here for some time. Figure 5.6 shows they're at historic highs, pushing forty weeks (almost ten months)!

What's worse, since this data was first collected in the 1940s, a post-recession bump in duration has tended to increase over time. Some of

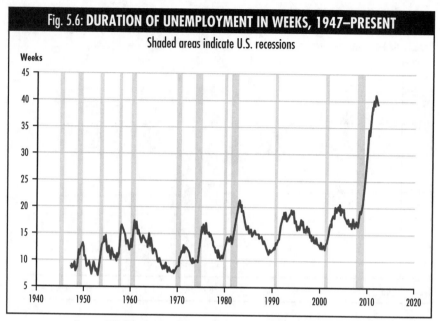

Fig. 5.6: **DURATION OF UNEMPLOYMENT IN WEEKS, 1947–PRESENT**

Shaded areas indicate U.S. recessions

Source: U.S. Department of Labor: Bureau of Labor Statistics | 2012 research.stlouisfed.org

Not only are jobs scarce, but workers are facing longer periods of unemployment between jobs. This is partly because of the job market and partly due to obsolete job skills.

that can be explained by an increase in the need for new worker training due to our shift from labor-oriented jobs to service-oriented and high-tech jobs. In the 1990s, America hemorrhaged factory jobs but created higher-paying white collar jobs in areas of information technology.

It's clear that the current rate of unemployment duration is well above any semblance of normalcy.

What does that mean? Well, jobs matter. So until this rate starts declining rapidly, an employment-based view of the economy will suggest tough times for the next several years.

Finally, let's look at t he absolute total number of workers in Figure 5.7.

While the long-term trend is up, the massive decline in jobs during the prior recession has created a flat decade for job growth. Compared to the slight dips or even flat-lining number of employed during prior recessions, this latest trend doesn't bode well for job seekers in the next few years.

Over the long term, we would expect this overall number of employees to rise along with the overall population. So, adjusted for

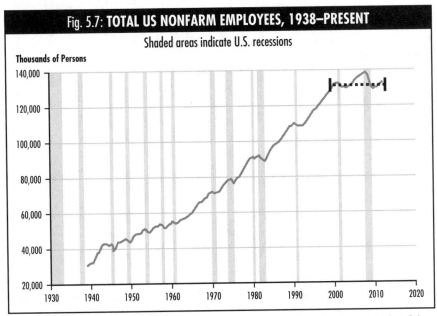

Fig. 5.7: TOTAL US NONFARM EMPLOYEES, 1938–PRESENT

Shaded areas indicate U.S. recessions

Source: U.S. Department of Labor: Bureau of Labor Statistics | 2012 research.stlouisfed.org

Looking over the long term, job growth has been flat over the past decade.

population growth in the past decade, we're far behind where we need to be in job creation to expand and grow the economy.

It's also worth noting here that the government started collecting this data in 1939, right as peak unemployment during the Great Depression started to wane. This starts the baseline data at a historical low point.

Consumer Price Index (CPI)

As we discussed in Chapter 1, a dollar doesn't go as far as it used to. While we looked at the growth of money supply, another way to look at purchasing power is with the consumer price index. This index is especially important because it's used to determine the official rate of inflation, as well as cost of living adjustments for government programs like Social Security.

Not surprisingly, this has perpetually been rising since this data was first tracked. But take a look at Figure 5.8.

Between 1970 and 1980, the CPI started to rise at a faster and faster rate. Then it started slowing in 1980. Arguably, the hard money

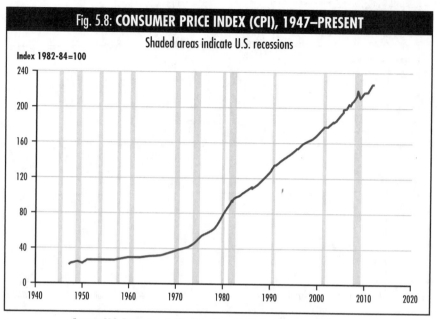

Fig. 5.8: **CONSUMER PRICE INDEX (CPI), 1947–PRESENT**

Shaded areas indicate U.S. recessions

Source: U.S. Department of Labor: Bureau of Labor Statistics | 2012 research.stlouisfed.org

The rate of inflation, as measured by the consumer price index, has been rising at an accelerating rate.

policies of then-Fed Chairman Paul Volcker raising interest rates to 20 percent in June 1981 helped to nip inflation in the bud.

But there's another story.

In short, when times get tough, CPI components get changed in a way that makes inflation appear lower than it truly is. When steak got expensive and drove up the price of food in the CPI, it was replaced with lower-priced chicken.

Because inflation appeared low, investors made decisions that gave more weight to fixed-income investments, leading to a thirty-year bond market rally. Yes, stocks rose too, aided by low valuations in the 1980s before the tech bubble popped and stocks peaked in real, inflation-adjusted terms in 2000–2001.

The biggest component of the CPI today is in housing. Using what's called owner-equivalent rent (OER), it's essentially a measure of housing as though a homeowner were simply renting their home rather than owning. The problem with this measure is that it understated housing costs, as measured by the Case-Shiller Home Price Index. While home prices rose an average of

15 percent per year between 2000 and 2005, OER rose an average of less than 5 percent.

While the CPI is a good "mainstream" metric to view the economy, be aware of its hidden dangers that understate inflation. Investors should look at the decades of changes in the CPI for what they are: a way to make inflation appear benign. The solution to this problem is to put more assets into investment that have a history of outperforming inflation.

An Inverted Yield Curve: The World's Premiere Recession Indicator

Inverted yield curves are one of the best leading indicators for a slowdown ahead. When the yield curve "flips" from normal to inverted, investors have anywhere from a few months to a few years to get out of markets.

Six of the past seven times, a yield curve has preceded a recession. That's an 85 percent successful track record, and a very easy-to-understand indicator to get out of markets.

The seventh case is often touted as the reason why the inverted yield curve is an inaccurate indicator. But really, it's a special exception.

That's because this inversion occurred in 1998, when a highly leveraged fund, Long-Term Capital Management, went belly-up. It took a massive, Fed-orchestrated bailout by all the major financial firms at the time to avoid systemic risk that *would* have thrown the economy into a recession.

Combined with the Asian currency crisis later that year, and it's clear that at least part of the world had huge setbacks in growth. In the United States, growth slowed, but the Fed's reduction of interest rates by 75 basis points (0.75 percent) kept the economy from "officially" entering a recession.

So what's the deal with yield curves anyway? Let me explain.

Yield curves are typically upward sloping. Investors who buy government bonds for longer periods of time require a higher premium for the increased uncertainty of their holding period. That's why a thirty-day bill tends to pay less than a two-year bill or a ten-year bond,

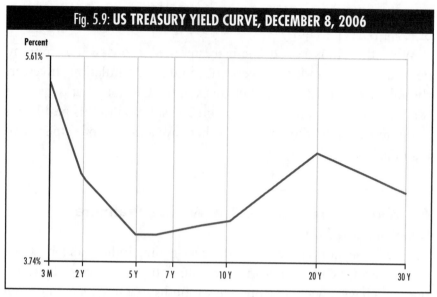

Fig. 5.9: **US TREASURY YIELD CURVE, DECEMBER 8, 2006**

Source: Stockcharts.com

In December 2006, the yield curve was "inverted." Such inversions are leading indicators that a recession is coming.

and investors who are willing to lock up their money with the government for thirty years want the highest yield of all.

But sometimes, fear hits the bond market. Bond investors fear a short-term economic slowdown. That means the Fed is likely to reduce interest rates, and thus today's rates won't last. They'll go lower. They need to lock in high rates now. In doing so, they drive long rates down. The yield curve flattens.

Rates have to rise on the short end of the yield curve to entice current lenders. The yield curve "flips," and investors receive a higher return for shorter rates than longer rates. Of course, at that point, most investors are still shunning the short end of the yield curve for the long end.

Compared to the way the bond market should operate, it's a big megaphone screaming to the financial community that chaos is afoot.

Now, here's why an inverted yield curve is such a great indicator of a recession: Financial institutions tend to "borrow short and lend long." They get low, short-term borrowing rates and then turn around and lend it out at higher rates. They make a fortune on the "spread." But now that spread is inverted. Financial institutions lose their incentive to borrow and make loans. Credit dries up. Thanks to financial alchemy, credit is essentially money.

Figure 5.9 shows what the yield curve looked like in late 2006, shortly before the average investor started to learn about subprime mortgages and derivatives.

This is what inversion looks like — essentially flat, perhaps with only a slight difference between short-term rates and long-term rates. Compared to a healthy yield curve (see below), however, it's much more clear-cut.

In short, an inverted yield curve is the alarm clock, waking up investors from the dream of easy credit and an expanding economy. Markets can hit the snooze button for a while — but not for long.

Just by checking the yield curve, you can get a good idea as to where the economy and typically stocks are going. Figure 5.10 shows that yield curves today indicate economic growth is likely to continue.

Fair warning: There may come a day when an inverted yield curve loses its accuracy in predicting recessions. It's also possible that yield curves will be unduly influenced by central bank purchases of government

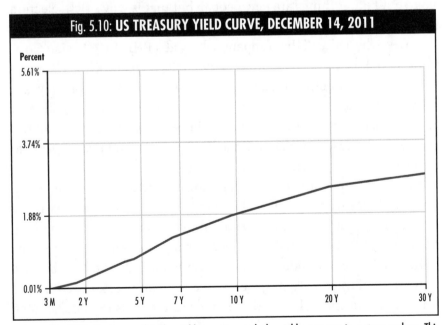

Fig. 5.10: **US TREASURY YIELD CURVE, DECEMBER 14, 2011**

Percent

5.61%

3.74%

1.88%

0.01%

3 M   2 Y   5 Y   7 Y   10 Y   20 Y   30 Y

In December 2011, five years after the yield curve inverted, the yield curve was in a steep upslope. This indicated that economic growth is likely to continue, even if it is at a modest pace.

bonds and that today's steep yield curve is thus misleadingly rosy. A sharply sloping yield curve may not be a healthy sign — but for the time being, an inverted yield curve is the market's best warning signal.

The S&P 500 P/E Ratio: The Market's Valuation Meter

In the long run, the biggest driver of a company's success, and consequently good performance in the stock market, is its earnings. A company can consistently grow its earnings over time increases its worth, increases cash flow, and allows for share buybacks or dividends.

So it should be no surprise that the price-to-earnings ratio (P/E) is the most common investment metric used by investors and analysts. The math is pretty simple to figure out too; simply divide the price of a company's stock into its earnings.

For example, a company that sells for $100 per share and produces $10 of earnings per share sells for a P/E of 10. A company that sells for $100 and produces $5 of earnings per share sells for a P/E of 20.

All other things being equal, a lower P/E ratio is simply better. Of course, all other things are *never* equal, but that is why stock selection is so important.

To see why, let's call the company selling at a P/E of 10 "Fusion Cola" and let's call the company selling at a P/E of 20 "Organic Cola." Now say that earnings for both companies stay flat at $10 per share for ten years.

In the case of Fusion Cola, it would take you ten years to make your money back from earnings (besides the resale value of your investment). In the case of Organic Cola, it would take you twenty years to make your money back just from earnings.

In this example, it isn't important *how* you make the money back. Some of those earnings might be paid in a dividend. Some earnings might go to a share buyback to reduce the common shares outstanding. Some will likely be reinvested in the company to ensure future growth.

In a static world, Fusion Cola is the clear winner. But we don't live in a static world. Fusion Cola might only be able to grow at 2–3 percent per year while Organic Cola sees demand for its products explode, and the company ends up growing at 20 percent per year. In that case, over the longer term, paying up for Organic Cola would provide the best returns.

So looking at the P/E ratio without any other data is a mistake. But, if you compare a company's P/E ratio relative to its peers (similar companies in the same industry), as well as the company's future growth rates, you may justify a higher or lower P/E ratio.

When it comes to the market as a whole, however, the P/E ratio in and of itself provides a relatively good snapshot for the overall valuation of the markets. Figure 5.11 shows the historical P/E ratio of the S&P 500.

When the P/E ratio of the S&P 500 drops under 10, investors should be backing up the truck! When the overall market is reaching P/E ratios over 25, it's best to be selling.

The mean and median for the P/E of the S&P 500 fall around 16. With a current ratio slightly above that, however, it would be best to sell companies trading above that level and to buy companies trading below that level, so that they rotate to the best value.

Of course, that's for the market as a whole. Individual companies may see their performance vary substantially, depending on the specifics of each business.

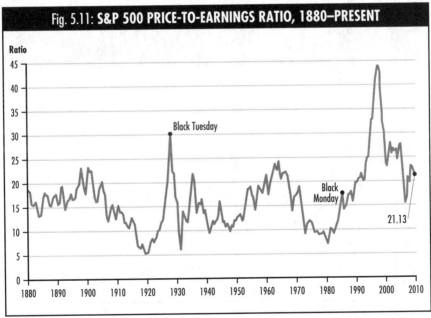

Published: May 30, 2012 | Source: www.multpl.com

Viewing the historic P/E ratio of the stock market makes it easier to determine if the stock market is at an extreme buying or selling point. Today, it is slightly above its historical average.

Fortunately, this measure provides a clear signal to buy stocks during a time when the markets themselves are at the peak of correcting. This is a sound metric for looking at the overall stock market during moments of chaos.

Mutual Fund Cash Ratio: Are the Market's Recent Moves Sustainable?

A market rally is driven by new cash entering the market. As the market rises, those who have been waiting on the sidelines start to dribble in. As a rally increases, more and more investors join in. Eventually, of course, it goes the other way: Astute investors first go to cash, followed by more and more as a sell-off intensifies. Looking at the cash ratio of mutual funds gives a quick way to track this trend.

Unfortunately, in the age of financial alchemy, newly created money can move into the stock market. Given the size and liquidity of this market, it makes more sense for institutions to choose stocks over

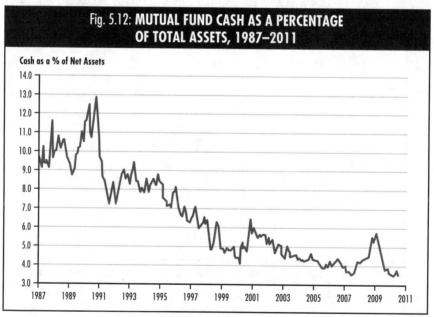

Source: BofA Merrill Lynch Global Research, Investment Company Institute

Since the start of the 1990s, mutual funds have reduced their cash holdings, removing a vital margin of safety.

bonds (as bond investments essentially represent a long-term loan on what could become a problematic business).

Figure 5.12 shows that cash levels have been on a long-term downward trend, suggesting the emphasis money managers have placed on being "fully invested" at all times . . . at least until there's a panic.

I Love Investing for Sentimental Reasons

Sentiment is a contrarian indicator. It's how everyone in the market "feels" in the market. And, when everyone feels the "same way' about a market, it's time to go in the opposite direction.

When everyone else is talking about blue skies, grab an umbrella. When the storm starts receding, be the first to determine bargains. In short, sentiment measures — and there are several — gives you a loose way of gauging the emotions of investors.

Of course, investment professionals would never want to say that they love a stock simply because it's been going up. Their name for this love is "momentum." Stocks that routinely make the top of momentum screens fall hard and fast once the love for the company stops. Sell these types of stocks when the euphoria hits and volume spikes. The market is littered with former momentum darlings.

On the other end of the spectrum, we find the unloved stocks — the ones routinely making the 52-week low lists, the ones that have faced one piece of bad news after another.

At some point, everything bad gets priced in, marking a true market bottom. When bad news doesn't push things any lower, then you know it's time to start looking at buying.

Emotionally, buying momentum stocks follows a risky pattern outlined in Figure 5.13, whereas buying unloved stocks follows the opportunity pattern. It doesn't matter if you're looking for income or capital gains. At the peak, you'll find little opportunity for both, and in the trough you'll be swimming in opportunity.

The advantage of this trend is that it can be seen daily on financial news. The emotional cycle is fed by reporters, analysts, and the like who talk up good news and downplay bad news during a market rally. But, when there's a correction, it's tough to get the feel from them

Fig. 5.13: **INVESTOR SENTIMENT DURING MARKET CYCLES**

Market Peak (Risk)

Euphoria

Thrill

Anxiety

Excitement

Denial

Fear

Optimism

Optimism

Desperation

Relief

Panic

Hope

Capitulation

Depression

Despondency

Market Trough (Opportunity)

Determining where markets are on an emotional level gives investors a key insight into prospective investment returns going forward.

that things will ever be the same again and that the great investment opportunities of the past will never resurface.

Watch enough of it, and you'll get cynical, because no matter which way the market goes, it's spun as an opportunity to buy stocks.

WRAP-UP
Invest with the Global Picture in Mind

- You don't go camping in the woods when it's going up in flames. Before making specific investment decisions, it's important to take in a wider view of the global economy by watching key indicators.
- No matter what kind of bargains you find in markets, the overall "big picture" is an essential check on your overall allocation to risky assets.
- Historically, countries like China and India have dominated global economic activity. The past few centuries have been an aberration from that trend. Expect global GDP to continue to

rise, with the caveat that it can be manipulated by government spending and the like.

- Employment changes and trends are key indicators for the overall health of the economy. If the rising tide isn't lifting all boats, something may be fundamentally wrong.

- The more indicators such as inverted yield curves or slowing GDP growth indicate an oncoming recession (or pullback in growth), the more one should "lighten up" on risky assets like stocks and commodities and more into cash and cash-generating investments.

- Even if the "big picture" sends an all-clear signal, other, more specific risks remain. In the next chapter, we hone in to items of more interest on the industry and sector level.

6

The Horizon
Honing in from the Forest to the Trees

---

*"It is only through labor and painful effort, by grim energy
and resolute courage that we move on to better things."*
— *Theodore Roosevelt*

WITH OVER A HUNDRED THOUSAND stocks traded worldwide, and even more bond issues, there's a vast amount of data for investors to sift through. In addition to a company's reported financials, there are a myriad of analysts coming up with their own future expectations. Fund managers will go on CNBC to talk about how great their latest holding is doing (after they've stopped buying, of course).

That's why you should begin your search for quality, rationally priced investments by filtering through all the obvious candidates that *don't* make the cut. As science fiction author Theodore Sturgeon postulated (what's now called Sturgeon's Law), 90 percent of everything is crud.

If 90 percent of investment opportunities are crud, then the next 90 percent of that remaining 10 percent is mediocre. A truly sound investment, one that offers the least prospect of losing money and a strong probability of outperforming the overall market over time, is a rare thing. It has to be found and then protected.

The rarity of fantastic investment ideas should be setting off warning bells. A good idea won't be touted in the pages of financial newspapers, magazines, or television shows. The best ideas will stay off the radar until well after investors who bought near the bottom are sitting on substantial gains.

That means if you have a good idea *don't brag about it* until after you're fully invested. Just keep it a secret.

Only one exception exists to the rarity of ideas: When markets have hit secular lows in a long-term bull/bear cycle. One such low occurred in 1980/1981. We didn't quite hit such lows in 2002/2003 or in 2008/2009.

Since the peak-to-trough period tends to last fifteen to twenty years, we're currently still in the bottoming process following the market's peak in 2000. The final bottom can happen in one of two ways: Stocks may fall below the lows set in early 2009, or higher inflation and a flat performance may simply drive valuations lower while nominal stock prices stay relatively the same.

When these lows are hit, attractive opportunities are so numerous that rational investors will wish they had more cash (while the average investors, gripped with despair, are finally cashing out of the market at a loss). Given the length of this trend, investors will typically only be able to take advantage of these extreme lows once or twice in their investment careers (perhaps three times if they start investing early and at the right point in the investment cycle). Therefore, the reality is that at any given time, excellent investment opportunities are substantially limited.

But that doesn't mean you should sit on the sidelines. Staying heavy in cash in the age of financial alchemy and chaos is the financial equivalent of suffocating yourself in quicksand.

Fortunately, investors today with an Internet connection can take advantage of a variety of free screening tools to find anything from stocks to funds to bonds that meet your specific criteria.

By identifying where the most attractive opportunities are likely to arise before starting your quest for the exciting handful of specific investments, you can spare yourself an often fruitless survey of the humdrum majority of available investments.

The research task does not end with the discovery of an apparent bargain. It is incumbent on you to try to find out *why* the bargain has become available.

Since most Americans are familiar with real estate as an asset, let's use a home as an example: Say that nice, four-bedroom homes in a given neighborhood are priced around $300,000. If you learned that a similar house was for sale for only $150,000, your first reaction would be pretty easy to guess: "What's wrong with it?"

You wouldn't have just gone out and bought the house because it was a bargain relative to other homes available.

This is *exactly* the kind of skepticism and inquisitive nature that you should bring to the stock market. Maybe there's a genuine bargain here, and nobody's looked at the house yet because the low price suggested there was something horribly wrong with it. Maybe not.

While the prices of securities are set by the market (or, more specifically, the individuals making decisions to buy and sell), the *value* of a business is based on its financial performance. That's why investors should read a company's financial statements. While that's something that every investor must absolutely do, bear in mind that accounting data is malleable.

In other words, there's no exact value that can be attached to a company. It can use all sorts of accounting rules to change its book value, earnings, cash flow, and the like. Beyond the numbers, be aware of how aggressive a company is when it comes to these subjective accounting terms.

And any investor should run, not walk, away from any analysis that's merely a future projection, especially if it depicts the world as full of flowers . . . but lacking in fertilizer. The real world is *never* so pretty. The real world brings out factors that can't be easily predicted, be they demographic, political, or macroeconomic in nature.

Quality In, Quality Out: A Caveat for Stock Screens

Like an old-fashioned gold miner sifting through pebbles and dirt for flakes of gold, so a well-constructed screen filters through the effluence of capital markets. It's important to create a screen that's tight enough to remove most of the garbage without being large enough to let the flakes of gold slip through.

But even then, the results of a stock screen might not be perfect. Before we look at some of the key criteria to screen for, we should first be aware of the shortcomings of using stock screens.

OUTDATED OR INCORRECT DATA

The Internet is fraught with numerous tools to screen for stocks. But these screens rely on the most recent quarterly data of a company. They won't take into account recent changes or developments. If a company shows up on a screen (or, better yet, on multiple screens for different criteria), it's best to review the data from the source: SEC quarterly filings. This is easily done by going to the SEC's database at *www.sec.gov/edgar.shtml.*

Sometimes the data itself is incorrect. In some instances, a missing or added decimal to some number can vastly over- or understate a key piece of information. Or the data is just plain wrong. Once while screening for small-cap companies, I found a firm whose market capitalization was understated by a factor of 20! By looking at the total number of shares outstanding and the current price, however, it was easy to see how this mid-cap company got lumped in with smaller firms.

NONFINANCIAL CONCERNS

A screen will only filter through selected financial data. It won't tell you if the company CEO just resigned, creating shareholder uncertainty. It won't tell you if billionaire investor Carl Icahn has bought a major stake and is looking for a few seats on the board to make changes you're uncomfortable with. Fortunately, any review of a company after it passes through a stock screen can reveal any publicly available concerns.

OFF-THE-RADAR METRICS

While an Internet-based stock screen can cover a lot of ground, not all metrics are available at this time. Even for services like Bloomberg, which runs thousands of dollars a month to access, not everything can be easily and automatically screened!

In some instances, for a particular industry, the absolute best metrics that can be used might not be available. In that case, one can usually construct a screen that approximates the missing metric. But if it's a particularly off-the-radar metric, it may be best to calculate by hand.

For example, when I'm calculating the value of timber-based real estate investment trusts (REITs), I like to calculate the amount I'm paying per acre of timberland. There isn't a screen for that, but the universe is small and the calculation is easy to determine. Of course, I recognize that not all acres are equal, but it provides yet another way of ranking these companies.

OFF-BOOK ASSETS AND LIABILITIES

A stock screen can't take into account any assets or liabilities of a company that are off-book or "hidden." Even then, such things don't have to be hidden in offshore limited liability companies (LLCs) like Enron used to mask their substantial debt. Many such off-book items can be found in the footnotes of a company's quarterly financial statements.

WHITTLING DOWN INVESTMENT IDEAS: FUTURE P/E

Most sources of data list a company's *current* price-to-earnings ratio. As investors, however, we're concerned about the future. Many companies will have a calculation of future earnings based on company reports and past trends made by analysts. While it's by no means 100 percent accurate, it's a good first step beyond looking at last quarter's earnings numbers, which are now obsolete.

Looking at the current P/E ratio of a company that recently reported a loss will show a null value, because you're dividing the price by zero. But, if there's been a one-time event leading to negative earnings, the future may rapidly change.

EARNINGS BEFORE INTEREST, TAXES, DEPRECIATION, AND AMORTIZATION (EBITDA) AND ECONOMIC VALUE (EV)

Earnings before interest, taxes, depreciation, and amortization (EBITDA), gives you a way to look beyond the basic earnings numbers and a P/E ratio. Essentially, this view of earnings backs out several pieces of data to arrive at a company's cash earnings. It's a widely used metric by creditors to determine the ability of a company to repay debts, offering a more conservative estimate of earnings.

Economic or enterprise value (EV) is the market value of a company less cash, plus debt. Dividing a company's enterprise value by EBITDA, investors get EV/EBITDA, or the ratio of enterprise value to a company's cash earnings, a quick measure of the company's overall valuation relative to its cash earnings. This is an important screen for companies with a lot of cash or business in capital intensive industries, such as oil exploration and production.

Typically, any EV/EBITDA number under 10 is ideal for a publicly traded company. Many private equity transactions for private companies use this valuation, paying at most five to seven times the EV/EBITDA to acquire an entire business.

HIGH PROFIT MARGINS AND RETURN ON EQUITY (ROE)

A company able to earn $1.50 for every dollar it spends will grow substantially faster and better over time than a company that earns only $1.10 for every dollar it spends. So, when it comes to looking at profit margins and return on equity (ROE), the higher the number, the better. As you'll see, in many ways they're intertwined.

A company with high profit margins offers investors a way to invest defensively in an increasingly commoditized world. Many small, niche companies have high profit margins, but they can't grow because of their niche.

That's where return on equity comes in. A company that can generate high profit margins with the money shareholders have invested (the definition of return on equity) and continually reinvest them can sustain a path of high earnings growth over time. Eventually, this will reflect itself in higher share prices. Anyone who has owned shares of Apple in the past ten years can attest to this fact, as the company reinvested its profits from the iPod into other products like the iPhone and iPad.

More importantly, companies with consistently high profit margins or return on equity often have a reason for doing so. This may include a powerful brand, a ground-breaking technology, a large portfolio of patents, or some other factor that creates a proverbial "moat" around earnings.

Looking at profit margins and ROE over time gives you a way to essentially identify likely moats without having to look at the minutiae of a company's assets.

It's little wonder then that ROE is one of the most important items that you can screen for in a prospective investment.

RETURN ON INVESTED CAPITAL (ROIC)

This ratio isn't as widely used as the P/E ratio or ROE, so not every stock screen today will let you look at return on invested capital (ROIC).

ROIC is essential to determine the prospects and profitability of a company that needs to invest substantial amounts of capital. That makes it a great way to look at the differences in performance between energy giants like Exxon Mobil and BP, than it does for less capital-intensive service companies like ADP or Qualcomm.

Essentially, ROIC looks at the cash-on-cash yield of a company. Simply divide a company's net profits after tax by invested capital. As with ROE, a higher ROIC indicates that a company is creating greater value for its shareholders.

PRICE-TO-EARNINGS GROWTH (PEG) RATIO

The price-to-earnings growth (PEG) ratio looks at how a company is priced relative to its ability to grow earnings over time. Generally, companies with low PEG ratios will outperform those with high PEG ratios over time. Why? Because a low PEG ratio means that you are paying less today for future growth.

The PEG ratio takes the P/E ratio divided by the company's expected rate of earnings growth. A number around 1 indicates a company where growth is currently "priced in." A number greater than 1 indicates that the company might be currently overvalued by the market, and a number less than 1 indicates that the market is undervaluating that company.

Again, that's all in terms of a company's expected growth rate, which may change substantially over time. For investors looking to grow their wealth over time, a PEG ratio offers a quick way to determine what companies might be currently undervalued by the market.

PRICE-TO-SALES RATIO (PSR)

This valuation metric divides a stock's price by its revenue per share. The price-to-sales ratio (PSR) works best when comparing companies within an industry, as it can vary widely. As with the PEG ratio, a smaller number is considered better than a larger one.

PSR is one of the weaker items to screen for, but it can be useful for industry comparison or when a company has no current earnings (and hence no current or future P/E ratio). This ratio is something used in evaluating technology companies that have huge prospective growth but low current revenue.

There's also a danger of using this metric with low-margin companies: Walmart has a PSR of 0.45, but that's because they sell a lot with a low profit margin. It doesn't indicate fast growth the same way a new company ramping up sales might.

BOOK VALUE

Book value, which looks at a company's assets minus its liabilities, is a way of looking at a company as though it had no ongoing future business that may allow it to grow.

That's why value investors flock to book value, which can be measured per share. The ability to buy a company below book value has been compared to buying a dollar for 50 cents. Over time, a portfolio of companies trading below book value will outperform a portfolio of companies trading above its book value.

It's straightforward, easy to calculate (or find on financial website), and takes a very conservative view of the overall business. Book value is a critical item for you to screen for in an environment where blind faith in growth has led most investors astray.

In a study of stock returns between 1963 and 1993 by Eugene Fama and Kenneth French, twelve hypothetical portfolios were created corresponding to different levels of book value. Companies with the highest book value gained an average of 3.7 percent annually, whereas companies with the lowest book value saw an average annual return of 24.31 percent.[23]

For strategic, long-term wealth creation, buying companies trading below book value is key.

One caveat: Book value numbers are historical, so they many not reflect current values for assets purchased decades earlier at lower prices. Items such as real estate come to mind here.

DEBT/EQUITY RATIO

If cash is king, a company with a high amount of debt relative to its equity is little more than a slave. Every dollar of debt has to be paid with interest, which affects the ability of a company to reinvest, grow, or pay shareholders.

In today's chaotic environment, the most critical use of this ratio is to compare a company with its industry peers as well as its cash flow. That gives an idea to the relative health of a company, as well as its ability to handle its debts.

While value investors might shun this type of investment, opting instead for a company with no debt and loads of cash, capital intensive companies and most financial companies require large amounts of debt to function.

Insider Purchases and Share Buybacks

Another way to screen for potential investment ideas is to look at companies with recent insider purchases. After all, understanding the business, its competitors, and its environment is the reason why management is getting paid in the first place. The Sarbanes-Oxley Act of 2002, an otherwise burdensome piece of legislation for businesses, requires insiders to report purchases and sales within forty-eight hours.

Insiders, company executives, or shareholders with a more than 5 percent stake have only one reason to buy: They expect higher share prices. But, on the flip side, they could have plenty of different reasons to sell: diversification of their total assets, funding college tuition or other big purchase, and so on.

Investors can track insider buying and selling easily, although it's not a typical "screen" in the formal sense. Insider purchases have been slim since mid-2010, especially when compared to insider sales. It's one quick way to get a very short list of investment ideas quickly and on a regular basis.

Buying a basket of companies based on major, recent insider pur-chases tends to beat the overall market as a strategy by anywhere from 4 to 10 percent per year, depending on the study.[24]

Alongside insider buys, a company's share buyback program can offer a "floor" to keep share prices from falling lower. With corpora-tions holding over $2 trillion in cash on the books at the close of 2011, buying back shares offers a few advantages that dividends don't, pri-marily the lack of double taxation.

Buying back shares essentially reduces the size of the "pie" out-standing, leaving remaining shareholders with a larger proportional stake in a company without having to acquire additional shares.

It's another way to reward patient shareholders. For a company with above-average rates of return and few opportunities for new investment, a share buyback might be the optimal way to return cash to shareholders.

While buybacks improve the per-share metrics of a company (due to a lower number of shares outstanding), it also lowers a company's total cash on hand.

Buyer beware: some companies that employ lavish executive com-pensation via stock options may employ buybacks to mitigate the amount of dilution that's being created.

The Product Life Cycle: Where Do This Company's Products Stand?

Every company has something to sell. Knowing where these prod-ucts are in a product's life cycle offer key insights as to future price performance.

Essentially, every product, once designed, created, tested, and approved, goes through four key phases, as shown in Figure 6.1.

First, it's introduced. During this phase, knowledge about the prod-uct is still spreading, and the first users, known as early adapters, begin to use the product. Second comes rapid growth, where sales volume kicks up tremendously and the product takes off. Third comes matu-rity, where the product reaches the peak of its life cycle. Typically, at this point competition picks up, the product becomes obsolete, or

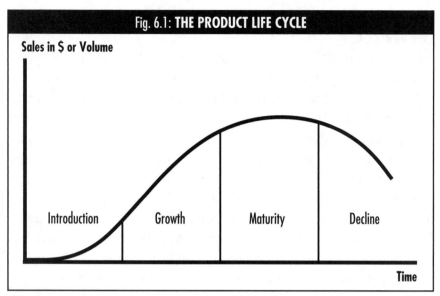

Fig. 6.1: THE PRODUCT LIFE CYCLE

Sales in $ or Volume

Introduction   Growth   Maturity   Decline

Time

All products see rapid growth as consumer interest surges. But no product's popularity lasts forever.

other factors come into play. Finally, sales volume declines as the product dies off.

Taking a page from Thomas Hobbes, this lifestyle is "nasty, brutish, and short" in industries with rapid technological advances and numerous competitors.

A product may change rapidly. In the ten years since Apple has released the iPod, the product has gone through numerous changes, most notably offering a larger storage size capacity in a smaller size. Nobody wants one of those bulky, original monstrosities today.

A product that's a fad might also be peaking right as investors are starting to follow the growth.

That was the case of Crocs footwear, as discussed earlier. By the time the company had its IPO, cheap knockoffs were bringing prices down, and everyone who wanted a pair of the company's unique product had one.

There are other important exceptions. A well-loved brand, say Coca Cola, has generational staying power. Utilities and railroads, which operate in capital-intensive and regulated environments, fit the bill as well. Look for these exceptions; you may be well rewarded!

The Business Cycle: Some Sectors Optimal Now, Others Later

As we've seen elsewhere, most investment trends move in cycles. Within a stock market's overall boom-and-bust cycle, several individual sectors will outperform at different places in a market's trend.

When stocks first begin to rise, companies in the financial and transportation industries may rise first, followed by technology and basic goods. Commodity-heavy industries tend to have a huge rise just before the top of the stock market cycle.

As markets correct, investors playing "defense" with their money will shift to consumer goods, utilities, and health-care companies. These companies tend to perform the best, although in a market correction, that often simply means they fall the least.

Figure 6.2 shows the disconnect between the stock market cycle and the economic cycle.

Additionally, the stock market is itself a leading indicator for the overall economy. So, when the stock market peaks, the peak in economic output before a decline will lag by several months. Conversely,

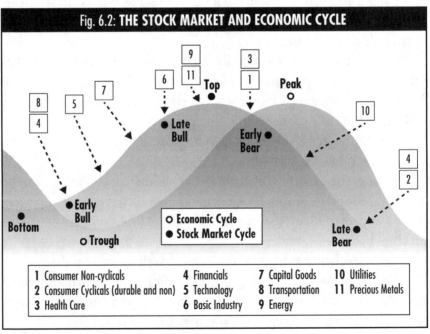

As a leading indicator, stock market prices will hit their peaks and troughs before the general economy.

when the economy finally hits the bottom of its most recent cycle, stocks will already be in an upward cycle.

A word of caution: There's no clear switch from one part of this cycle to another. So the present location of where we're at in this cycle is always up for debate, making a precise sector allocation difficult.

For instance, in 2012, are we continuing to see modest and uneven economic recovery? Or do we still have several more years of bouncing along the bottom ahead of us? Only time will give us a sure answer.

WRAP-UP
Screening Data

- By being able to efficiently and effectively screen critical data about a company, you can easily put together the data you need to sort from the vast universe of investment opportunities to a few candidates.
- While screening software has advanced to the point where nearly any investor can analyze any aspect of a company — or screen multiple criteria at once — every company's unique situation and every industry place a different emphases on each piece of data.
- Of course, not everything of importance can be screened for. Quality of management, shareholder activity, and new product developments won't show up on any stock screen yet available. You'll have to dig into SEC filings and other corporate reports.
- Economic cycles influence the performance of industries differently at different times.
- In the next chapter, we'll take data from stock screens and use it to further hone and analyze an investment decision via a checklist.

7

The Trees
Fundamental Analysis of Individual Companies

———

"He that cannot reason is a fool. He that will not is a bigot. He that dare not is a slave."

— *Andrew Carnegie*

FUNDAMENTAL ANALYSIS GETS TO THE ROOT of investing: the selection of specific assets within the investment universe.

Many assets, such as real estate and bonds, can be valued in a reasonably simple manner. You can value these assets by focusing on cash flow potential (measured against the prospect of future inflation and repayment for bonds and future rents and appreciation for real estate).

For stocks, that means analyzing the underlying company based on quantifiable metrics in their financial statements. It also includes subjective measures such as future prospects for returns, management's ability to create value, and possible "off-book" assets and liabilities.

Make no mistake: Fundamental analysis is somewhat backward looking. It has to be. By the time data is compiled on a company, it's out of date. But this data can be used to create a forward-looking view of a company.

But where do you start? Some say, start with the news. See what the financial talking heads are saying, follow up on their advice, read a few investment articles online, and start from there.

Frankly, I think that's a huge problem. Here's why.

Dogs Chase Cars, Irrational Investors Chase the News

Imagine you heard someone say, "We absolutely have to get in on this investment now. We shouldn't wait for more data. We should buy shares of this company *immediately*. Obviously the news from the Chinese is only going to get worse, so we have to get in now."

Watching an investor make trades based on news events is like watching a dog chase cars.

There's little rationality behind it. There's a high probability of a painful failure, and even if you're successful, odds are luck played a substantial role. In reality, you were just fortunate that some greater fool was willing to come along and buy more.

Maybe you find that one talking head has better ideas than the others so you just blindly follow him or her, ignoring the fact that nobody is 100 percent right forever.

Either way, you let your emotions get into the investment process from the get-go.

This is why rational investors analyze stocks with a keen eye on the fundamentals. It takes a lot of the emotion and "luck" out of investing. It also helps keep emotion in check, so when things work out, it's because your *process* was right and not because you're God's gift to equity markets. It also means you're able to stay the course when things go awry — as they always do — without blaming everything and everyone but yourself.

While you, the rational investor, might not chase the latest big news story or high-beta darling, it also means you're more likely to consistently make money investing over the long haul. Simply reducing mistakes alone means that you're always increasing your capital rather than suffering setbacks. Over time, that will more than offset the loss of substantial capital gains on a few risky ventures that shoot to the moon.

The other advantage of fundamental analysis is clear: the entire market doesn't need to be trading at a discount to its true value, only a few companies need apply for you to take advantage of any market condition (although bargains abound after a crash).

I'm not saying you should *never* follow the financial advice of what you read or see on television. Just remember Sturgeon's Law! The talking heads on TV are doing what they do to entice viewers like you into watching. If anything, it can give you an idea of investments that the great herd of investors is following right now.

There's nothing wrong with learning about the markets while being entertained, but at some point you have to hit the mute button and do your own work.

Separating Financial Jesters from the Herd: A Close Inspection of a Company's Financials

You would be wise to begin a company analysis with the most recent quarterly statements and most recent annual report. Unfortunately, that's usually a bit daunting for most investors. Annual reports often run over a hundred pages, and it's all too easy to just read the part up front written by the CEO or Chairman of the Board (or both).

Typically, that section is designed for the lazy investor. It's in full-color, full of glossy graphs, unrelated photos of smiling children, and words like "success," "optimal," "opportunity," or, if it's been a bad year, "challenge" or "turnaround."

Reading these letters from the CEO may give a good overview, but you must go deeper. As a shareholder, or even potential shareholder, you're just seeing the freshly painted front door and marble lobby. You need to go beyond the curb appeal to make sure the foundation isn't rotting.

Frankly, reading through annual and quarterly reports, rather than relying on what the CEO says in the most recent conference call, will give you more knowledge about a company than what 90 percent of market participants look at.

A company's financials are broken down into three statements: the income statement, the balance sheet, and the cash flow statement, more often referred to as sources and uses of funds.

Most analysts focus on the income statement, which looks at reported revenue, expenses, profits, or losses, taking into account a myriad of accounting techniques. I prefer to start with the cash flow statement in today's age of economic chaos.

Cash Flow Is King

As an individual, you're prone to thinking about cash flow all the time. How much money do you have coming in each month? Any dividends? Perhaps even rent from that condo you can't sell? That's all money coming in. What you spend at the grocery store, on your mortgage, and, yes, even on taxes is cash flow going out.

Looking at your personal cash flows each month, it's easy to see if your net worth is increasing or decreasing (do you spend more than you bring in?). For companies, it's much the same way.

You should start your research with net income, then add back in the noncash charges (primarily depreciation and amortization). This gives a clearer picture to the cash-generating ability of the business, as it eliminates areas where accounting changes are prone to help a company meet analyst expectations each quarter.

For companies that have pensions, calculations will need to be made to adequately estimate the true costs. Typically, companies underfund their pensions because they assume a higher rate of return than can actually be expected. Ideally, a company won't have pension expenses so this calculation won't be necessary.

But, more often than not, companies with superior cash flow are in mature industries that have legacy pension plans in place. On the plus side, mature industries tend to have limited growth potential.

Yes, that's a good thing. It means that capital doesn't have to go back in to the core business. The company can expand elsewhere, buy back shares, or pay a hefty dividend to its shareholders. In other words, score one for "stodgy" companies when it comes to creating the kind of stable, predictable, and large amounts of free cash flow.

Balance Sheet Blues

The balance sheet identifies exactly *what* the business owns and uses. The assets of a company form the "engine" that powers its returns. These assets may include tangible items like cash, property, and equipment, or it may include intangible items like goodwill from acquisitions.

Meanwhile, the balance sheet lists liabilities as well. These include sources of funding, such as bank loans or bonds outstanding. A high level of short-term debt (including long-term debt due within a year) may indicate trouble in the event of an unforeseen problem (especially if there's little or no cash or other liquid assets).

So, looking at both the assets and liabilities of a company gives you a "snapshot" of the overall financial health. As an individual, it's akin to looking at your net worth every quarter.

Your assets would include the value of your investments, real estate, and so on (and you could always include the "depreciated" value of things like electronics and furniture based on an estimate of what you could sell them for). Your liabilities would include car payments, mortgages, credit card debt, and so on.

As an investor, reviewing changes to the balance sheet over a long period of time allows you to see how the company has either improved its financial health or whether it's on the decline. This information is easy to find online, and Morningstar offers the ability to look at the balance sheet constituents over a ten-year period.

It's rare, but the balance sheet can often show you huge opportunities that might not be revealed by income/earnings or cash flow. In early 2003, investors purely looking at the balance sheet of Apple Inc. (NASDAQ:AAPL) would have found that the company was trading at a discount to net cash.

In other words, if the company went immediately bankrupt, each share was worth more than what it could currently be bought for. And that's to say nothing of Apple's brand, which was just starting its amazing transition into the consumer tech powerhouse it is today!

There's a tremendous opportunity here, because most analysts look at earnings (part of the income statement), then cash flows, and then, if there's time, the balance sheet. But subtracting the value of from a company's market cap can often show that a company's price-to-earnings ratio (the most-used metric for valuation), is artificially high.

Changes in the balance sheet aren't always good. Here are three potential ways the balance sheet can give you early warning signals about a company whose profitability and competitive position are declining even when it's reporting increased profits:

- **Did the company borrow more or pay down debt?** The balance sheet will answer that basic question on a quarterly basis. Healthy companies should be generating cash and gradually paying down debt over time. A company that needs to increasingly borrow money to fund general operations has a problem that might not be "visible" when strictly looking at earnings per share.

  The poster child for this phenomenon is General Electric (GE). GE essentially created the commercial paper market to ensure enough short-term funding was available. As a result of low interest rates and the short term of commercial paper, GE has been able to expand its debt to over $450 billion dollars against a market cap of only $175 billion.

- **Was a company profitable but has a big buildup in inventory?** Ideally, a company isn't just profitable, it can't keep the store shelves stocked with its products. When a company's inventory increases consistently, that's not a good sign. Eventually the inventory has to go, and chances are, if it's not selling already at full price, it'll have to be steeply discounted.

  In 2011, Hewlett-Packard (HP) couldn't sell its tablet device, the TouchPad. After a substantial buildup of inventory, the company went ahead and discounted it to $99 — a major loss for each unit sold.

- **Does the business always have to make big capital expenditures?** A business that continually needs to invest in new properties, plants, and equipment must prepare for these large purchases by accumulating cash for the eventual purchase. It dries up money available for reinvestment or payouts to shareholders.

  In this area, utilities fit the bill. Large power plants must be continually maintained or upgraded. However, this is regulated to ensure a modest profit, so some investment opportunities may be available depending on market pricing.

The best bargains in investing are companies with a favorable balance sheet and strong cash flow, even if earnings are misleadingly low.

A company that's cheap may stay cheap for a while before markets figure it out.

But a company that's trading below what it would get in bankruptcy, especially if it has some kind of competitive advantage, offers one of the best investment opportunities of a lifetime. That's not to say its stock will surge 500 percent; rather, the prospect of further downside is limited.

That's rational investing. It's like buying a house for $100,000 that comes with a Picasso painting or a safe full of diamonds.

Income Statement: Wall Street's Quarterly Hoops for a Company to Jump through

Compared to the balance sheet and cash flow statement, the income statement is more widely followed.

Earnings per share is the critical number. There are estimates, forecasts, "whisper" numbers, and then the actual number. It is a recurring ritual on Wall Street to go through all these numbers. Performances are available every thirteen weeks.

Income statements break down sources of revenues and expenses over a specific period, typically quarterly for stocks, although some foreign firms may report monthly, semiannually, or annually.

The income statement can be useful: It can provide a quick and easy way to see if a company is making money or not. Are expenses greater than revenues? Are there sources for revenues or expenses coming from an area outside the "core" business that accounts for a large percentage?

Remember: The income statement doesn't provide a breakdown between whether or not cash came in. A company may freely lend credit to its customers, book revenues, and then have a rising accounts receivable (so as a potential investor, you would want to look at the balance sheet as well). Rising revenues combined with rising accounts receivable may indicate that a company is having problems, even though it's still reporting some great revenue numbers!

Financial "Yellow Lights" to Consider

Just looking at numbers and finding a favorable trend isn't enough to declare the financial analysis done and call it a day.

That's because financial statements alone are no substitute for common sense. Here are some common accounting shortfalls to look for:

- A company's inventories may be rising because they have too many obsolete products.
- Accounts receivable may be uncollectible, and thus assets are overstated.
- Some liabilities may not have been recorded.
- Some assets may have their values or depreciation methods overstated or understated.

Finally, all the best calculations of the future may be rendered moot rather quickly if the company's business model is unsustainable, if management moves outside its core competency, if hidden liabilities or some other unforeseeable problem suddenly comes to light.

Beware Information Overload . . .
and Intellectual Laziness

Too much information and analysis might put some to sleep or induce some other emotional state. It's important to remember a fundamental lesson of economics: diminishing marginal utility.

Think about eating a pizza one slice at a time. If you're starving, the first slice takes away the burning hunger. The second and third slice will too, but with less of an effect. End up eating another four or five slices, and you'll probably go from being full to feeling sick.

It's the same way with information. As an investor, you want to be better educated on a company's prospects without going overboard. You need to know what's coming up in terms of new products and services, potential regulations, and management changes. You don't need to know the childhood pets of everyone on the board of directors.

We've looked at some of the major ways to analyze a company — but we've hardly scratched the surface. There's no one single way to analyze a company. There's *no single metric* that can consistently point to where the best opportunities lie. There's a lot of data, and a myriad of ways it can be interpreted.

Intangible Sources of Wealth: Competitive Advantages

Reviewing a company's financials may overlook other sources of a company's wealth, namely *competitive advantage.*

Over the long term, companies that can build, maintain and keep a competitive advantage will perform remarkably well. A competitive advantage is nothing more than an aspect of a company that allows it to earn above-average profit margins for its industry.

The brand of Coca Cola is a competitive advantage. Microsoft's dominance of the operating system market is a competitive advantage. Walmart's supply chain superiority and consequential lower price relative to other retailers is a competitive advantage.

(It's little surprise that companies with this kind of advantage tend to become big, as their competitive advantage allows them to grow faster or stay in business while competitors go bankrupt.)

These sources of wealth tend to be qualitative rather than quantitative. And yet, they do contribute meaningfully to the bottom line. The best place to look on a company's balance sheet is goodwill, where intangible items often end up as an asset. Otherwise, another key area is a company's profit margins. There's a reason Coke's profit margins are consistently north of 25 percent (brand power!), whereas, even benefitting from $100 barrel oil, ExxonMobil's profit margins are a slim 9.6 percent (only a commodity!).

There's no hard or fast rule for what a competitive advantage is — or how long it will last. Disney has lobbied (successfully for now) to extend copyright law to protect its trademark mouse. A pharmaceutical company has to deal with expiring patents on medication. Walmart can't drive prices to zero.

A Tale of Two Companies: The Role of Competitive Advantage and Sound Accounting

To better understand the role of competitive advantage, let's compare two companies, Company A and Company B.

Company A is the largest company in its sector. It controls 51 percent of its domestic market for its core product, and other secondary products have as much as 80 percent of their respective markets. It has the world's largest finance company, yet it's the largest consumer of the US banking industry, thanks to its cash-rich position but need for short-term financing. Its competitive "moat" lies in its brand, respected for its quality, as well as its industry, which requires substantial capital to enter.

Many other industries serve this company's financial, supply, and marketing needs. Its cost-control systems are the envy of the world. Despite its large size, management strives to balance between the centralization of operations and decentralization, trying to ensure that divisions have independence.

Executives are rewarded through a lucrative bonus plan, and low-level employees flock to this company for a long-term, steady career that guarantees them a comfortable position in the middle class and a secure retirement.

Company B is overleveraged to the hilt, but nobody knows how much, thanks to the accounting measures undertaken to ensure that the total debts remain unknown. All that can be said with certainty is that this company was so deep in debt that it had *annual interest payments of $16 billion*. In the company's best year, the most they ever made was $7 billion, so they were now borrowing more simply to make interest payments. That's pretty bad!

This shouldn't have come as a surprise: Revenues and market share have been on the decline for over twenty-five years. It was easy to blame low-priced foreign competition, although the company's products certainly didn't have the kind of reputation and prestige that many of its competitors had.

A large, bureaucratic executive structure ensured that there was no final responsibility for the company's rampant spending habits. Lower-level employees were, in some circumstances, even paid not to work! To be fair, those employees were unlikely to realize the full benefits in retirement that were promised by the company.

Company A is General Motors (GM) prior to its restructuring in 1958. Company B is General Motors prior to its bankruptcy and seizure by the US government in 2008.

What a difference half a century makes!

What does this teach us?

First, one thing is clear: Competitive advantages can disappear, especially ones based on brand when the quality declines. Sound accounting principles and conservative financing can end up on the slippery slope to overleverage, especially if they're originally undertaken to boost short-term results in a declining industry.

In one time period, GM may have been a sound investment at a reasonable price. But by 2007 it certainly wasn't. The determination of investing is always a function of *both* what you're getting and the price you're getting it at. If it's a great asset, it's worth more. If it's garbage, run for the exit.

General Motors is an extreme example of an untenable financial situation. However, if a company is selling off to bargain basement levels based on a problem and its problem is solvable in the long term, it might be worth a closer look. At present, the sovereign debt crisis in Europe may be presenting an opportunity to buy quality European companies.

Changing Accounting Rules: Why Cash Flow Matters in the World of Make-Believe Accounting

To focus purely on earnings is misleading. Yet that's exactly what most Wall Street analysts do. Today's Wall Street analysts focus on quarterly earnings numbers. Companies beating their estimates see their shares soar for a day or two, while talking heads wax philosophic about what a long-term winner this company will be . . . based on one ninety-day period.

Companies that miss their estimates see shares sell off steeply (although this is not always the case, because analysts may set the bar so low that most companies in trouble can often "trip" over the estimates).

This focus turns investing into a short-term horse race, exactly what speculation is and exactly the opposite of reasonable behavior and analysis.

With a focus purely on earnings, management has an incentive to resort to accounting gimmicks to report the numbers that analysts want to hear.

For example, for nearly two decades, General Electric managed to beat analyst expectations by a mere penny or two. Close scrutiny into specific divisions often showed companies reporting numbers with a 0.5 or 0.6 at the end, so that they'd round up to the nearest whole number. While these "managed earnings" were — and are — still acceptable accounting practices, GE's pervasive use of them cost them $50 million in fines from the SEC.

This brings up a bigger point that bears repeating: reported earnings are not the same as cash flow, due to accounting standards and noncash events that often occur.

If you were asked to be a private investor for a friend starting a company, you'd undoubtedly ask several key questions, such as "How much?" "What rate of return can I expect?" or "When will you start paying me back from the cash flows?" If an investor were to take this approach with publicly traded businesses, they would carefully scrutinize cash flows first.

This is especially important in today's world of financial alchemy. The Financial Accounting Standards Board (FASB) has determined that companies can list assets on their books for what they paid, not necessarily what they're worth. By suspending the rule of marking assets to their market value on a regular basis, there are more opportunities for investors — and more pitfalls.

Buyer beware: this rule was suspended to help ensure the solvency of marginal companies in the middle of the credit crisis.

A company loaded with real estate bought at the peak of the market that it can't get rid of might not look like such a bargain. But a company that bought assets decades ago that have substantially appreciated in value might be an unseen bargain.

One Equation to Rule Them All:
Discounting the Future to Determine Current Value

It's time for some math. Let's say you've looked at the historical numbers of a company, looked at potential future developments, and are confident that their $1.00 per share of free cash flow today will increase by 10 percent per year. Table 7.1 shows what free cash flow (FCF) should look like over the next 10 years.

If those calculations are correct, by Year 9 cash flow will have more than doubled. Not bad! But what does that tell us about how to value that free cash flow today? For that, we need to determine present value. We need to decide what we'd be willing to pay *today* for those dollars *in the future*.

(What level of discount should you make? Hint: Since we're in an age of freewheeling and print-happy central banks, it better be higher than zero to handle inflation! Most estimates of discounting are based on the return of a low-risk asset, such as ten-year

Table 7.1: FREE CASH FLOW (FCF)	
Year 1	$1.00
Year 2	$1.10
Year 3	$1.21
Year 4	$1.33
Year 5	$1.46
Year 6	$1.61
Year 7	$1.77
Year 8	$1.95
Year 9	$2.14
Year 10	$2.36

Treasury yields, plus a kicker for additional risk. I usually use 10–15 percent for companies with consistent earnings, and 20–25 percent for companies with a more cyclical outlook, although those are just general rules of thumb. The logic here is that if your projections are accurate, the rate you discount at should at least equal the rate you earn.)

It's a simple calculation. Present value is equal to the original amount (in this case cash flow, although you can also use this for dividend payouts or the accounting-rule-driven earnings per share), divided by the discount rate minus the growth rate, or $PV = c/(k-g)$, where *PV* is present value, *c* is the coupon, *k* is the discount rate, and *g* is the growth rate.

Let's say this company has a decent "moat" so cash flow is likely to stay pretty steady around a 10 percent increase every year. Using a conservative 15 percent discount, we get $1.10 (free cash flow at the end of the first year) divided by (discount rate of 15 percent minus growth rate of 10 percent). Crunch the numbers, and we come up with a present value of $22.

Will a 15 percent discount rate always be appropriate? In most cases, yes, although the rate can be lower in the event that returns are "steadier." But at the very least 15 percent should compensate you over and above inflation as well as above all historical measures for the "average" stock market return over time.

Remember that $22 is the present value of those discounted cash flows. It's sort of the "fair value" price you as the investor would pay today to obtain shares.

We want to take an additional discount to that price, so that we have our margin of safety (after all, we're making a lot of assumptions about what could happen to a company for the next ten years and beyond). Adding in another, say, 25 percent discount for safety's sake, and we'd *only* want to buy shares of this company if the price was lower than $16.50.

Let's take a look at two examples: one for a company trading well below what I calculated to be a reasonable intrinsic value and one for a company trading well above such a level.

Real-World Example #1: Intel Corporation (NASDAQ:INTC), June 2011

In June 2011, Intel Corp, one of the world's largest makers of computer chips, sported earnings per share of $2.14. Let's say I expect those earnings to grow at around 10 percent per year for the next ten years and then 5 percent thereafter. Their competitive position is strong, their product is respected over competitors, and they have a healthy balance sheet and growing dividend.

Using a conservative, 15 percent discount, the discounted cash flows come up with a "fair value" price for the stock today: $31.30.

Taking an additional 25 percent discount to this discounted value for a margin of safety, I come up with a maximum price I'd be willing to pay for shares: $23.48.

On the day I made this calculation, shares traded for $22.65 — a modest discount to my estimate of the company's true value, even with a margin of safety added in! So I considered it a good buy.

Real-World Example #2: Green Mountain Coffee Roasters (NASDAQ:GMCR), June 2011

In June 2011, GMCR was a high-flying stock whose shares have quadrupled within a year. Is this kind of move justified? Is there still value left? Revenues have been doubling for the past few years. Let's run some more conservative numbers and find out.

Let's assume this company's growth will slow from its current levels to *only* 40 percent per year for the next ten years, before leveling off at 15 percent after that. With trailing earnings of $0.79 per year and using a 25 percent discount rate due to the company's inconsistent cash flows over the past few years, we come up with a fair value of $43.74 per share.

Adding in a 25 percent margin of safety, we get $32.81.

However, in June, shares traded at $80.27. Clearly, you should wait on this opportunity (or find better ones) unless the company can truly keep its substantial growth clip. If you disagree with the idea that the company's rapid growth will continue, you would have been wise to short the stock.

As a high-flyer that's had a huge move in less than a year, they might not have to wait long. What goes up quickly tends to come down faster!

Comparing Intrinsic Value to the Market Price

The most important thing with this equation is to pick a conservative estimate. That way, even if you're wrong, your margin of safety should still protect you from a downslide in any event.

Remember: It's easy to make a forecast. The math isn't that difficult. You can do it without a financial calculator, a complex spreadsheet, or a team of researchers. It's the accuracy of the forecast that matters. And it *will* be inaccurate no matter how well the future can be predicted.

But there's consolation: Each layer of financial analysis, if done conservatively, acts as a defense against a loss. Understanding the business is the first step. Understanding the company's history of cash flows is another. Discounting a conservative estimate of future cash flows adds to that. Finally, adding in a margin of safety creates a buffer that should reduce, if not outright eliminate, the prospect for losses.

There's one additional advantage to calculating a company's intrinsic value. Once bought, the rational investor has a specific price point in mind at which they should look to sell shares (adjusting the intrinsic value as new data comes out). This goes a long way to answering one of investing's most difficult and emotionally fraught questions: when to sell.

Given the tendency of markets to move from undervaluation to overvaluation, reaching the intrinsic value doesn't *always* mean an automatic sell. But, at the very least, it's a strong indicator to prepare to sell and go on the hunt for the next opportunity. This kind of fundamental analysis based on discounted cash flows is dependent on owning shares the irrational investor is too busy chasing what's hot to truly think about risks and returns.

WRAP-UP
Price Doesn't Equal Value

- Rational investors evaluate the opportunity to invest in a company based on the predictability of the business and on an objective calculation of its expected future return.
- Never invest without careful scrutiny of a company's finances, and never invest only relying on the financial numbers. Be sure to account for off-book assets and liabilities, the competency of management, competitive advantage, what competitors are up to, and any other potential catalysts that haven't been priced in.
- Sort data for relevance. There's a lot of noise out there, and this can easily lead to data overload. Of course, it's a balancing act to make sure that you consider enough information, including the effect (and financial health) of competitors, new technologies, possible regulations, and so on.

- Most valuation is based on backwards-looking data, but you must look forward. The more predictable a company's past cash flows, the easier it is to make a conservative estimate of future value.
- The price you should pay for a stock should always be at a discount to any estimate to true value, because, despite the math, investing isn't an exact science — it's art with numbers. At best, calculations will directionally reflect reality, although they might not be perfect.
- Any company can be valued to some extent, although companies with more complex products that can become obsolete quickly need a steeper discount, often well below the high valuations that they typically trade for.
- Discounts to true value, and the emotional fortitude to stick with them, are critical in the age of financial chaos.
- The irrationality of markets ensures that there are always some bargains out there, although there will be lean years (before major crashes) and fat years (after market crashes).

8

The Case for Inflation . . . and the Case for Deflation

"I do not think it is an exaggeration to say history is largely a history of inflation, usually inflations engineered by governments for the gain of governments.**"**

— *Friedrich von Hayek*

THE CASE FOR INFLATION logically proceeds from what we've seen so far: The Federal Reserve's easy-money policies, designed to stimulate economic growth, could spark a huge jump in inflation rates. The Federal Reserve's track record since 1913 has shown that, despite their commitment to "price stability," the value of the dollar has fallen by over 98 percent.

Although so far we've focused on the most obvious source of inflation, an excess creation of fiat money, other problems remain.

Given the huge increase in money supply and the Fed's easing policies, why has inflation remained relatively modest?

Most people overlook this, but inflation isn't just that new money is created. It has to then get into the economy, allowing participants to bid up the prices of goods and services that, in the short run, are relatively fixed.

Typically, when the Fed lowers interest rates, that doesn't mean that a printing press starts running around the clock somewhere in the bowels of the Treasury Department. Rather, lower rates are supposed to encourage borrowers to take on more loans.

Since banks make loans, newly created loans effectively serve the same purpose of freshly printed paper money. But, as you'll recall from Chapter 4, banks are hoarding cash or investing the excess with the Treasury by buying bonds rather than making loans to consumers.

From a balance-sheet perspective, it's a safer bet for the bank. Despite a downgrade in America's credit rating, the Federal Deposit Insurance Company (FDIC) and the Fed have assured banks that Treasury debt can still be carried on its books with no risk. That's in stark contrast to loans, although the suspension of mark-to-market accounting, which requires updating an asset's value based on its current price rather than original purchase price, means that a $500,000 loan can be listed on the books for the full value, even if it's defaulted and the property securing the loan is only worth $250,000.

Thus, while inflation is still a monetary phenomenon, it still won't come into play until that excess money actually gets into the economy. Printing trillions of dollars and leaving them in a vault somewhere does nothing for the economy. However, if it manages to get out to a wide enough population to bid up prices, we'll see inflation return with a vengeance.

Nonmonetary Explanations for Inflation

While I lean strongly toward the monetary view of inflation, whereby money printing is the root cause of inflation, the so-called Keynesians are still with us. With the financial crisis came the resurgence of Keynesian economics, a branch of economics that views the government as a needed element to balance insufficient demand during periods of recession.

In the Keynesian worldview, nonmonetary factors can and do contribute to inflation rates.

The first of these factors, *demand-pull inflation*, occurs when there's an increased demand for goods and services themselves from consumers or the government.

Since strong demand for a good will encourage the private sector to step up production, Keynesian economists view this type of inflation as a good thing, since more goods are being made and more workers are being hired.

The second Keynesian explanation for inflation is *cost-push infla-tion*, which is when the total supply of a good suddenly drops. If a crop of oranges in Florida is ruined by frost, for example, then prices of orange juice will rise in the short term. Thus, cost-push inflation is viewed as negative. Society has to spend more money on the acquisi-tion of a reduced amount of a good.

Finally, Keynesians explain inflation by way of the fact that it's simply "built-in" to the economy. Essentially, this view of inflation is that prices rise because people expect it to rise. Workers may receive annual cost of living adjustments of a certain extent expect the prices of everything to go up by a certain extent.

Velocity: The Gas Running the Economic Tank

Outside of Keynesian and monetary explanations is the concept of *velocity*. This refers to how often a given dollar changes hands.

If the economy is a car, then the Federal Reserve's influence on inter-est rates is akin to stepping on the gas pedal when lowering rates and hitting the brakes when raising rates. Yes, this affects the speed of the car (the growth of the economy). But the actual engine needs gas to run, and these pedals merely affect the flow. Velocity is the gas in the tank.

Imagine a dollar bill in your wallet. Not just any dollar either, but a specific one that's perhaps dog-eared and torn at one corner.

If the economy is humming along, you might spend that dollar at a farmer's market in the morning. The farmer may then go and spend it on lunch at a nearby café. The café may then use that dollar to pay out the day's wages to its busboy, who then goes to a corner store and buys a loaf of bread. The store owner uses that dollar in change to a businessman, who hands it off to a homeless man on the street.

In other words, that one unit of currency is used in a frequent num-ber of transactions. Ultimately, the supply of money is irrelevant, as long as the same unit can be used often and repeatedly.

But velocity peaked in the late 1990s. It dropped like a rock during the financial crisis, as seen in Figure 8.1.

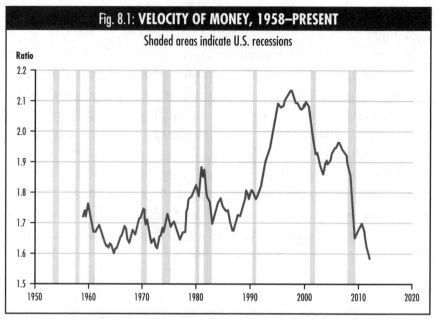

Fig. 8.1: **VELOCITY OF MONEY, 1958–PRESENT**

Shaded areas indicate U.S. recessions

Source: Federal Reserve Bank of St. Louis | 2012 research.stlouisfed.org

Money velocity has slowed to a halt. This means that efforts to flood the financial system with cash won't be particularly effective.

Here's why: Instead of going to the farmer's market, you buy food in bulk at the grocery store and pay with your credit card. You put your excess cash under the mattress . . . just in case.

If velocity were zero, the money supply could be infinite, and there'd still be no economic activity. That's like having a car with a bone-dry gas tank.

When velocity rates kick up, so will inflation rates. But inflation still ran at a rapid rate during the period between 1998 and 2008, even as velocity slowed. So it's not a perfect measure of inflation. But, if inflation rates rise while velocity starts to tick up as well, that should send a clear signal that it's time to shift investment allocations to assets that perform well during higher rates of inflation.

Risks to the US Dollar: Loss of Reserve Currency Status

As inflation rages, the US dollar will increasingly join the role enjoyed by the Japanese yen as a "carry trade" currency. That means traders will borrow dollars at a low rate of interest to buy currencies, stocks, and bonds that carry a higher rate of interest.

While it likely won't become as strong a carry trade currency as the yen was through 2007, it still bodes poorly for the dollar. This means that actual deflation is highly unlikely, as even Japan grew its money supply enough to keep deflation low in the past twenty-five years.

The fiat currency regime is still in relative infancy. The final tie to gold was severed in 1971 when President Nixon took us off the gold standard. With perpetually low interest rates to keep the recession from spiraling downward and further breaching Great Depression territory, dollars are going to be cheap to borrow for years to come.

We simply can't tell how it will play out in terms of time or severity — but it won't end well for the dollar. It's a simple matter of incentives. You take care of a car you own, but you never wash a rental car. It'll be the same thing with the dollar — it's become a sort of "rental currency."

But there's a great way to profit off of all that. You see, by borrowing dollars today at a low, fixed rate, you can let inflation repay down the line.

It's a term I like to think of as "penny dollars." You borrow dollars today and pay back essentially in pennies tomorrow, courtesy of the Fed's loose monetary policy.

If you think about it, a couple who bought a home in 1965 with a thirty-year, fixed-rate mortgage (through 1995) did quite well under the "penny-dollar" scheme. That fixed rate stayed the same throughout stagflation of the 1970s, double-digit interest rates of the 1980s, and a decline in the dollar's value of over 50 percent. (Okay, so in shorter periods it's more of a 50-cent dollar, but it's still a good deal.)

Even better, inflation works across the board, increasing the value of hard assets. It certainly doesn't hurt companies that have the kind of pricing power and competitive advantage to raise prices in excess of inflation either.

In other words, inflation means you should be in every anticash position available — even currencies in countries with more responsible central bankers and less fiscal shenanigans. Let's take a look at specific investments for periods of high inflation.

The Best Investments for High Inflation

- Invest in gold and silver. During the 1970s when inflation rates exploded to double digits, inflation rose 112 percent. Gold, however, returned over 2,300 percent. Granted, this includes a time when Americans were finally allowed to own gold again, so there had been some pent-up consumer demand. So let's look at a more recent decade.

  From 1999 through 2007, the dollar lost over 25 percent of its value due to inflation, but gold rose over four-fold from its most recent cyclical bottom.

  Silver will likely have greater returns, as it has during prior periods of high inflation, but it will have a more volatile ride.

- Nonmonetary commodities have also performed well during periods of high inflation rates. No matter what happens, people still need energy, food, and other basic materials. Investments in this area include oil, natural gas, copper, and agricultural commodities.

- You can do well with real estate during periods of high inflation, especially on rental properties. Rents can be increased annually, and, if you lock in a fixed-rate mortgage, you can pay it off with depreciated dollars.

  In addition, the tax benefits of real estate offer some shelter from rising nominal income that may occur during periods of high inflation.

- Dividend-paying stocks in companies in a dominant industry position should fare well. If inflation drives up a company's costs, it can simply pass on higher prices to consumers. But companies with a dominant position will fare best overall.

  Let me explain. Consumers buy certain brands despite changes in price. Essentially, whether a six pack of Coke costs $1.00 or $1.50, consumers won't change their demand. That's not true when the alternative is between chicken and steak, where consumers will change their purchases depending on the overall price.

- For the risk averse, Treasury Inflation-Protected Securities (TIPS) offer partial protection against higher rates of inflation.

That's because interest and principal payments on these bonds are tied to the Consumer Price Index (CPI). Effectively, the principal is designed to increase with inflation. Since interest is paid biannually at a fixed rate, an increase in principal means an increase in the interest payment.

However, the CPI often understates the true rate of inflation. That's why TIPS only offer partial protection

- For the extreme risk-taker, currency investments offer high potential returns, especially in exotic currencies like the Mexican peso or South African rand. These currencies tend to strengthen with the prices of oil and gold, respectively.

The Case for Deflation

Before World War II, one hallmark of a "recession" was the fact that prices were falling, as well as production and unemployment. And yet, in every recession since World War II, prices, especially consumer goods prices, have been rising . . . we have suffered through several "inflationary recessions," where we get hit by both inflation and recession at the same time, suffering the worst of both worlds.

— **Murray Rothbard,** dean of the Austrian school of economics, which holds that inflation is purely a function of excessive money creation, whether paper or electronic[25]

Let's face facts. Today's media on-the-airheads would be able to spin the Great Depression as a "jobless recovery." In fact, when looking at employment, wages, and housing prices, there's a strong case to be made for deflation right now.

During the Great Depression, the lack of new job creation wasn't the problem — it was the ongoing and pervasive job destruction over the span of a few short years. It culminated in 1935, when one in every five workers was unemployed. Figure 8.2 shows the official unemployment rate, as well as alternative employment rates based on calculation methods used prior to the 1970s.

Naturally, government stepped in. 1946 saw the passage of the Employment Act, making full employment an official government policy.

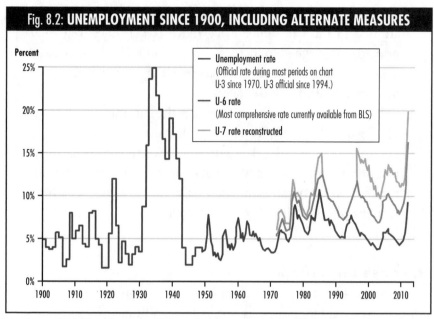

Fig. 8.2: **UNEMPLOYMENT SINCE 1900, INCLUDING ALTERNATE MEASURES**

Source: BLS | All numbers except U-7 reconstruction are seasonally adjusted. U-6 data from 1970-1993 (and U-7 from 1970-1982). Interpolated from yearly BLS data. U-7 reconstruction since 1994 is U-6 plus smoothing to "want a job now" dataset.

At the height of the Great Depression, one in five workers was unemployed. Based on old methodologies, today's unemployment rate is closing in on that number.

But politicians can only generally think in terms of pairs. What does the government use as a policy tool to offset unemployment? Inflation.

And as it stands today, inflation is still a major concern for the Federal Reserve. With unemployment officially flirting with double-digit rates, the highest level since the early 1980s, inflation will definitely take a backseat to employment for the time being.

And that means the Fed will hold interest rates down and print more money than we will ultimately need if it can get folks back to work. Yes, even if it means digging ditches and filling them back in (a move that's literally out of the Keynesian playbook).

It's an easy argument to make. Credit destruction from the failure of thousands of banks from 1929 through early 1933 was deflationary. The Fed had a tight monetary policy in the early years of the crisis. Some consider that a "mistake" that shouldn't be repeated again.

Federal Reserve Chairman Ben Bernanke is one of them. Flooding the system with money by keeping rates low is supposed to prevent deflation. In reality, deflation can't be prevented. But print enough money, and you can certainly hide it with enough inflation elsewhere.

Case for Lost Decade

The proactive policies of government and central banks today mirror the deflationary experience Japan had in the 1990s — the so-called "Lost Decade."

First off, the name's misleading. Japan's decline is entering its third decade. In the United States, stocks are in their second Lost Decade.

The initial start of Japan's Lost Decade should sound familiar. Loans were made out on rapidly rising real estate prices rather than on more conservative metrics such as cash flow. The easy lending policies led to further price appreciation in land.

At the start of the Lost Decade, the value of all real estate in Tokyo alone was reputed to be worth more than the value of all real estate in the United States.

Think about that for a minute. A few hundred square miles of highly urbanized land carried a greater nominal value than a few hundred million miles of land diversified by vast resources and a mix of everything from undeveloped land to farmland to forests and mines to the highly developed and urbanized.

Hindsight tells us now what common sense should have back then: Japan had some serious problems it needed to acknowledge. But the point of the Lost Decades is that Japan has been taking the easy way out, refusing to acknowledge the reality of its excesses.

And that behavior is already starting to play out in the United States and other Western nations in the past few years. We've already seen the start of it in the stock market, which quickly wiped out a decade of gains in less than eighteen months during the 2008–2009 crash.

While the same thing happened in Japan — it continued getting worse. Figure 8.3 shows Japanese stocks have declined to the lowest levels since 1982, almost entirely unwinding their huge rally that started in the 1970s.

Fig. 8.3: **JAPAN'S NIKKEI 225 INDEX: 1970–PRESENT**

Source: Bank of Japan

Over the course of nearly twenty years, the Japanese stock market slowly unwound the speculative excesses of 1982–1990.

The Best Investments during Periods of Deflation

The dollar has benefited for decades as the world's reserve currency. And, with the rise of other nations and a general unease over the Fed's inflationary policies, that's about to gradually come to an end. Perpetually low interest rates compel a higher purpose for the dollar than a store of wealth. Already, other countries led by the likes of China and Russia are clamoring for a new world reserve currency.

But, if the deflation argument holds, the US dollar will do something unexpected: it will strengthen.

Think about it this way: Say you go to the grocery store and buy a can of soup for $1. But, one week, there's a sale where you buy one, get one free. Suddenly your $1 buys you two cans of soup. That's a bit of a simplification, but it demonstrates purchasing power increasing. The same amount of money buys more goods.

Ironically then, if there's persistent and ongoing deflation, then the economy will grind to a halt. That happens when nobody wants to buy anything because they expect even lower prices in the future.

During times of deflation, cash will become the best asset to own.

The next-best asset to own will be fixed-income investments that generate cash. Why? Because every payment in dollars during a period of inflation, even if it's a fixed amount, will throw off more purchasing power each time.

Of course, thanks to deflation, bonds may fall in price over time as well, leading to such a loss that you have to sell them. So, even though they're the next-best way to profit from deflation, they're a distant second.

It'll also be a boon to savers, who will see their purchasing power increase. Anyone with substantial debts will have to bear a burden, however, as it means that their real payments, when adjusted for deflation, are increasing.

Ultimately, that's why deflation is unlikely. Our economy is based on debt. Interest rates drive the incentive to take on a mortgage, secure a car loan, or start a new business. When people want to borrow, this extra money gets into the system.

Right now, the extra money is not in the system. People don't want to borrow, and banks have opted to lend money to the government by buying US Treasury debt. That's why it's easy to find evidence of deflation in so many places right now.

The possibility that we face a deflationary trend akin to that of the Great Depression is possible but remote. Nevertheless, it's important to remember that deflation, as with inflation, is a monetary phenomenon, created by the political process and an accommodating central bank.

As Milton Friedman pointed out, "The Great Depression, like most other periods of severe unemployment, was produced by government mismanagement rather than by any inherent instability of the private economy."

Conclusion: The "Sweet Spot" of Investing

There are a lot of working parts, and weighing each factor correctly or incorrectly will impact investment returns. Of course, it could also work out better than expected — at least until it doesn't.

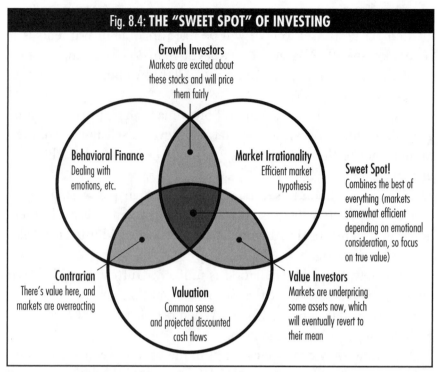

For most investors, the important thing is to hit the sweet spot where the best elements of various investment styles combine in a way that minimizes their shortcomings.

So how do you balance the different perspectives we've looked at? Very carefully. Analyze the market for news. Are you looking to invest in a "hot" sector? If so, you may have to worry more about behavioral finance. Are you looking to buy a company trading for less than its net cash? If so, you may be weighing your decision based on the irrational pricing of the market.

On the whole, when done right, your investment portfolio should hit a "sweet spot" that captures the advantages of key market techniques and mitigates the disadvantages as much as possible. I've outlined the key points in Figure 8.4.

WRAP-UP
The Case for Inflation — and the Case for Deflation

- Modest amounts of inflation have been the norm; however, there have been some periods with above-average inflation rates.

- Outside of pure money printing, a general level of price increases can happen due to other means.
- The velocity of money is important but doesn't completely correlate to inflation rates. Nevertheless, a period of high inflation may see higher velocity levels.
- To best preserve and grow your wealth during periods of increased inflation, gold, silver, commodities, real estate, stocks, Treasury Inflation-Protected Securities (TIPs), and currencies make for the optimal investments.
- However, high unemployment rates, stagnating income, a lost decade in the stock market and declining housing prices point to a possible deflation scenario. In short, deflation remains possible, but unlikely.
- While a short bout of deflation may occur, it my serve as an excuse for further easing measures to juice inflation — leading to higher inflation rates over the long term.
- Ultimately, investors will have to spend the next few years with a careful eye toward either outcome. Over the longer term, however, inflation will prove to be the inevitable consequence of today's low interest rates and government easing.

9

Cash and Cash Equivalents in the Age of Chaos

"That clinking, clanking, clunking sound
is all that makes the world go 'round**"**

— Cabaret

HAT ROLE DOES CASH — or any other low-yielding but highly liquid investment — play in today's unprecedented world of quantitative easing? The fast and easy answer might be to mention cash investments as a footnote of investment history and move on.

After all, there's little to no yield in holding cash, and the era of quantitative easing (making money out of thin air) ensures that the government will prop up other assets.

But, alas, the world is more complicated than that. It always has been. Granted, unprecedented government involvement has brought new challenges with it. Those challenges are simple: the endless string of crises to shake confidence in the world's easy-money policies.

Whether it's a debt crisis in Europe, the world's fourth-strongest earthquake in Japan, or unrest in the Middle East and North Africa, each new crisis shakes the underlying reality of a market heavily influenced by meddlesome politicians and central bankers.

But cash is important. It's vital. It represents the savings necessary before you can make investments. And that's why cash has a substantial role to play for you as a sensible investor, no matter what takes place in the world.

The role of cash remains threefold: first, against the unlikely (but possible) prospect of deflation; next, to prepare for unforeseen consequences of extraneous crises that roil markets; and, finally, to keep some "dry powder" on hand to take advantage of market mispricing.

Deflationary Spiral: Unlikely but Possible

Deflation, the bane of central bankers everywhere, was on a lot of minds in the early days of the collapse of the housing market.

But here's the funny thing: deflation used to be a normal state of affairs!

You see, back when markets were closer to a purely laissez-faire capitalism, rising output, and a relatively stable supply of gold and silver meant that the amount of goods available in the economy rose greater than the money supply. More goods relative to the same amount of money mean prices should fall.

However, inflation has always been the rule except for three periods since the creation of the Federal Reserve: immediately after World War I, the Great Depression, and now 2008/2009.

That's quite the contrast! Indeed, the Fed's ninety-eight-year track record is one of abysmal failure when compared to its stated goal of "keeping prices stable." In terms of purchasing power, the dollar has lost 98 percent of its purchasing power since 1913, as seen in Figure 9.1.

Central bankers say two contradictory things: First, that they must fight the perceived evil of deflation. Second, they say it's their goal to keep prices stable. But the historical record tells a different story.

Prior to the creation of the Federal Reserve in the United States, inflation was much more inconsistent. It was certainly not today's traditional view of perpetually falling rates of inflation that the average American today has had to deal with over the past thirty years.

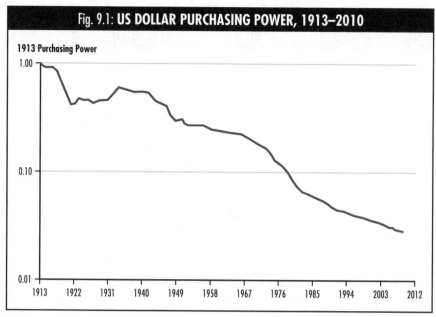

Fig. 9.1: US DOLLAR PURCHASING POWER, 1913–2010

1913 Purchasing Power

Source: Global Financial Data

As a result of decades of persistent inflation, the US dollar has lost 98 percent of its value since 1913.

Periods of rampant inflation prior to the Fed's founding in 1913 tend to cluster around times of massive government spending. During the Revolutionary War, inflation was so rampant on the Continental, the paper currency, that the phrase "not worth a continental" was coined. The War of 1812 and the Civil War saw similar results.

But, as governments paid off their debts (a key difference between a responsible republic and an empire that eventually falters), prices that went up tended to come back down. This gave way to periods of deflation as an expanding economy led to the rapid expansion and quality of goods and services, which drove prices down.

One such period of deflation, from 1873–1896, was originally called the Great Depression before the title was stolen by the events of 1929–1932. During this first so-called Great Depression, rapid economic expansion in railroads, new technologies, and farming methods allowed prices to fall but at a huge benefit to society.

As Figure 9.2 shows, real gross national product (GNP) per capita exploded by over 50 percent during this period, even though falling prices gave it the "feel" that times were tough.

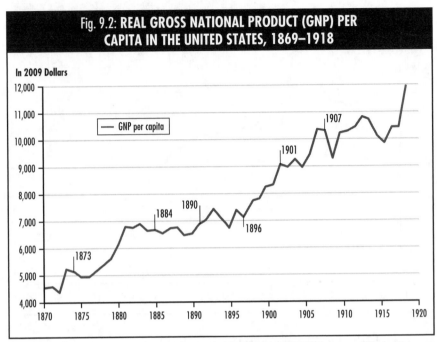

Fig. 9.2: **REAL GROSS NATIONAL PRODUCT (GNP) PER CAPITA IN THE UNITED STATES, 1869–1918**

Published: May 15, 2012 | Courtesy of ShadowStats.com

Despite being considered the greatest depression before the Great Depression, real gross national product per capita surged over 50 percent in the United States between 1873 and 1896.

Large cash holdings during deflationary periods eventually offer the kind of substantial investing opportunities that legends are made of, as purchasing power allows for more assets to be picked up on the cheap.

Then the government took control of the money supply. That culminated with the creation of the Federal Reserve in 1913. Since then, the Fed has created the myth that deflation is an evil bogeyman that must be stopped at all costs and that some slight inflation would actually benefit us all!

The deflation we saw in 2009 wasn't the result of a monetary collapse. The Fed and Congress saw to that with easy-money policies. Housing is one major component of deflation, as banks went from issuing mortgages to anyone with a pulse to only issuing mortgages to buyers who practically had enough assets and income on hand to buy them outright!

But another trend helped with deflation as well: The modest decline of prices in 2009 can be partially explained as the result of shifting consumer preferences. Instead of loading up on unhealthy amounts of debt to finance a consumerist lifestyle, we're seeing a shift to a healthier financial diet that focuses on cutting out debt and watching the balance sheet much more closely.

This is reflected best in the trend of rising personal savings rates, which strongly rebounded during the crisis as consumer debt outstanding fell as well. What a contrast from only a few years ago when the savings rate went negative! Data from the Federal Reserve, outlined in Figure 9.3, shows the spike in savings rates that has already started to come back down.

The negative savings rate in late 2005 was the worst savings rate since the Great Depression. Of course, back then, 25 percent unemployment and lack of social nets compelled many to draw down their savings.

Today unemployment isn't as bad (if you use the official government numbers), but social nets like unemployment insurance have lulled average Americans into a false sense of financial security. They've been unprepared for the severity and duration of today's unemployment.

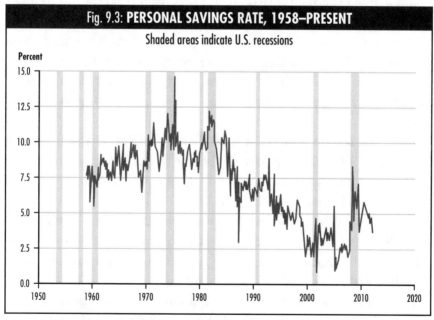

Fig. 9.3: **PERSONAL SAVINGS RATE, 1958–PRESENT**

Shaded areas indicate U.S. recessions

Source: U.S. Department of Commerce: Bureau of Economic Analysis | 2012 research.stlouisfed.org

After reaching record lows earlier in the decade, Americans are starting to save again. However, the 5 percent savings rate is still too low to ensure financial security, much less a retirement.

Today's personal savings rates are far below the typical rate that most Americans saved even during the high-inflation years of the 1970s!

In 2005, when savings went negative, nearly all asset classes were on a tear. That includes the growing bubble in real estate, commodities and stocks. Unemployment was in the 5–6 percent range, a surprisingly healthy number.

Of course, we know how this story ends. Artificially low interest rates led the world on a buying spree in real estate, where perceived increases in wealth translated into more consumer goods, more investments in stocks, and so on.

By keeping rates low, the Federal Reserve compelled money that could have gone into safe cash positions into other, riskier areas. Indeed, in the housing market, "no income, no job" loans became commonplace as lending standards declined below a rational level.

The real estate bubble was fantastic for creating the illusion of prosperity: We saw real assets being built. We saw a flurry of construction and real estate jobs, which in turn helped keep unemployment low.

But a home is not an ATM. The returns from real estate and stocks entail substantially more risk than cash-related holdings. What may appear to be a sure thing is more likely to be a huge investment mistake if incentives are distorted, such as by artificially low interest rates.

Who would have really bought houses they couldn't afford if interest rates were higher and banks actually had underwriting standards? Nobody.

Interest rates are lower now than they were in 2005 and likely will be for some time. Yet with so many people burned or scared by plunging equity, housing, and job markets, there is now a widespread urge to clean up personal balance sheets.

It's likely that we'll see weak consumer spending for *years*, possibly as long as a decade. Consumers will continue to shun high-interest rate credit cards and move toward earnings- and savings-based spending rather than debt-fueled spending.

Even with the modest decline in prices in 2009, the long-term trend is clear: Deflation remains unlikely barring some massive, unforeseeable event. Staying cash-heavy out of fears for deflation is the wrong reason to keep your investment portfolio cash-heavy.

Fortunately, there are better reasons to keep a good 10–20 percent of your portfolio in cash and cash equivalents at all times. And that's because, even though central bankers and politicians have stepped in to promise stability, the real world is a different place. Radical changes can and do happen frequently. Often, some of these changes are largely unknown.

Prepare for Unforeseen Consequences

Cash provides another unique role in investing besides personal savings and the accumulation of capital. Simply put, cash allows you to invest when unforeseeable events drive prices to bargain levels.

Even if the current macroeconomic environment is primed for one investment to soar, and even if that investment has fundamentals that suggest strong strength, something unexpected can still happen.

Someone who invested in BP in March 2010 would have been in the same position.

Macroeconomic conditions were favorable for rising prices in oil and natural gas. The company had a fat dividend payment and traded at a slight discount to other major oil producers.

But that didn't last. One month and a major spill in the Gulf of Mexico later, and the stock took a 40 percent hit in value.

For most, this was the time to panic. For others, it was an opportunity. Once BP's total liabilities for the spill were reasonably known, it was simple to crunch the numbers and determine that shares had sold off far in excess of any liabilities. Consequently, that was the time to put some cash to work and buy shares.

There's always some kind of BP-style event happening somewhere in the markets. Keeping cash on hand allows you to take advantage of these common, but short-term, opportunities.

Keep the Powder Dry, but Know When to Use It

We know that the Fed's money creation will likely cause substantially higher levels of inflation at some unknown future date. Perhaps even hyperinflation will occur as a result.

But let's be rational and face reality. Most of the cash that's being created isn't getting into the economy in the form of new loans, capital investment, or jobs — it is being used to shore up balance sheets, at the moment, of the bailout banks.

Indeed, courtesy of the Fed's quantitative easing and Congress's 2008 Troubled Asset Relief Program (TARP) plan, nearly one trillion dollars of excess bank reserves is sitting in bank vaults and with the Fed (where they conveniently earn interest). Figure 9.4 shows the spike.

The problem isn't interest rates right now. It's risk.

And here's the key thing: If it's too risky, banks simply *won't* make the loan. They'd rather pile into a no-risk asset, like Treasury bonds, rather than make a loan right now.

Alas, we don't live in a world where money supply is regulated by the individual decisions of billions going about their daily business. But think about it this way: in the long run, deflation now would be healthy for the economy.

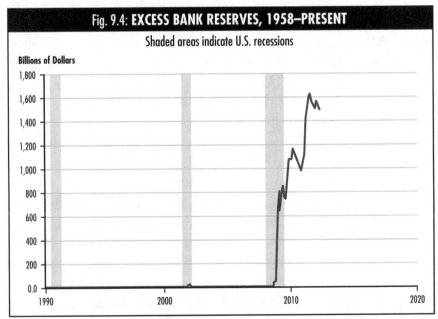

Source: Board of Governors of the Federal Reserve System | 2012 research.stlouisfed.org

After reaching record lows earlier in the decade, Americans are starting to save again. However, the 5 percent savings rate is still too low to ensure financial security, much less a retirement.

It would stop forestalling the inevitable. Losses would have to be taken on bad economic choices. Businesses saddled with unserviceable debt would go bankrupt or get bought out at prices far below current levels.

The upside, however, is that the recovery process would be much quicker. Bad economic choices would indeed have bad consequences. This would make a repeat of the previous debt excesses less likely (at least in the *near* future). Best of all, it wouldn't monetize the problems or grow the size of government in the process.

Delaying the liquidation of bad banks in the 1930s helped prolong the Great Depression. The Fed pursued a policy of deflation in the 1930s by hiking interest rates and contracting the money supply.

But that deflationary policy was more than offset with Keynesian-style public works projects, modestly under Hoover and substantially under Roosevelt.

Today, pumping money into banks is all the rage, and government spending is going through the roof. We would have a set of worrisome conditions.

If that suddenly were to come to an end, then investors would no longer assume that prices will be propped up indefinitely. That could lead to some profit taking, meaning investors with cash on hand can pick up quality assets on the cheap.

In later chapters, we'll look in more detail at investments that can prosper during periods of higher inflation and hyperinflation, as well as investments that can prosper during a prolonged period of deflation.

When a Mattress Just Won't Do: The Best Ways to Store Your Cash

Eventually, running the printing press will have inflationary results, assuming, of course, that such money makes it into circulation.

Right now, propping up the banking system with excessive reserves is keeping a lid on bank loans, keeping new money from circulating. Add in the fear of average consumers in the light of a weak housing market and substantially high unemployment rates, and it's clear that the inflationary boost will eradicate any *real* gains on cash-related investments.

While we're seeing rising food and energy prices, the drag on housing is keeping "official" measures of inflation low. And following a two-year rally in many paper assets, there's nothing wrong with going the low-risk route.

Now, how much of your portfolio you reserve for cash will depend on a lot of factors such as your age, income needs and risk tolerance. Given the uncertainty of the world, it would be rational to keep 10–20 percent of your net worth in cash and cash equivalents.

It's small enough to ensure that you're invested in assets that can provide the best inflation-beating return but still leave you enough to make meaningful investments when the opportunity arises. While a sizeable chunk of cash will lower your risk, it doesn't mean you have to give up yield.

In the age of chaos, there are two key reasons to stick to cash. The first is to avoid and mitigate losses. When assets like stocks and commodities crash, they do so in dollar terms. Cash doesn't suffer a loss.

Secondly, keeping cash on hand is critical to take advantage of the lower prices that are available *after* a crash. Every dollar can now buy more than it could before, thanks to the selloff.

If you're looking for short-term vehicles to park your cash, there are plenty of opportunities.

The iShares Lehman Brothers 1–3 Year Treasury ETF (SHY) and iShares Lehman Brothers Short Treasury ETF (SHV) are better than using cash to firm up your mattress or insulate your home. SHY sports a 3.3 percent yield; SHV has a lower, 1.7 percent yield. While these rates are low, there is the advantage of better liquidity than directly buying and selling bonds.

A forward-looking play for future inflation protection can be achieved through the *iShares Barclays TIPS Bond ETF (TIP)*, a US government bond that's designed to pay a higher rate in the event of inflation. It's certainly better than most government bonds, which provide a substantially low return right now and will more likely provide a net *negative* return once higher inflation is taken into account.

Foreign currencies can provide a higher yield than the dollar. Some countries have been largely unaffected by high levels of debt or are resource rich and have recovered sharply since early 2009. We'll delve further into the role of currency investing in the age of quantitative easing in a later chapter.

However, outside currencies themselves, higher-yielding debt from governments outside the United States can provide a way to stay cash-heavy without having to lose all gains to inflation. One such fund is the **Aberdeen Asia-Pacific Income Fund (NYSE:FAX)**, which has a substantial 6.2 percent dividend yield with monthly payouts.

WRAP-UP
The Role of Cash

- Although deflation is unlikely, it is not impossible. During periods of deflation, cash represents the best store of value, as cash can be used to buy an increasing amount of goods and services.
- The market can be disorderly when unforeseen events occur. Having some cash on hand allows for opportunities to avoid the worst and invest when the clouds begin to clear.
- Markets can misprice assets, and keeping cash on hand allows for rapid deployment to those opportunities without having to leave other profitable investment opportunities on the table.
- In today's world of money printing, cash can be kept in select bond funds for a better yield than the pittance in savings and money market accounts.

10

Generating Cash in a Low-Yielding but Turbulent World

———

"Do you know the only thing that gives me
pleasure? It's to see my dividends coming in.**"**
— *John D. Rockefeller*

I NCOME HAS ALWAYS BEEN the key to making money in investments
throughout history.

Don't get me wrong, stock appreciation is great too. There's
nothing like speculating on a stock, being right, and banking profits
of several hundred to several thousand percent.

But you can't count on being able to persistently make those kinds
of gains. For every "ten bagger," the stock that rises tenfold, there are
many more stocks that don't go anywhere, decline, or go bankrupt.

Ultimately, preserving capital is key for reaching retirement goals.
As you get older and closer to retirement, the last thing you want to do
is risk your money on the next big thing, only to see it blow up.

In fact, a great way to think of risk is the likelihood of **permanent
loss of capital**. By owning assets that produce income, you lower the
risk substantially compared to chasing the latest "fad" stock.

In the days before the 1929 market crash that brought about the
SEC and other regulations, investors looking at stocks relied *entirely*
on the income. They demanded higher dividend yields than seen in

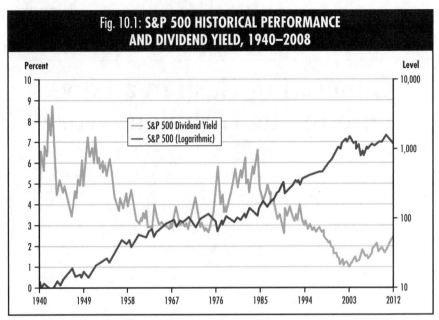

Fig. 10.1: **S&P 500 HISTORICAL PERFORMANCE AND DIVIDEND YIELD, 1940–2008**

Dividend yields on the market hit a record low when stocks hit an inflation-adjusted record peak in 2000. But, it now appears that dividend yields are on the rise.

markets today. Indeed, early stocks often had a set par value and were more often bought for the high dividends than capital appreciation.

Why? Because the regular payout of cash to shareholders proved that a company really brought in cash to begin with.

That's a huge contrast when compared to today's stock chasers, looking for fat capital gains and little, if any, dividends. Since the "great stock market bull run" began in 1980, the average dividend yield on the S&P 500 has dropped from 6 percent to under 2 percent today, as seen in Figure 10.1.

When fast-moving stocks get crushed, most stock chasers watch as their portfolios are decimated. Even if they did manage to take profits off the table, it doesn't mean the next hot stock will be a winner — it could just be the next company to announce financial shenanigans, like Groupon (NASDAQ:GRPN) did in early 2012.

There's a substantially better way to consistently make money in stocks than chase the markets. This was confirmed in a ground-breaking study made by Wharton School of Economics professor Jeremy Siegel. In his 1994 book *Stocks for the Long Run,* Siegel's research showed that over a long enough time period, the returns on stocks with the dividends reinvested beat every other asset class hands down.

For his follow-up book, *The Future for Investors*, Siegel examined the individual stocks in the S&P 500 that had the best performance since the late 1950s. His results were *astonishing*: due to the power of reinvested income from dividends, the best performing stocks in the S&P 500 were the "stodgy" companies in the index that were never replaced with high-flying growth companies.

The best performing stock was tobacco producer Philip Morris (now Altria Group, NYSE:MO), with nearly 20-percent annual returns. That includes a period where tobacco stocks were hit with multibillion dollar lawsuits, saw their advertising banned, and were vilified more than banks are today!

The primary reason for Philip Morris's amazing return in spite of these headwinds was the reinvestment of dividends. Philip Morris continued to raise its dividends annually, so when new tobacco litigation slammed the stock's price, each dividend payment would buy more shares (or fractions of shares) than it would have at a higher price.

This left investors with a substantial number of shares, each spinning off ever-rising dividend income. As Siegel put it, "Although the earnings, sales, and even market values of the new firms grew faster than those of the older firms, the price investors paid for these stocks was simply too high to generate good returns. These higher prices meant lower dividend yields and therefore, fewer shares accumulated through reinvesting dividends."

A few other stocks performed almost as well as the tobacco producer. Siegel found that the top twenty highest returning companies in the original S&P 500 were dominated from the consumer staples, pharmaceuticals, and energy sectors.[26]

Replicate Siegel's Research with Dividend Growth Stocks

If you have a long-term outlook and you don't need current income, the best approach to building a large pool of retirement income is to find quality, dividend-paying stocks and reinvest the capital for a prolonged period.

Focusing on companies with a history of growing their dividend over time will be even more lucrative when it comes time to stop reinvesting and start living off the dividends. This is especially true for tax-deferred accounts, where the 15 percent tax rate on dividends doesn't come into play.

Many lists are available online showing companies that have increased their dividends annually. Studying these lists shows a few key differences between a dividend grower and other types of companies:

- First, the company has a "moat." That means it has some kind of advantage over its competitors. Walmart's distribution system gives it an advantage over other retailers. Kraft's brands are more trusted than lesser-known food products. Coke's brand and bottling network can't be replicated by a startup today. It can even include intellectual property, like IBM, a company that creates hundreds of new patents each year.

- Second, the company needs to generate substantial cash-flow. These are the types of companies that benefit from recessions and credit crunches. They've got the balance sheets to stay in business and even expand when their weaker competitors go out of business. A company that can consistently bring in large amounts of cash also has the financial reserves available to pay out dividends every year.

- Third, the company has a parasitic relationship with inflation. What do I mean by that? It's simple. The company has the power to raise prices and pass higher inflationary costs onto their consumers. Whether it's a service company like Automatic Data Processing, or a consumer goods producer like McDonald's or Hershey's, when prices go up, they can respond with price increases (or in the case of consumer goods makers, decrease the quantity of their product per serving).

It's no surprise that companies meeting these simple criteria for dividend growth are well-known, large-cap household names. These companies know they can't rapidly grow the size of their business like they have in the past, so they now focus on paying a dividend.

And, as we've seen from Siegel's research, reinvesting these dividends is the key to higher returns, even if the share price moves nowhere.

You can do well by investing in dividend achievers, companies with a history of growing their dividend over time. But a few advanced income strategies can help turbocharge your income, a necessity in today's low-yield world.

Advanced Strategies to Supercharge Your Income

STRATEGY 1: SIZE MATTERS — HIGH YIELD TRUMPS RISK OVER TIME

Think all yields are alike? Think again. A lot of people believe that if one investor is getting 10 percent and another 5 percent, the person getting 10 percent is getting double the return. That may be true for the first year, but over time the person with the higher yield will do *substantially* better, thanks to reinvesting those dividends. Here's how it works: Consider the case of Jack, a low-risk investor who buys $10,000 worth of bond funds earning 5 percent per year. By reinvesting, Table 10.1 shows how he performs over thirty years.

Table 10.1: JACK'S STRATEGY						
Year	Shares	Share Price	Amount	Annual Dividend	Total	Total Profit
1	1,000	$10.00	$10,000	$500	$10,500	$500
2	1,050	$10.00	$10,500	$525	$11,025	$1,025
3	1,103	$10.00	$11,025	$551	$11,576	$1,576
4	1,158	$10.00	$11,576	$579	$12,155	$2,155
5	1,216	$10.00	$12,155	$608	$12,763	$2,763
10	1,551	$10.00	$15,513	$776	$16,289	$6,289
15	1,980	$10.00	$19,799	$990	$20,789	$10,789
20	2,527	$10.00	$25,270	$1,263	$26,533	$16,533
25	3,225	$10.00	$32,251	$1,613	$33,864	$23,864
30	4,116	$10.00	$41,161	$2,058	$43,219	$33,219

Jack manages to more than triple his money over thirty years. Not bad! He's also getting dividend payments of over $2,000 per year — that's more than 20 percent of his original investment.

But thirty years is a long time. More than enough to see financial markets through some boom times and bust times.

Every thirty-year period in the market has seen some amazing transformations. An investor in 1900 saw a panic in 1907, the creation of the Federal Reserve in 1913, a stock market closure during World War I, a phenomenal postwar boom, and finally a major crash.

An investor who started in 1930 saw the same crash, a global depression, a global war, the beginning of the nuclear age, and the start of one of the most powerful demographic changes of all time. Over that period, even an investor who went all-in at the top of the 1929 market came out ahead, even during the period where most investors shied away from stocks.

An investor starting in the 1960s saw the emergence of the Nifty Fifty ("the only stocks you'll ever need"), their subsequent crash, and a twelve-year period of high inflation where stocks went nowhere before the start of one of the biggest and longest bull markets in history.

You get the idea. Over time, incredible changes in demographics, technology, hope, fear, and greed all tend to fall by the wayside.

Consider Jack's neighbor, Jill, who also starts investing $10,000 at the same time. However, Jill knows that over thirty years, it'll pay off to take some bigger risks. So she invests in some beaten-down investment funds offering a 10 percent yield.

Since Jill's initial yield is double that of Jack's, it stands to reason that she'll do at least twice as well, right? That's certainly true for the first year, but over time Jill comes out *much, much* better off. Jill's performance is summarized in Table 10.2.

By shooting for a higher yield, Jill manages to amass a nest egg that's five times greater than Jack's nest egg. Best of all, by the thirtieth year, Jill is getting income payments of nearly $16,000 — more than her original stake, each year!

Granted, Jill took on more risk than Jack did. But Jill recognized that the traditional concept of "risk" wasn't as important over time.

Table 10.2: **JILL'S STRATEGY**						
Year	Shares	Share Price	Amount	Annual Dividend	Total	Total Profit
1	1,000	$10.00	$10,000	$1,000	$11,000	$1,000
2	1,100	$10.00	$11,000	$1,100	$12,100	$2,100
3	1,210	$10.00	$12,100	$1,210	$13,310	$3,310
4	1,331	$10.00	$13,310	$1,331	$14,641	$4,641
5	1,464	$10.00	$14,641	$1,464	$16,105	$6,105
10	2,358	$10.00	$23,579	$2,358	$25,937	$15,937
15	3,797	$10.00	$37,975	$3,797	$41,772	$31,772
20	6,116	$10.00	$61,159	$6,116	$67,275	$57,275
25	9,850	$10.00	$98,497	$9,850	$108,347	$98,347
30	15,863	$10.00	$158,631	$15,863	$174,494	$164,494

What did matter was the final size of her nest egg — and how much income it was spinning off.

In both the case of Jack and Jill, we assumed that the share price went nowhere. But let's say Jack's investment also saw its share price increase an average of 5 percent per year. Taking into account that growth and subsequent dividend reinvestment, by Year 30, Jack acquires a nest egg with a total value of $95,670, more than twice the original $43,219 he originally owned.

Jill still comes out ahead even if her investment never appreciates in price.

Ideally, however, investors should get both capital gains and dividend growth. If Jack invested with an initial 5 percent yield but saw a 5 percent share appreciation every year *and* his investment dividends rose by 10 percent per year, he'd soon surpass Jill after the first few years.

By the end of thirty years, his investment in that scenario would have a total value of $1,162,746.93. He'd own 26,903 shares, having received over $904,090.63 in income. His annual return would work out to 17.18 percent, far above his 5 percent yield.

There are two conclusions: Yield counts, but dividend growth counts even more.

STRATEGY 2: UP, DOWN, OR SIDEWAYS, INCOME INVESTORS COME OUT AHEAD

Income investors don't need to worry about the direction of the market. In fact, a prolonged bear market is a golden opportunity!

Most investors focus on capital gains. Typically, around 80 percent of stocks trade in the direction of the market. So most investors want the market to rise. But, as a good income investor, you don't need the market to rise to make money.

In fact, a falling market is ideal. It means that dividend yields increase. If dividends are being reinvested, they'll buy a larger stake every time.

If you bought Johnson & Johnson (NYSE:JNJ), for example, you wouldn't have seen much appreciation in share price over the past ten years, as Figure 10.2 shows.

But if you reinvested your dividends in the health-care titan, you would have managed to eke out a 60 percent return over the past decade — while most common stocks have gone nowhere (or have even gone negative once adjusted for inflation)!

Why? Between 2000 and 2011 alone, the company nearly quadrupled its dividend payment from $0.62 per share to $2.28. On a

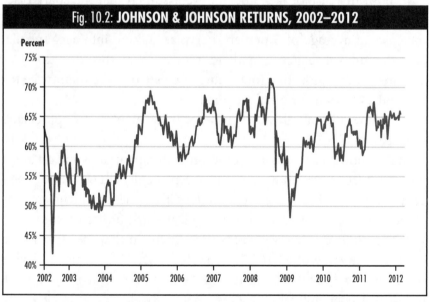

Fig. 10.2: JOHNSON & JOHNSON RETURNS, 2002–2012

Source: Yahoo! Finance

Johnson & Johnson isn't an exciting stock. But when investing for dividends, its flat share price still allowed for a 60 percent return as the dividend increased over 216 percent.

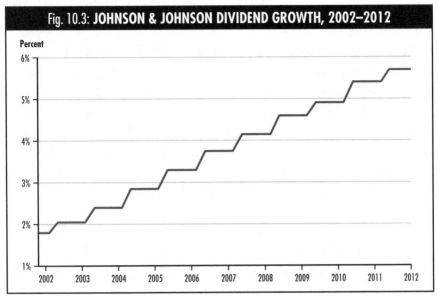

Fig. 10.3: JOHNSON & JOHNSON DIVIDEND GROWTH, 2002–2012

Source: ycharts.com

Finding an investment that can make consistently rising payments is the key to taking substantial risk out of investing. Johnson & Johnson's steadily rising dividends are a surefire way to grow your wealth over the long term.

quarterly basis, the company's $0.57 dividend has increased over 216 percent in the past ten years, as can be seen in Figure 10.3.

So, it doesn't matter if an investment goes up, goes down, or stays sideways. What really matters is getting an increasing cash flow.

Ironically, most investors don't take their investing that serious. They'd rather try to get on the ground floor of the "next" Intel, Walmart, Apple, or Google. They see a stock taking off or one that's been "hot" lately and try to go along for the ride.

Instead you can use an approach that's more likely to create value: Buy quality stocks on sale. When you're shopping at the grocery store, do you buy more or less steak when the price goes up? Probably less. You'd opt for chicken instead. Conversely, when a grocery store is having a buy-one-get-one-free sale, you load up.

Sound a lot like value investing? That's because it is. Income investors know that the price they pay is important. The initial price sets the initial yield. That can make a huge difference over time.

Of course, investors who try to buy an asset class when it's unloved and falling tend to do best over time. That's the philosophy behind the investment legends like Ben Graham, Warren Buffett, and Sir John Templeton.

Right now, the one market that fits the bill for a continued decline is housing. Nationwide housing prices are moving downward again. Lending standards remain incredibly tight after years of staying incredibly loose. In some states, the backlog of foreclosures could take *years* to unwind.

For anyone interested in becoming a landlord, the "yield" on real estate continues to get better and better. An investor who bought a $200,000 house and rented it out in 2005 might have gotten a paltry $10,000 in income or a 5 percent return on their investment.

A house in the same neighborhood today might go for half that in some devastated parts of the country like Las Vegas, Florida, or southern California. Let's say the rents are the same (and studies have shown rents have remained relatively stable): $10,000 in annual rental income. For the number of Americans that have gone back to renting, this seems like a pretty reasonable assumption.

For a $100,000 home price, that gives you a 10 percent return on your investment. Figure 10.4 shows that price-to-rent ratios have declined significantly.

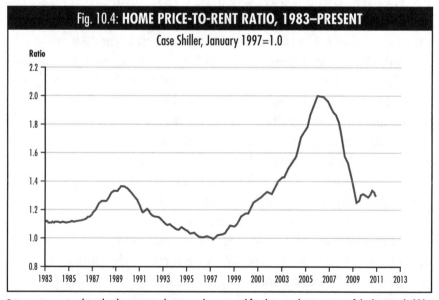

Fig. 10.4: HOME PRICE-TO-RENT RATIO, 1983–PRESENT

Case Shiller, January 1997=1.0

Price-to-rent ratios show that home prices have mostly corrected for the speculative excess of the housing bubble. However, every housing market is different. Some may still be overpriced, while some may be bargains.

This explains some of the optimistic signs amidst the real estate slump of 2011: Foreign buyers are scooping up comparatively cheaper properties in the US price-to-rent ratios in some markets make owning more compelling than renting, even before taking into consideration the tax benefits of home ownership.

In fact, a recent survey by *The Economist* lists US real estate as slightly undervalued (by the Case-Shiller Home Price Index) relative to other first-world countries.

Real estate is definitely worth a closer look right now, even though many real estate investment trusts (REITs) haven't fallen as much as individual housing.

The dividend yield on REITs is still substantially better than most common stocks, and REITs can invest in properties that individual investors might not have the knowledge to invest in, such as industrial and commercial properties.

Either way, most of the news about real estate is ugly. That should be your first clue that there may be some opportunities in there.

This isn't just true of real estate. Any dividend-paying stock that goes down in the short term just ends up benefitting from reinvesting those shares over the long term.

STRATEGY 3: STABLE INVESTMENTS IN AN UNSTABLE INVESTMENT WORLD

Income investors might not be willing to admit it, but when done right, income-focused strategies can lead to substantial capital gains.

Share prices also tend to rise over time along with dividend payouts. Think about it this way: The dividend yield on companies like Altria, Proctor & Gamble, and Johnson & Johnson would be over 100 percent if the company's share price had *never* moved up over the decades during which each of these companies has been paying a dividend.

Many investors look at these companies from time to time and find them "boring" because they barely move compared to other stocks — and their yields tend to be the same.

For example, let's compare a company associated with frugal, home-cooked meals, Kraft Food Group (NASDAQ GS:KRFT), with a fast-growing casual dining chain, Panera Bread (NASDAQ:PNRA).

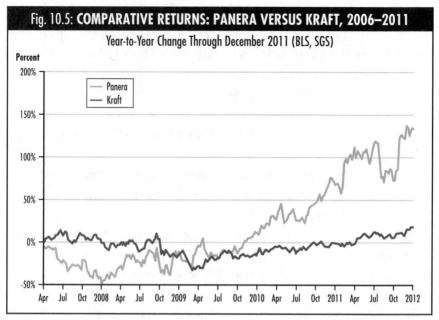

Fig. 10.5: **COMPARATIVE RETURNS: PANERA VERSUS KRAFT, 2006–2011**
Year-to-Year Change Through December 2011 (BLS, SGS)

Source: Yahoo! Finance

While some companies will always comparatively perform substantially better than others, such performance often ignores the effects of dividend payments.

Over the past five years, Panera investors have seen shares double, while Kraft has been left in the dust, as shown in Figure 10.5.

But such charts can be misleading. Panera doesn't pay a dividend. Kraft investors have the freedom to take the cash or reinvest shares. Over time, Panera's growth will slow. As a "mega-cap" company, Kraft is already priced by the market as a company with little growth prospects.

As a result of the market's expectations, Panera must continue to grow, or it will sell off sharply as growth investors look elsewhere. If Kraft reports a few weak quarters, the market won't be as harsh, because dividend investors own these shares. There are two different types of investors at work with each of these companies.

Take a closer look at the chart though, and you'll notice another trend: Kraft's range is narrower. It has less extreme movements. If you're an investor who doesn't want to take on a lot of risk, Kraft is the clear winner here. As any long-term investor will tell you, as an investment strategy, "boring" is where the best deals are.

Proctor & Gamble (NYSE:PG), for instance, tends to trade in such a way that its dividend yield is usually in the 3 to 4 percent range. Let's think of that as the company's "historical yield range." Since the company is increasing its dividend over time, its share price continues to gradually rise to the point where its dividend yields stays within that range.

Granted, there will be some events, like a 1987 or 2008 crash that sends the stock significantly down. But in that event, it merely makes dividend paying stocks a screaming buy, because they're now on the low end of that range. They will eventually get back to their average historical yield range.

This worked well for "stodgy" companies like Unilever (NYSE:UL), where shares fell nearly 40 percent during 2008–2009 only to quickly rebound. We can clearly see in Figure 10.6 that investors who waited until the company's dividend yield was above its historical average managed to snag some amazing capital gains (for a blue chip company) along the way!

Fig. 10.6: **UNILEVER SHARE PRICE, 2006–2011**

Buyers of Unilever in the circled range below were able to obtain a yield above the company's historic average — A real bargain!

Source: Yahoo! Inc. © 2011

Investors who wait to buy a company when its dividend is above its historical average are able to lock in an initial high yield — and let it grow from there.

If you have a long-term outlook, you can do well investing in companies that "only" offer a dividend yield of 2 to 5 percent today, but only if those companies have a history of raising their dividend payouts.

Alas, not all income investments are the same. Investments with higher payouts might not be able to increase payments over time. If you need more current cash flow, these high–income investments will generate the income that today's cash and bonds simply can't.

Be cautious with companies that pay out their dividend based on earnings, such as master limited partnerships (MLPs) and REITs. The payouts may be higher, but they might not always be as consistent with increasing their cash flow and dividends over time.

STRATEGY 4: REDUCING THE TAXMAN'S BITE: BOOST YOUR INCOME RETURNS WITHOUT BOOSTING YOUR RISK

To a man with a hammer, every problem looks like a nail. It's the same in investing. There's a veritable toolbox you can use to minimize your tax burden. Here is a broad overview of how you can reduce your annual tax burden and still receive income payments:

- Beware the bite of the short-term capital gain. For income investments, any period under a year can be problematic. That's because the current short-term rates are taxed as ordinary income (whatever your tax bracket for the income tax is) up to 35 percent.

     Long-term gains, however, are currently maximized at 15 percent. That's a huge difference. If you're an income investor, the long-term rate will mostly apply because you'll likely be more concerned with receiving dividends (four times a year for quarterly payouts, twelve times a year for monthly payouts), rather than making a quick capital gain and cashing out.

- Do yourself a favor and reduce your taxable income with contributions to retirement accounts. This includes a 401(k) plan with your employer (be sure to check to see if they do a "matching" amount — for most workers, it's effectively a "bonus"), an IRA, or a Roth IRA. Although a Roth IRA doesn't reduce your taxable income in the present, investments in Roth IRAs face no capital gains or dividend taxes, making them optimal for growth over time.

- If you have a choice to buy a dividend stock in a Roth IRA or a regular account, consider buying it in your regular account. Ironically, retirement accounts like IRAs should be used for companies with large capital gain potential over time. That's because investors can defer being taxed on capital gains in IRAs, and dividend tax rates remain lower than capital gains taxes at this time.

- Income investments are optimal for regular investment accounts because dividends are tax advantaged already compared to capital gains. There's a 15 percent tax rate on dividends and a 35 percent on capital gains, depending on your tax bracket and whether or not the gain is short term or long term.

- Investments that offer payments that are considered "return of capital" can help reduce tax payments from income investments. This includes most partnership investments, such as MLPs (as discussed in the *High Income Guide* available from Newsmax). These high income investments are optimal in a regular account.

- Covered-call writing on dividend paying stocks can pay off handsomely over time. Since these stocks tend to have lower volatility, the chances are excellent that a significantly out-of-the-money option will never get called. This strategy also reduces the chances that investors may sell as a knee-jerk reaction to falling markets.

- Over a long enough timeline, a covered-call strategy can allow you to obtain their original investment back, giving you a "zero cost basis," the holy grail of investing (something for nothing). Add in the power of rising dividends over time, and this strategy can turbocharge your income over the long haul.

- Although it's a worthy goal to reduce your taxes, don't do so at the expense of your investment portfolio. If a company's investment rationale no longer holds, sometimes it's just best to take the profits and move on. Don't invest in a high-yielding venture just because of the potential tax break it offers. Always check the underlying fundamentals first. On the plus side, selling a loser may offset some of the capital gains taxes you would have to pay on a winning trade that is also closed out in the same year.

- Finally, don't be afraid to pony up some money to get advice from a qualified accountant. Every individual has different needs, which may entail more specific information than what can be provided here.

WRAP-UP
Why Income Matters More than Capital Gains

- Investing for income is a critical, if not the most critical, aspect of investment returns.
- Numerous stocks with a history of dividend increases will trounce market indices if you simply put in your initial capital, reinvest the proceeds, and do nothing else. (Remember Jill, who trounced Jack's reinvested bond investment.)
- Although the stock market is currently trading well below its average historical yields, plenty of companies exist that can pay a respectable dividend.
- Over a long enough timeline, a higher yield will more than compensate you for higher risk.
- Whether the market goes up, goes down, or stays sideways, over a long enough timeline, income investors come out ahead.
- Income investments offer lower volatility, a definite plus in the age of monetary and political chaos.
- With the right structure, income investments can have favorable advantages over other investments when taxes are taken into consideration.
- For more information regarding income investments, see the **High Income Guide** available from Newsmax.

11

Tangible Assets in a Fiat World
Commodity Investments

———————

"Capital is money: Capital is commodities."
— *Karl Marx, Das Kapital*[27]

NLIKE STOCKS, WHICH represent fractional ownership of a business, or bonds, which represent debt obligations, commodities are, simply put, stuff. More specifically, commodities are natural resources like copper, oil, gold, silver, wheat, corn, soybeans, and more than a dozen other resources.

While the stock market has had no traction since the start of this century, commodities have been on a tear. Figure 11.1 shows historical commodities going back to 1749, where you can see a massive explosion in commodity prices in the last forty years.

The primary mechanism for determining commodity prices isn't the "spot" market, as it is for stocks and bonds. Rather, it's the futures market. And it started over a hundred years ago when America was primarily an agrarian nation.

Futures historically developed with commodities as a result of volatile prices for goods in a given year. By locking in prices for their goods at the beginning of a season, farmers would be able to know with confidence that their crops would fetch a certain price in the

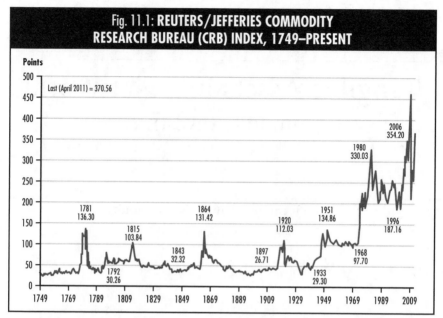

Fig. 11.1: **REUTERS/JEFFERIES COMMODITY RESEARCH BUREAU (CRB) INDEX, 1749–PRESENT**

Commodity prices remain substantially above their historical averages going back to the middle of the eighteenth century. This trend is likely to continue over the long term, with short-term bumps along the way.

future, even if the price of that crop was wildly different from what was speculated.

In short, the original goal of the futures market was to create future certainties so that farmers could grow their crops more effectively.

Of course, as we also saw in Figure 11.1, a much more stable picture for commodities before central banks came to rule the world. Since the start of the fiat money system, wilder swings in commodities have occurred, as inflation has eradicated the price deflation from better crops, technology, and farming methods.

Also, the rise of central banks and fiat money made speculation easier. One of the most profound changes in commodity investments began quietly in 1991, as oil prices were devastated following the first Gulf War. Prior to 1991, commodity trades were limited to parties who had a genuine need to hedge production.

Once the first financial institution, Goldman Sachs, was allowed to trade in the futures market by creating a derivative product in commodities, others eventually followed. The industry was largely still deregulated in 1999.

When oil prices ran up to $147 a barrel in 2008, any investor looking strictly at supply and demand for oil would have been wondering why. The answer was supplied by the Commodity Futures Trading Commission (CFTC), which noted that during the 2008 speculative pop in oil prices, a full 81 percent of trading volume was done by financial institutions.

Rather than oil companies looking to hedge their production or airlines wanting to lock in a price for future delivery, then were institutions with no intention of ever taking delivery of the large volumes of oil that they had bought contracts for.

In fact, speculative trading in commodities has grown so large that in some instances the size of the "paper" market of outstanding derivatives trades exceeds the available supply of the physical market! Figure 11.2 shows the explosion of the commodity futures market.

Simply put, increasing volatility (and prices) in commodity prices are another side effect of financial alchemy and monetary chaos. It's also a trend that currently has no slowdown in sight. Investors in commodities will assuredly face an extremely volatile roller-coaster ride in the years to come.

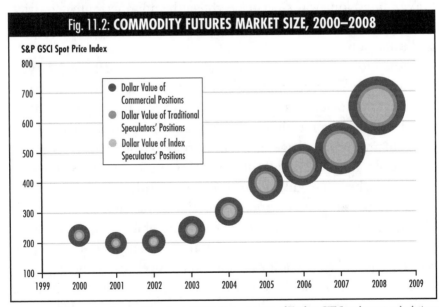

Fig. 11.2: **COMMODITY FUTURES MARKET SIZE, 2000–2008**

S&P GSCI Spot Price Index

- Dollar Value of Commercial Positions
- Dollar Value of Traditional Speculators' Positions
- Dollar Value of Index Speculators' Positions

Source: Bloomberg, CFTC Commitments of Traders CIT Supplement, calculations

The commodities futures market has exploded over the past ten years, leading to more volatility in commodity prices.

Also, commodities have patterns of highs and lows occurring around twenty years apart. As a result of these cycles, we can use a simpler way to make investments at the strategic level, by seeing where commodity prices are and whether they're in an uptrend or a downtrend.

Within the commodity universe, there's a rough divide between the so-called "soft" commodities and "hard" commodities. Within the soft commodities are items like rice, wheat, cotton, and corn. Hard commodities include items like copper, gold, and silver.

The commodity universe is rapidly changing, but if you're looking to benefit from the age of monetary chaos you should focus on three key areas: agricultural commodities, energy, and precious metals.

Amidst the chaos of monetary crises and the struggle for global growth, these three groups stand out as the best investment opportunities over the next few years. They can be purchased easily through common stocks of companies, options, futures, and funds.

The Case for Agricultural Commodities

We've come a long way since the eighteenth and nineteenth centuries, when most Americans were simply farmers and didn't really hold a traditional job.

Thanks to economies of scale and advances in technology, most people have been freed from life on the farm for labor that's less backbreaking, and society has the chance to thrive beyond mere sustenance.

But we have become highly dependent on aging infrastructural networks to produce, package, and transport food from where it is grown — generally from the middle of the country in the United States — to the coasts where the bulk of the population resides.

We saw the first hint of trouble with this infrastructure in the middle of 2008. As gas prices skyrocketed, prices of food rose as trucking companies added "fuel surcharges" and the energy required to process agricultural commodities remained relatively constant.

The prospect of our food delivery infrastructure hitting a major snag — to say nothing of collapsing — would be considerably scarier than anything coming from the finance industry. That's completely outside our demand for food, which rises with the population.

Secondly, 2011 marked the year that America used more corn for fuel than for food. But those yellow kernels aren't just missing from your plate. Corn makes up 60–70 percent of the cost of raising livestock, as it's used as the primary ingredient for feeding chickens, pigs, cows, and even turkeys.

In the United States, corn crop production has surged, but the increase in output has gone into corn ethanol as an additive in gasoline. Ultimately, that means we've developed the ability to stretch our supply of fossil fuels with a renewable additive.

But it comes at a price, namely, the fact that the more we put in our tank, the less we can put on our plate. No wonder corn prices, shown in Figure 11.3, have already surged past their 2008 highs!

The "food versus fuel" debate about using agricultural commodities as a source of energy continues to rage on. It will (and should!) continue for as long as there are humans starving. But, in a world where fossil fuels have passed the point where they're incredibly easy

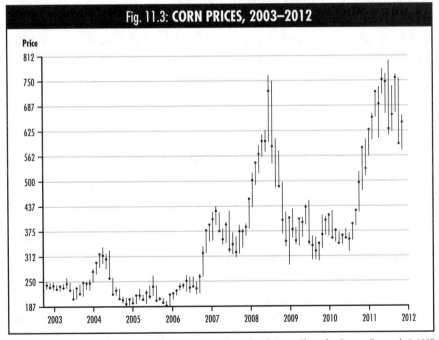

Fig. 11.3: CORN PRICES, 2003–2012

Created with SuperCharts by Omega Research © 1997

Thanks to subsidies that turn corn into ethanol for fuel, corn prices are substantially higher, even though corn's use as a fuel is marginal at best when acting as a substitute for oil.

to reach and global demand is still rising, the answer is that we will probably continue to use both.

That means agricultural commodities will likely continue their long-term uptrend for years to come. That still doesn't take into account the fact that agricultural commodities stand to benefit from any effort at currency debasement. These commodities are essential to sustaining human life. And they rise in price everywhere the mechanism they're priced in — US dollars — loses value.

For most investors, the simple way to invest is to buy shares of the **PowerShares DB Agriculture Fund (DBA)**. Originally an equally weighted mix of only four agricultural commodities, the fund now contains over forty. It offers the best way for you to profit from rising agricultural prices without having to dabble in the futures market.

The Case for Energy Commodities

Three trends will weigh on energy prices: surging global demand for energy, a static supply, and commodities priced in a weakening dollar.

Added into this mix is the increased investment demand for commodities in general, in which the paper markets often disconnect from the reality of supply and demand in the physical markets.

Surging Global Demand: The Strongest Catalyst for Oil's Rise

It's almost a cliché to say that emerging markets will fuel the rise of oil prices. But they will.

Countries like China are spending billions of dollars each year to urbanize their populations. Bringing their population from low-income, labor-intense rural farms to better opportunities in the cities will spur economic growth.

But, more importantly, this trend is a boon for oil: an urban population uses substantially more oil than a rural population.

Whether that extra oil use comes from increased private transport, personal transport, or construction operations doesn't matter — the

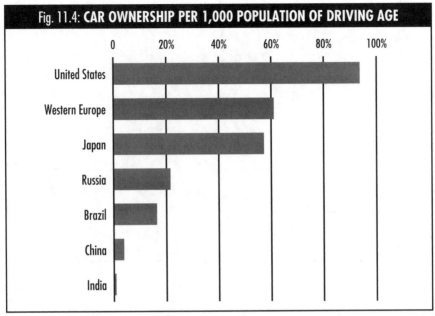

Source: Morgan Stanley

Less than 20 percent of the adult population of Brazil, Russia, India, and China own a car. As these countries modernize and more embrace the use of cars, oil consumption will rise.

trend is clear. And, for countries like China and India, with billions of impoverished workers moving to middle class digs, it's better to pay up for oil rather than face a population stuck in backwards, third-world rural jobs.

Despite all you've heard, growth for oil in emerging markets is just beginning. After all, in China, Brazil, and India, less than 20 percent of the adult population has access to a car, as seen in Figure 11.4. If citizens in these countries became as dependent on the automobile as the average American, the price of oil could become devastatingly high for anyone with a long daily commute.

That's why even the most mainstream, benign estimates for growing oil use in China and India show heavy growth. Of course, this won't happen overnight but rather over the course of decades. Many analysts have already said that China's infrastructure outside of Beijing and other major cities is too vast for current consumption levels, where five-lane highways are filled with perhaps twenty cars per hour.

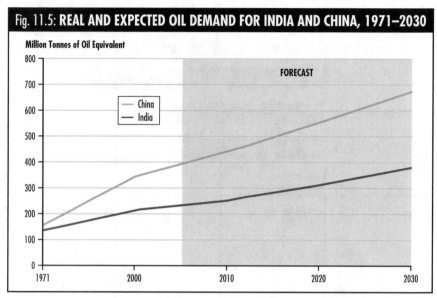

Fig. 11.5: **REAL AND EXPECTED OIL DEMAND FOR INDIA AND CHINA, 1971–2030**

Source: IEA

Oil demand is expected to rise by over 50 percent in both India and China in the next twenty years.

Figure 11.5 illustrates potential future demand for oil in China and India, the two fastest-growing, highly populated "emerging market" countries.

Static Oil Supply Will Keep Market Tight (and Gas Prices High for US Consumers)

As demand rises, however, another problem emerges. It's the lack of major new discoveries of oil deposits that are sufficient in size to offset current use. In other words, we're using more oil than we currently discover in new finds each year. That means supply is expected to generally decline, even as demand continues growing.

How bad will this deficit be? That depends on many factors. Depending on who you talk to, you'll get a different answer. Proponents of "peak oil" insist that we've already passed the point where supply outstrips demand, whereas other economic predictions view rising oil prices as a rationing mechanism, whereby consumers seek alternative energy sources and scale back on their oil use.

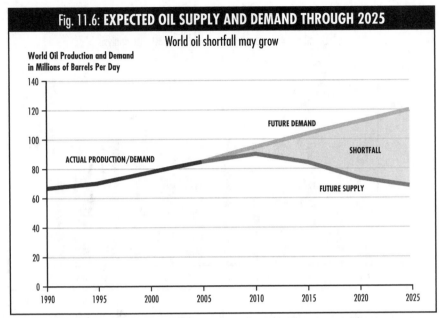

Fig. 11.6: EXPECTED OIL SUPPLY AND DEMAND THROUGH 2025

World oil shortfall may grow

World Oil Production and Demand
in Millions of Barrels Per Day

FUTURE DEMAND

ACTUAL PRODUCTION/DEMAND

SHORTFALL

FUTURE SUPPLY

Sources: World Oil Production: U.S. Energy Information Administration. Future Demand: Reference Case — International Energy Outlook 2005 — U.S. Energy Information Administration.Future supply: Projections by The Association for the Study of Peak Oil & Gas, April 2006.

Future supplies of oil are expected to be less than expected future demand. This means oil prices are likely to rise through the roof.

But, any way you slice it, you won't find anyone out there predicting surges in supply and declining demand anytime soon. That means that the overall trend for oil prices remains positive over the long term, even if we see the world economy slide into a recession again within the next few years. Figures 11.6 and 11.7 outline the growing imbalance that we may be facing even today.

We've seen that demand is surging — and supply is starting to dwindle. But there are still other catalysts that could cause oil to surge. The next area isn't a global trend at all, but one squarely centered in the United States. It's the weak dollar.

Weak Dollar to Weigh on Oil's Price
Oil is priced in dollars globally. That's true whether you're a Texas oilman selling to Singapore or a Saudi Arabian sheik selling to a European conglomerate.

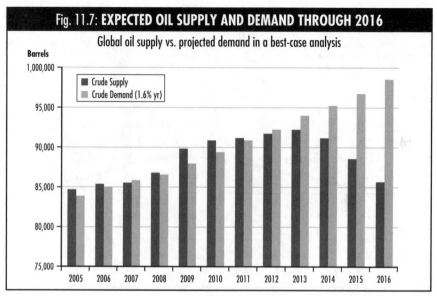

Fig. 11.7: **EXPECTED OIL SUPPLY AND DEMAND THROUGH 2016**

Global oil supply vs. projected demand in a best-case analysis

Source: Peak Oil Consulting

Demand for oil continues to grow faster than supply. If these trends continue, oil prices will continue to rise.

Well . . . that's *mostly* true. You see, thanks to the decline of the dollar, some countries are starting to sidestep the dollar when trading in oil and using their own currencies instead. That trend is just starting, so most oil transactions are still held in dollars.

As you may recall, however, the dollar isn't what it used to be. It used to be a symbol for America's financial might . . . and now it's little more than a stark reminder for our copious debt and the Fed's constant weakening of the dollar to prop up asset prices.

Since oil is an asset, and it's still overwhelmingly priced in dollars, it's clear that the Fed is working overtime to keep oil prices up (along with real estate, stocks, and so on).

We've already seen this play out in oil prices. In terms of the euro, oil prices had a wild ride but ended up at about the same price after six months. In terms of dollars, oil prices made a huge gain in the same time period, as Figure 11.8 shows.

If oil had moved higher both in dollar terms and euro terms, we would know that the primary change in price was due to rising demand. Rather, it's safe to say that the big move during this time came from the dollar weakening.

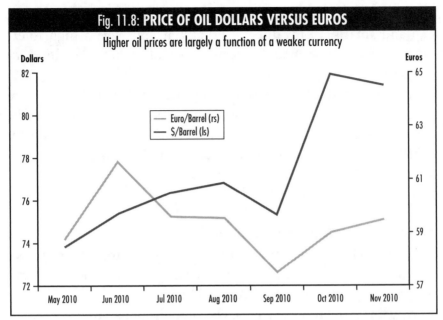

Fig. 11.8: PRICE OF OIL DOLLARS VERSUS EUROS

Higher oil prices are largely a function of a weaker currency

Legend:
- Euro/Barrel (rs)
- $/Barrel (ls)

Source: DOE & DB Global Markets Research

Because oil is priced in dollars, investors must remember that any substantial change in the dollar relative to another currency can have a major effect on its price over the short term.

This should be a wakeup call to the average American investor, especially if you have all your assets denominated in dollars. Investing with an eye on oil, rather than the dollars that it is currently priced in, makes more sense.

By diversifying into international oil companies, you can diversify out of the dollar. But even domestic oil companies can provide you with some protection from the ever-weakening US dollar.

With a wide universe of options, there's no single "slam dunk" energy play. That's because every company has its unique challenges, costs, and has to deal with a myriad of local laws, no matter where they are in the world.

If you're an investor with a low tolerance for risk, focus on **major integrated oil companies** and *infrastructure* like **pipelines** and **service companies** (the proverbial "pick-and-shovel" providers). All of these areas include both common stocks, along with exchange-traded funds (ETFs) if you don't have sufficient time to research specific companies.

If you have a moderate tolerance for risk, add in some **mid-cap** and **small-cap producers**. Finally, if you have a high tolerance for risk, research and invest in a small basket of exploratory companies.

A note on natural gas: Recent discoveries in the United States are likely to create a glut of natural gas for at least the rest of this decade. Prices should remain low. If we can achieve a large-scale conversion of vehicles to natural gas within the next generation, this should somewhat offset rising oil prices.

The Case for Gold and Silver

In the first chapter, we reviewed the case against the US dollar. We looked at its long-term decline and the failure of the Federal Reserve to achieve its stated goal of price stability.

Why this instability? In part, it's because the dollar lost the backing of gold and silver over time. So let's invert what we know about the dollar from Chapter 1 and see how things played out with a closer look at the role of gold.

How does this removal of some mere metal allow for governments to rev the engines of chaos? It's simple. It's because precious metals like gold and silver are rare, durable, easily divisible, and portable. (That's the very definition of money, by the way!)

Also, new quantities of gold and silver are brought to the market via mining companies, not the whim of a central banker.

After suffering from years of poor performance and disrepute as the 1990s bull market raged on for global stocks, gold has finally turned the corner since 1999. In the summer of 2011, it hit an all-time nominal high of $1,900 per ounce and closed in toward $2,000.

A combination of declining supplies caused by soaring input costs, rising long-term inflation spurred by unprecedented government bailouts and rescues and booming government deficits all point to much higher prices for gold and silver over the next few years.

Also, the exchange rate system remains mired in a state of flux as countries continuously devalue against each other. *Since 2005, gold has outpaced all major currencies — not just the American dollar.*

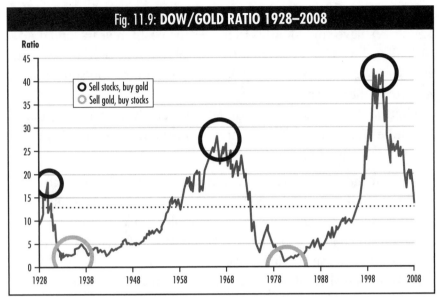

Fig. 11.9: **DOW/GOLD RATIO 1928–2008**

Source: BullionVault.com

The Dow/gold ratio is near its average but is still in a downtrend. This means investors should favor gold over stocks until the ratio drops below 5.

Indeed, gold is in a long-term boom and should continue to out-perform stocks for the foreseeable future. That's because, as Figure 11.9 shows, the Dow/gold ratio is currently in a downtrend, which favors gold.

Simply put, when one ounce of gold nears the price one "share" of the Dow Jones Industrial Average (DJIA) — the two are trading close to a 1:1 ratio — it's time to buy stocks; this happened at the bottom of the Great Depression in the early 1930s and during the inflation-adjusted stock market bottom in the early 1980s.

Conversely, when the ratio is above 15 (meaning it takes more than 15 ounces of gold to buy one "share" of the DJIA), it's time to sell stocks and buy gold. This was the case in 1929, as a high-flying stock market was incredibly overvalued relative to gold.

It was also the case in the late 1960s as stocks hit a nominal peak just as inflation started perking up (charting the course for the rise of commodity prices in the 1970s). Finally, it was the case as the stock market peaked in the late 1990s and gold bottomed around $250 per ounce.

Today, gold and silver are halfway through a multi-decade bull market. Prices have consistently risen over the past ten years, and gold is well off its lows. But the cycle isn't fully played out. Gold prices could peak between $5,000 and $10,000 per ounce if inflation spirals out of control in the next decade.

Gold and silver, as commodities, are perceived as having higher investment risk than owning shares of common stocks. But here are a few factors to bear in mind:

- **Gold and silver don't have credit risk.** When the United States lost its precious AAA credit rating in the summer of 2011, markets sold off, sending investors, ironically to investments with a perception of safety, such as the US dollar and Treasury bills. It's no surprise that gold also rallied.

- **Gold and silver don't have a business model.** Some analysts criticize gold and silver on the grounds that it doesn't generate any income, such as interest or dividends, so it makes more sense to invest in stocks. But many companies don't pay out cash to shareholders either.

  Furthermore, companies that have a business model that's eventually revealed as flawed, such as Netflix in the fall of 2011, will see a sharp selloff. Gold and silver don't have to worry about analyst expectations. They don't have to worry about competitors or their services becoming obsolete.

- **Gold and silver just sit there and do nothing.** This pronouncement, made famous by Warren Buffett's quote that gold is simply dug up somewhere and put in another hole somewhere else, makes the whole notion of investing in gold and silver sound silly.

  But sometimes the best course of action in investing is to do nothing. Every action of every business is immediately judged by the market. Gold and silver face no such risk.

  It's almost a cliché to say that the world is facing rapid changes. But, despite those changes, it still needs physical commodities, and gold and silver still represent true value and shelter from fiat currencies whipped up at government whim. If gold is not an "investment," as some have argued, then it is still real money and has been so for five thousand years.

- **Gold and silver don't have counter-parties.** Many investments involve a counter-party, someone on the other "side" of the asset with an obligation. For example, someone who owns bonds in General Electric (GE) requires GE to earn enough cash to cover its obligations. A shareholder needs management to continue delivering value in the form of sales and earnings.

    Currencies are ultimately valued by the whims of governments that may have a political need to manipulate the value of its currency relative to others. In short, gold and silver are monetary assets that don't have someone else on the other side of the trade with the potential to cause devastation.

Those are just unique characteristics of gold and silver outside their fundamental supply and demand. It's absolutely essential for you to hold some gold bullion, as well as gold stocks, over the next several years to inoculate their wealth from the monetary madness of central bankers and turbulence created by the policies of desperate governments.

Investors who have never touched a gold investment in their lives have missed out on recent market innovations to make owning gold easier. One of the easiest ways to invest in gold is with the **SPDR Gold Shares Trust (GLD)**.

GLD is the sixth largest holder of gold in the world, exceeding even the reserves of countries like Switzerland and Canada.

The price of GLD tracks 1/10 of an ounce of gold. This makes investments in small increments easy and with a significantly lower premium than purchasing the same quantity of physical gold. For those worried about liquidity, this is the optimal gold investment.

The major drawback to the SPDR Gold Shares is the inability to exchange the shares for physical bullion. GLD also has to sell gold in order to pay for its custodial fees — diluting the amount of gold backed per share over time. Nevertheless, if you're looking for ways to go long (or short) on gold for *small periods of time,* you can use GLD to quickly increase your exposure with the advantage of liquidity to boot. However, you should still own some physical bullion.

Similar funds to GLD include the Sprott Physical Gold Trust (ETV) and the Central Fund of Canada (CEF). Both also primarily hold physical bullion, although individual investors can't redeem shares directly for the metal.

If you're interested in seeing bigger gains from gold's long-term bull market, you can better leverage their positions with gold stocks. The **Market Vectors Gold Miners ETF (GDX)** offers a convenient way to hold all the major gold stocks of the world, offering instant diversification among gold miners.

WRAP-UP
Commodity Bull Has More Room to Run

- Commodities are hard assets. In the age of chaos, these real assets will generally appreciate in value.
- Among commodities, agriculture, energy, and precious metals pose the best opportunities and offer the most choices to investors.
- An aging infrastructure and soaring demand for use of food crops in fuel production will keep agricultural prices on the rise.
- Supply remains tight for traditional fossil fuels, and declining usage in some places is more than made up for with surging usage elsewhere.
- Ultimately, monetary commodities like gold and silver will soar in nominal value as fiat currencies are continually devalued.

12

Forex in the Age of Currency Devaluations

"Paper is poverty . . . it is only the ghost of money, and not money itself."
— *Thomas Jefferson*[28]

FOREIGN CURRENCY TRADING offers inherent profit potential, limited time exposure, and in some quarters, limited regulation. That's why traders from around the globe now enter positions for weeks, days, hours, or only seconds. The Forex (FX) market can have explosive moves, steady flows, and like all markets, the inevitable flat periods.

Money changes hands quickly on the Forex markets for a staggering daily average of about $4 trillion and growing. There are no geographic or temporal boundaries any longer. FX is a twenty-four-hour market open to all eligible players.

A Quick Look at the Evolution of Money

Have you ever wondered how those little pieces of green paper in your wallet came to be used for everyday transactions? Why is it that we accept mere paper, or in many cases electronic transfers of mere numbers, as something of value? More importantly, why does it take more and more of these pieces of paper to buy the same thing?

Many would like to ignore these questions. If they're not asked, nobody has to think up a clever way to dance around the truth.

But the answers to those questions are pretty simple. The money in your wallet and bank account, of all currencies, are money *today* because it they were used as money *yesterday*. More importantly, the purchasing power of that money *today* is based on what it could purchase *yesterday*. Logically, *tomorrow's* value will be based off of *today's* value.

This idea about the evolution of money can be worked backwards to give us an idea about where we've been, and more importantly, where we're going. There's even a name for this concept: *the money regression theorem*.

In 2012, currencies are ruled by the printing press, with no link to a commodity (or any item of tangible, fixed value) to keep their value in check against inflation.

Fiat money is fundamentally misleading, because it tends to hold its value from one day to the next. But, over time, it gradually erodes in value. While there may be the occasional devaluation, like the British pound in 1992 or the Belarus ruble in May 2011, it's an exceptionally rare event.

Usually devaluation is gradual. It isn't noticed over small day-to-day periods. It's only over the long haul when you can stand back and see how destructive fiat money truly is to your purchasing power.

With the world's currencies all free-floating, they can jockey against each other every day as people exchange money. Traders in the Forex market, supercharged with substantial levels of leverage, can move trillions of dollars around a day trying to catch a few pips of profit wherever opportunity allows. With or without leverage, it's one way to try and preserve, if not increase the value of your wealth, relative to one currency.

All currencies today are fiat, or backed by nothing more than government will. Even the so-called "commodity currencies" like the Canadian and Australian dollars are purely fiat. Currency investors instead look to the natural resources of these countries as something of a loose commodity link to the currencies.

The last time a major currency was linked to gold (or any commodity for that matter) was the Swiss franc. This final tie to gold was finally cut in 2002.

So, if you wanted to completely escape all the "printing press" currencies of the world, you'd have to move your wealth into silver and gold. Why? Just look at how money has evolved historically.

Older readers and collectors may be familiar with a silver certificate. It has the same size and general design of a dollar bill, but it has blue trim, and states that the Treasury of the United States of America (not the Fed) has $1 in silver in its vaults backing up the certificate. This is an intermediate step for currency, known as *representative money*.

Simply put, instead of having to carry around $1 in silver (about 1/20 of an ounce of gold during the gold standard era and 1/35 until silver was no longer used in US coinage), you could carry a certificate that's convertible into silver that is portable and convenient.

But a funny thing happens when you have a situation with representative money. Say I have ten thousand ounces of gold in a warehouse and I prefer to issue certificates in payment in lieu of handing over my gold.

If anyone who accepts my certificates knows I have the gold, they may prefer the ease of trading the paper certificate around to others who know I have the gold.

It's lighter, and the certificates are easier to divide amongst different creditors than a quantity of gold. In other words, it's much more convenient.

Let's say I notice this and hatch a devious scheme to enrich myself at the expense of others. I issue a few more certificates, so there are now certificates outstanding for fifteen thousand ounces of gold. I've increased my wealth 50 percent — but only (and literally) on paper.

Should all the certificates outstanding be turned in at once, the fraud would be evident. I would either end up with a free trip to jail, or some other unwanted outcome would befall me (and rightly so)!

If I'm devious enough and don't make it apparent that I'm flush with extra (fraudulent) wealth, I can probably keep the fraud going nearly indefinitely.

If I go overboard and people start to suspect that there are more certificates in circulation than gold outstanding, they will rush to get out of the certificates and take possession of the physical gold instead.

In other words, any fraudster with a printing press has to strike the right balance between enriching themselves and not going overboard in doing so.

Still, you can see the utility of having a rare commodity as a form of money — it prevents the sort of fraud and artificial wealth creation that I described. It also gives you an idea of why governments love fiat money: it removes their restrictions on what they can spend and provide.

As long as they're the first recipients of the new, unbacked money, they can make promises, and for a long time, fulfill them. In so doing, the new money will eventually move throughout the financial system. As more money chases the same number of goods, prices have to rise.

Suddenly, we find persistent inflation, rather than the occasional periods of inflation and deflation that tend to average out over time. Those holding only cash may find that there's little change day to day, but over time the loss of purchasing power is immense.

This sort of fraud with representative money wouldn't be possible with a tangible commodity like gold or silver.

In addition to gold and silver, a variety of other items have been used for money. In colonial Virginia and parts of the southern United States, items like tobacco and cotton have been common and durable enough to serve as money. In World War II prisoner-of-war (POW) camps, cigarettes also acted as a form of money.

Let's move back another big step in the regression theory: Why does a commodity become money? For that, we have to go back to the barter system!

The barter system screams for a better alternative. A shoemaker can't trade with a butcher if the butcher doesn't need shoes. An attorney can't trade legal services with a farmer who has no need for them. What goods and services need is something that can act as a clearinghouse. That's where money comes in. A barter system is inefficient to supply a myriad of different wants and needs.

Surprisingly, some people say the same thing about paper money in an electronic world today.

Incidentally, where *are* we going today? For some countries, like China, India, and Russia, the answer is a partial rejection of the "printing press" currencies. They've been building their gold reserves, encouraging their population to save in gold and silver, and are calling for an end to the global supremacy of the US dollar, which has been the world's reserve currency since the end of World War II.

The US dollar enjoyed widespread use in part because it was backed by gold in international transactions until 1971. But substantial government spending and a growing welfare state caused nations to demand gold for their dollars, and ties to gold were cut.

Fast forward to the present: we've moved from a barter system, to a commodity-backed monetary system, to a representative system, to a fiat system.

In the forty years before Nixon took dollars off the gold standard, US money supply roughly doubled. In the forty years after the gold window has been "shut" money supply has risen over twenty-fold! No wonder we keep getting caught in increasingly larger and more economically dangerous investment bubbles. That money has to go somewhere.

So, what happens from here?

We are, perhaps, at the beginning of the end of the first act of a global fiat system. It's likely in the years ahead that the US dollar will continue to decline in prominence, as other national (and multinational) currencies will become more widely held, traded, and used in financial transactions.

For the next few years ahead, you will be able to strategically act to preserve and expand your purchasing power by investing in sound currencies. Over the long haul, there's nothing to stop a fiat currency from dropping to zero, so any grand strategy involving alternative currencies should also involve a close scrutiny on political and monetary developments in those countries and regions.

Forex Trading: The Nuts and Bolts

The foreign exchange market has been regarded as the last "frontier" of capital markets, although recent regulation has given the Commodity Futures Trading Commission (CFTC) more oversight and reach.

The Forex market is the largest and most liquid financial market in the world, with an estimated daily turnover of over $4 trillion in 2010, with bank trading turnover surging 42 percent between 2007 and 2010.

Despite its size, this market actually has no fixed location! It operates twenty-four hours a day, seven days a week, relying on what's known as over-the-counter trading. There are three kinds of transactions in the foreign exchange market: spot transactions, forwards, and swaps.

Spot trades are foreign exchange transactions that trade based on the current (or "spot") price of a currency. This is the traditional type of trade most people think of when it comes to Forex trading. In the spot market, traders employ leverage and technical indicators to make tactical, short-term trades. These transactions account for about 35 percent of daily volume in the foreign exchange markets.

Forward trades are transactions that settle on a date beyond spot and account for 12 percent of the reported daily volume. Essentially, two parties agree on the exchange rate between two currencies today and lock in that rate. It's not the goal of either party to make or lose money then; it's to ensure that a wide swing in a currency doesn't adversely affect a business transaction or the like.

Swap transactions account for 53 percent of volume. In a swap transaction, two parties exchange two different currencies on one or more specified dates over an agreed period and exchange them again when the period ends.

Swaps allow different companies or individuals to easily access foreign exchange without going to the spot market, and in some cases such as in the United Kingdom, avoid currency controls.

There also are transactions in currency options, available through a variety of exchanges, although volume is still too light to justify it as a viable investment opportunity for most investors.

The foreign exchange market offers different opportunities to different groups. Multinational corporations and importers need foreign currency to do business abroad, whether buying or selling goods or services.

Individuals need to diversify out of their home currency. This is especially true for most US investors, as the US dollar represents the lion's share of the world's currency market.

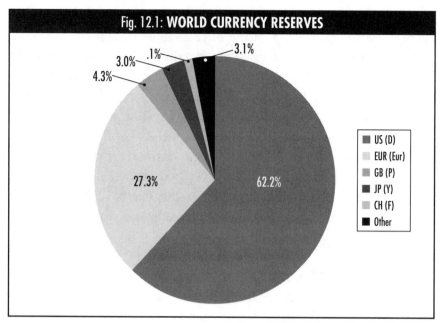

Fig. 12.1: **WORLD CURRENCY RESERVES**

3.1%
.1%
3.0%
4.3%

27.3%   62.2%

- US (D)
- EUR (Eur)
- GB (P)
- JP (Y)
- CH (F)
- Other

Source: IMF, own calculations © Lighthouse 2011

Most currency trades and central bank assets involve the US dollar, with the euro and British pound rounding out the top three positions.

As you can see in Figure 12.1, world currency reserves are still heavily concentrated between the US dollar, the euro, the British pound, and the Japanese yen.

Strategic Forex Plays

For most investors, the best strategy with currencies and Forex trading is to first start by diversifying out of your home currency. For American investors, that means selling dollars and investing in foreign bank accounts or foreign currency certificates of deposits (CDs).

This helps ensure that the long-term decline of the US dollar won't trash your portfolio's true value after inflation. In many cases, it means higher interest rates and payments. It means international diversification and a way to invest in strong currencies while essentially shorting weak ones.

Although they might not end up as a reserve currency, currencies tied to commodities such as those in Canada, Australia, and New

Zealand should perform well as the US dollar declines and the prices of commodities rise over a period of years if not decades.

These currencies are an excellent starting place to diversify their cash out of US dollars. With CurrencyShares ETFs, investors can diversify with a simple phone call by picking shares of the Australian Dollar Trust (FXA) or Canadian Dollar Trust (FXC). For more exotic currencies, however, you may need to look elsewhere.

The ultimate goal with one's strategic currency investments is to beat inflation over time, not make leveraged bets on short-term currency movements. But, in the age of monetary chaos, such short-term, tactical Forex plays can provide a much needed portfolio boost.

Tactical Forex Plays

Over the short term, corrections may occur that deviate from the long-term trend. Typically, when markets revert to fear, investors clamor for the US dollar as a safe haven, causing the dollar to appreciate versus other currencies. Sometimes, the Swiss franc and Japanese yen also fulfill such a role.

Short-term, central bank interventions and surprise interest rate announcements can provide short-term profit opportunities.

Shorting the overbought Swiss franc ahead of their central bank's decision to peg the currency to the euro in mid-2011 was one such opportunity. Japan is infamous for making interventions to weaken the yen, although such interventions often prove short lived, lasting anywhere from several hours to a week.

The ultimate goal, then, is to study recent central bank interventions. Central bankers that are prone to cut rates or institute other easy-money policies should have their currencies shorted. You should look to go long currencies where central bankers are strengthening by raising rates or, at the very least, have a laissez-faire attitude as opposed to a willingness to intervene.

Specific recommendations are impossible, given the rapidly changing news environment.

Currency du Century

For those with an exceptionally long-term outlook, consider investing in the "currency du century" for the long haul. What do I mean? It's simple. Just about every century sees one dominant, world currency.

Simply put, a dominant world currency is one that's widely used outside its borders and is regarded as the best liquid store of value. It also goes by the term *reserve currency*.

Records of currencies gaining widespread, global usage dates back over twenty-five hundred years to 500 BC, to the silver drachma coins of ancient Athens. These were later replaced by gold *aureus* and silver *denarius* coins used by Rome. As Rome expanded into an empire and coin clipping became more common, those coins eventually lost value.

In the sixth and seventh centuries, the world reserve currencies came from the Middle East, first with the Byzantine Empire's gold solid coin and later the Arabian dinar. As the world succumbed to the Dark Ages and commerce waned, no clear reserve currency came into place until coins issued by Florence and Venice in the thirteenth and fifteenth centuries.

When commerce returned to the world, the Dutch prospered in their financial and commercial interests to such an extent that their coins, *guilders*, came into dominance. With the vast wealth of the New World, Spain initially benefitted from the discovery of large silver deposits, only to waste it and suffer vast inflation.

The British pound carried the mantle as the island nation became a global empire and served the role as the world's reserve currency throughout the nineteenth century. The twentieth century had the US dollar take over the role from the decaying British Empire. Although this didn't completely happen until the conclusion of World War II, the pound never fully recovered from its devaluations during World War I.

As you can see, each of these countries gained entry into the international currency club by being the greatest creator of economic value at the time. It lost it with declining trade, the rise of new economic power, and mismanagement of domestic finances.

Who will take up the mantle in the twenty-first century (and possibly beyond)? Let's start with the countries that won't succeed: those that have defaulted on their sovereign debts.

Since 1900, twenty-six European and Latin American countries have defaulted on sovereign debts a total of one hundred times, not counting defaults by Asian and African nations.

Greece could be considered the poster child of outright sovereign default. They defaulted on government bonds in 1826, 1843, 1860, 1893, and again in 1932. They are in technical default again today.

Austria has been an even worse deadbeat, defaulting or rescheduling sovereign debts six times in the nineteenth century and twice in the twentieth century.

In the 1990s recent defaults by Mexico and Argentina, and fears of a slowdown in Asia among the "Asian Tigers" of Hong Kong, Singapore, South Korea and Taiwan caused their currencies to face a huge correction relative to the US dollar.

Even the US government has a long history of defaulting on its IOUs. The United States defaulted after the Revolutionary War on Continental dollars, certificates promising payment in silver to soldiers who served in the war. In 1933, Franklin Roosevelt defaulted on the gold backing of US gold notes and voided all gold clauses in contracts.

In 1968, President Johnson announced that silver certificates could no longer be redeemed in the metal, and silver was removed from coinage. On December 31, 1970, President Richard Nixon ended the Bretton Woods financial system, breaking the US promise to foreign central banks that they could redeem dollars for gold.

Indeed, sovereign defaults are commonplace. But outright default isn't the method anymore. It's all about further quantitative easing (or whatever else they choose to call the next iteration of it). That means printing more currency, causing its value to decline relative to other countries.

Over the long term, the US dollar will continue its decline, as will the currencies of Europe and Japan — the kings of fiat currencies. Asian economies, with a strong emphasis on frugality, savings, and gold, however, will likely see their currencies appreciate.

That's why the likely currency du century will likely be centered in Asia. The Chinese yuan is often touted as such a replacement currency. Perhaps it will be, but China will first have to overcome its recent slowdown in growth and internal lending policies, in addition to its policy of keeping the yuan loosely pegged to the value of the US dollar.

India, with an eye for slower, steadier growth, may be the eventual winner. If you have a long-term outlook, you should look at both the yuan and the rupee.

A smaller contender may be the city-state of Singapore, whose dollar has remained strong for the past several years. Despite its small economic size, the country has never seen a banking system failure and has a stronger procapitalist stance than either China or India.

WRAP-UP
Currencies in the Age of Currency Devaluation

- Today's fiat currencies are the result of centuries of development away from scarce commodities.
- Fiat currencies can be easily manipulated by printing press or computer accounts, a far cry from the relatively fixed supply of a commodity over the short term. That's why no currency today has a tie to any tangible asset.
- Considered the last "frontier" of capital markets, the foreign exchange market today allows investors to make extremely leveraged bets on minute fluctuations between fiat currencies.
- The US dollar still dominates trading, but other currencies are gaining in appeal.
- On the strategic level, the US dollar will continue to decline, so it's best for American investors to diversify into other (and higher yielding) currencies.
- On the tactical level, you can take advantage of today's monetary mayhem and economic chaos by shorting the currencies of weak economies and going long the currencies of strong economies.
- Over an incredibly long term, a country offering the best prospect for the creation of economic value will become the world's reserve currency. The US dollar is on the way out, and several potential candidates are on the way in.

13

Real Estate
Opportunity Boom amidst Credit Bust

Buy land, they're not making it anymore.
— *Attributed to both Mark Twain and Will Rogers*

EVERYONE HAS AN OPINION on real estate these days. Odds are, however, that such opinions *understate* the role of the chaotic investment age we live in . . . and also understate the devastation that could occur should attempts to prop up real estate come to an abrupt end.

As the most recent burst bubble, real estate opinions run into two camps. In the first, it's opportunity. In the second, plenty of investors still fear the next "downleg" in real estate prices, as defaults across residential and commercial properties rise and the market continues to be flooded with listings.

Let's take a look at each argument in more detail.

The Optimists: There's Always Money in Burst Bubbles!
Whether it's tulips, real estate, or technology companies, the survivors from burst bubbles tend to not only survive — they tend to thrive. In the case of stocks, it's much clearer because weak competitors have been wiped out.

To value investors, that sounds a bit like today's real estate market. There's nothing wrong with individual properties per se, so much as the lending system that nearly froze during the credit crisis in 2008. Add in the end of the speculative side of real estate, personified by various property "flippers," and you've got a true buyer's market.

On the residential side, the Federal Housing Authority (FHA) now backs 90 percent of all mortgage originations. You can lock in a low fixed rate below 5 percent with as little as a 3 percent down payment. Add, in banks saddled with foreclosures that need to be cleared, again, the market favors buyers.

On the commercial side, lenders have become much more conservative, requiring larger down payments and higher operating cash flows to justify loans.

The Pessimists: Always Waiting for Another Shoe to Drop

Alas, on the other side of real estate are the eternal pessimists. They're likely represented by folks who were burned during the real estate crash.

But they're not entirely wrong. Lending remains weak. Unemployment is stubbornly high — and after a while depleted savings can't go toward the mortgage anymore.

More importantly, after logging a mild gain in 2010, the Case-Shiller Home Price Index looks poised to start declining again. Pessimists refer to this as the dreaded "double-dip."

Home Prices Stopped Their Major Drop in 2010, but the Trend Is Negative Again

Indeed, the pessimists who look at the macrolevel housing data have a point. The Case-Shiller Home Price Index is at 140, but some argue that an index level of 100–110 is warranted given the surging number of foreclosures. That means housing prices are back at their 2003 levels but should really be trading at 1998 levels — well before the real estate bubble truly took off.

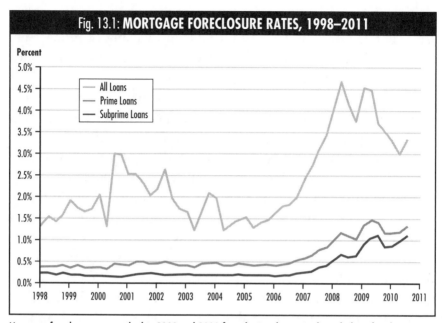

Fig. 13.1: **MORTGAGE FORECLOSURE RATES, 1998–2011**

Mortgage foreclosure rates spiked in 2008 and 2009 for subprime loans. As those decline, foreclosure rates for more traditional loans have started to rise.

And it's tough to deny the facts: Real estate foreclosures are still on the rise, as attested in Figure 13.1. And as long as they're on the rise, there's a strong argument to be made for weak, if not outright negative, pricing.

There's a considerable backlog of physical properties beyond those currently being foreclosed on. In some areas, such as New York, the foreclosure backlog is now up to 18 months — a considerable amount of time to live somewhere rent free!

While real estate can prove to be a great investment at today's prices, it's clear you don't need to rush to get a good deal. They are plenty of opportunities.

Other solvent parties aren't coming to out to invest in this sector (yet), so stay patient. Always be prepared to walk away from a deal, no matter how good it looks. You're the buyer, and it's your market.

Even with the horrible price decreases in the real estate market, the Case-Shiller Index shows that housing prices are still at 2003 levels. While that's hardly bubble territory, it's still substantially higher than prices were in the late 1990s, when the index was at 100 and well before speculation really took off.

Ultimately, these two sides look only at the valuation of property in terms of sale prices, and don't fully take into account cash flow from rentals or the numerous legislative benefits built into real estate such as depreciation deductions on income taxes.

In the age of quantitative easing, real estate may be a prudent way to lock in today's artificially low interest rates and purchase an asset that may appreciate when higher rates of inflation hit down the road.

Treating a property like a stock — buy today to flip it later at a profit — overlooks the true value to real estate. Given the illiquidity of real estate and the costs to hold (often without rent, if making improvements), there's hardly any benefit to flipping property unless you are a professional and that is your core business. Even then, it's risky.

To sensible investors, real estate can be a sound investment, depending on several factors. The most important factor is the price, which includes not only the purchase price but the terms of financing. In today's low-rate world, being able to lock into a fixed-rate loan may be the best speculation of all, although it won't be apparent for a few years' time.

So, yes, real estate can be a solid investment. But, with rising foreclosure rates, it's likely that excellent values will be had for the next few years, even if interest rates start to rise. If you're looking to invest now, you can bide your time in a few different ways.

Real Estate Strategies for the Investors in Today's Markets

Real fortunes are made in bear markets. And, despite over $1 trillion in support from the Federal Reserve and the Treasury, real estate remains in a bear market.

But, for investors with a long-term time horizon (at least five years or more, ten years through forever would be better), small rental properties may provide positive cash flows. Small properties also give you the prospect of significant gains in home value in the event of higher inflation and tax benefits.

What constitutes a rental property? Anything from single-family homes, duplexes, triplexes, and fourplexes. This size is manageable for individual investors, even those with full-time work elsewhere. As a side note, my family has had rental properties off and on for three generations. In 2012, we're off . . . but looking.

Larger unit properties require full-time management and typically are more difficult to finance. It's a lot of work, and there are other was to invest, such as REITs, which are discussed later in this chapter.

Done correctly, a small portfolio of a few properties can offer a different type of returns than in the stock or bond market alone.

Danger: We're Still Busting

Houses nationwide have fallen 20 percent from their peak, according to the Case-Shiller Index.

Since bottoming out, prices have slightly bounced, gone flat, and are now going down again — the dreaded "double dip." This is an astounding and unprecedented move. Unlike the stock market, where a 20 percent pullback isn't particularly uncommon, a 20 percent decline in home prices nationwide is an historic first.

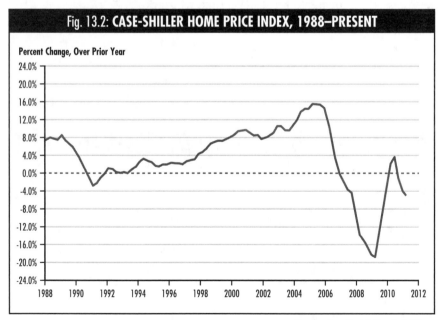

Fig. 13.2: **CASE-SHILLER HOME PRICE INDEX, 1988–PRESENT**

Percent Change, Over Prior Year

Source: Standard & Poor's & FiServ

The Case-Shiller Home Price Index shows that housing prices are still, on average, falling.

Of course, that 20 percent pullback is just the average among real estate markets across America. Some of the best-performing markets during the housing boom have fallen even harder, with the worst facing a 50 percent decline.

"We've never had a decline in housing prices on a nationwide basis," boasted Ben Bernanke in 2005.[29] Bernanke assumed that housing markets were local. But, with easy financing, it was possible for homeowners in, say, Ohio to buy properties in California or Texas and flip them — sight unseen. Which they did. And from which, they profited. And then the music stopped playing.

Since 2008, the readjustment of interest-only "teaser loans" which reset at higher rates and the substantial rise in unemployment have resulted in a staggering number of foreclosures.

So here's the ultimate downside: two million more homes facing foreclosure could move from bank balance sheets to the real estate market over the next few years.

In short, with expectations of a further decline, a huge overhang in housing inventory, and banks cutting back on lending to individuals with less-than-perfect credit, it's a buyer's market.

Cash Flowing like a Broken ATM

While most investors in housing considered capital gains as the ultimate objective, the pendulum is swinging the other way. If you're

Table 13.1: AMERICA'S HARDEST HIT REAL ESTATE MARKETS AND CASH FLOW			
Metropolitan Area	**2007 Median**	**2011(Q2) Values**	**Change**
Las Vegas-Paradise, NV	297.7	97.2	−67%
Los Angeles-Long Beach-Santa Ana, CA	593.6	167.8	−72%
Miami-Fort Lauderdale-Miami Beach, FL	365.5	137.3	−63%
Phoenix-Mesa-Scottsdale, AZ	257.4	100.3	−61%
Tampa-St. Petersburg, FL	226.6	127.1	−44%

(Source: Standard & Poor's and Fiserv)

considering real estate today, you should look at cash flow, specifically the price-to-rent ratio. Since some markets command higher rents than others, they can command higher valuations.

A prudent investment in properties that provide monthly positive cash flow (there's money in your pocket each month after paying the mortgage, maintenance costs, insurance, and taxes) can provide a consistent source of income, akin to a monthly paying bond fund.

Table 13.1 illustrates a before-and-after snapshot of some of the hardest hit markets, which can now provide you with positive cash flow following major declines.

In bombed-out parts of south Florida or the Inland Empire in southern California, the price-to-rent ratio is low enough to provide large cash flows, *even if the properties never appreciate in value.*

Of course, it's not going to command the kinds of rent someone would pay in New York, Los Angeles, or Washington D.C. In south Florida, a modest two-bedroom/one-bath home in a working-class neighborhood will pull in around $900 in monthly rent. That works out to $10,800 a year.

The average price for such a home right now is around $70,000. That works out to a price that's 6.5 times the annual rent. Historically, it's better to buy a property than rent when the price-to-rent ratio is under 10. So this property more than passes that test.

If you buy such a property all in cash, you can expect expenses and vacancy losses to account for about 60 percent of the total annual income. The remaining 40 percent, or $4,320, is about a 6.2 percent annual "yield" on the original $70,000.

Even if the property never appreciates, you're getting about the average long-term return of the stock market! Inflation or a recovery in the credit market down the road could add in some modest capital gains over time. But compared to the current yields on anything from thirty-day bills to thirty-year bonds, cash-flowing real estate — bought at the right price to rent — wins hands-down.

If you can get financing, however, the numbers look even better.

When Leverage Works for Your Benefit

Let's say you get a $56,000 mortgage (80 percent of the purchase price) at 5 percent interest for thirty years for the same $70,000 home.

Subtract the $374 mortgage payment from your $900 in monthly rent, and you have $526 in monthly cash flow, or $6,312 a year. Back out 60 percent for maintenance and expenses, and you end up with $2,524 per year.

Since your initial cash investment was just $14,000 ($70,000 minus the $56,000 mortgage), you're starting out with a cash yield of 18 percent! That's a three-fold difference in returns on cash outlay compared to paying all cash.

Assuming no increase in the value of property, this 18 percent yield can increase over time as rents go up. You can also pay down the principal of the mortgage, although a 5 percent interest rate in a world where *true* inflation is running in the 8–10 percent range offers you the opportunity to pay off a dollar's debt today for pennies on the dollar later.

Of course, having a mortgage gives you leverage if prices do end up rising. But the most important use of leverage is to increase the current yield relative to the amount of money allocated to real estate. After all, when you put 20 percent down, you're leveraged five to one, but that isn't a problem if the cash is coming in.

Other Advantages of Physical Real Estate

There are other advantages to owning some rental real estate. For instance, in some areas, properties are selling for less than replacement value. Many who overextended themselves in homes during the boom are now being forced to rent.

A renter's market needs buyers — and it also means that rents are likely to stay strong, even in an overall weak housing market.

From a tax perspective, you can enjoy deductions on the mortgage interest and depreciation and tax deferment with the 1031 exchange, which allows you to defer capital gains when trading real estate. I wish I could do that with stocks!

Moving toward the Intangible: Stay Liquid with Real Estate Investment Trusts (REITs)

Next, there are real estate investment trusts (REITs). They're liquid, especially relative to physical properties. Compared to common stocks, they tend to pay higher dividends.

The downside is the lack of incentives versus owning actual properties. You won't get to enjoy the gains of leverage as much as you would with a mortgage. But, considering the liquidity and low transaction costs relative to owning and operating actual buildings, they're a great proxy. There is a wide range of choices among the REITs, so choose carefully.

For an investor who doesn't mind tying up money for a few months to a few years, you can also invest in tax liens. Essentially, you're paying the delinquent taxes on a property now, and the owner has to pay fat interest rates (often as high as 20 percent) on those back taxes owed. And, if they can't make payments, the house defaults to you . . . for only the price of the outstanding tax bill!

Buyer beware: Tax liens are very illiquid. Unlike stocks, which can be easily bought or sold once markets are open, the resale market on tax liens is nonexistent. In many cases, the liens are in place for at least two years before the property can default to you, the lien holder.

In the age of quantitative easing, the ability to quickly convert an asset to cash, gold, or other assets is a key factor. So, if you're looking to profit off of real estate you might just want to stick with highly liquid REITs.

Caveat: While I think there is substantial opportunity for individual investors to benefit from a real estate investment by locking in a 30-year, fixed-rate mortgage at under 5 percent today, there is further market risk to real estate values when (not if), we get a large increase in interest rates. This is true whether you invest via REITs, tax liens, or physical housing.

WRAP-UP
Opportunity Booming as the Market Stays Soft

- As with any asset, real estate moves in cycles. Right now it's in the process of bottoming in its down cycle. Whereas real estate was a beloved investment years ago, today prices are in some places more than 50 percent off their highs. That makes it one of the best opportunities, even amidst the age of monetary chaos.

- Real estate includes real assets purchased with borrowed money. This allows you to take advantage of likely future inflation by making a purchase today and paying off with depreciated cash over time.

- Real estate investing can come in many forms, but for today's bottoming market the optimal route involves cash flow. Buy properties where local rents can more than pay for the mortgage and expenses. You should get an immediate cash flow, and over a long enough time, capital appreciation.

- Investors today (and for the next few years) will likely get an increased value for purchasing physical real estate. Due to its illiquidity, many investors don't want to own actual properties right now but have no qualms about owning real estate via real estate investment trusts (REITs).

- Real estate still offers tax benefits for owners today. Additionally, today's ultralow interest rates, fueled by the Federal Reserve's attempt to stem off a deflationary collapse, offer one of the best opportunities to purchase a physical, cash-flowing asset.

14

How to Select the Best Stocks (Beyond Sound Fundamentals)
Mitigate the Effects of Uncertainty with a Checklist

"Checklist routines avoid a lot of errors. You should have all this elementary wisdom and then you should go through a mental checklist in order to use it. There is no other procedure in the world that will work as well."

— *Charlie Munger*

T HE BOEING MODEL 299 was considered "too much airplane for one man to fly."[30] That's a sign of the impressive technological changes. The year was 1935, a mere generation after the first flight at Kitty Hawk by the Wright Brothers.

As part of a US Army aircraft evaluation, the Boeing Model 299 was put to the test along with other new aircraft. However, the Model 299 stalled during takeoff, turned on one wing, and crashed, bursting into flames as it did so.

Due to the complexity of the new aircraft, it wasn't simply enough to familiarize a pilot with the plane's equipment. Pilots needed a way to determine the plane's safety before takeoff. From that, came the checklist. Four, actually — one for takeoff, flight, prelanding, and landing. Checklists provide a clear, simple safety test. Either something works, or it doesn't. And if something's wrong, you don't fly. It's that simple. Once the checklist was employed, sales of the Boeing Model 299 took off, thanks to zero accidents. The government ended up buying 12,731 B-17 bombers from the company.

Checklists have become a critical tool outside of aviation. When they started using checklists for intensive care unit (ICU) intravenous lines to ensure equipment was sterile, cross-infections in ICU lines dropped to near zero!

These checklists aren't too complex. Today's modern planes, for example, might have only a dozen items to check off during a takeoff. Today, a hospital's ICU checklist contains as few as four steps.

As an investor, a checklist can provide you a key, objective overview on an investment's prospects and help keep your emotions in check. The most important thing it does is give you the chance to pause, reversing our instincts to fight or flee without thinking.

Unlike the aviation or medical industries, however, a thorough investment checklist will be self-defeating. After all, if we're too stringent on what we're looking for, we'll pass on everything!

All investments have risks, and a checklist, such as the example provided in Appendix C, will help you weed out the ones with the most red flags. Some yellow flags may remain. Indeed, some should remain, since those concerns may lower the price enough to justify an investment.

Think back to the biggest investment mistakes you've ever made. Did you invest in a company without looking at the fundamentals?

Some start-ups or resource companies might not have positive cash flow or an excellent price-to-earnings ratio to screen for. In this case, rather than peg a specific number based on past earnings, you should base your decision on expected forward earnings.

Did you lose money during the credit crunch by investing in a company that employed too much leverage? A checklist for a specific debt-to-equity ratio may take out a lot of solid companies, such as banks. In this case, it would be prudent to state that a company should have a low ratio *relative to its industry*.

In short, you need a checklist, but it must have flexibility. It must balance quantitative and qualitative data about the underlying business, as well as a quick check on the price and possible market activity that may adversely affect the price (that's where technical analysis comes in).

Core Checklist Criteria

While most full-time investors will need to develop an elaborate (or at least long) list based on their needs, goals, and risk preferences, you can use some of the criteria below to start building your own checklist:

Can you explain the business to a kindergartner?

This one's pretty self-explanatory. If you can't explain what a company does, how will you know what's really going on? Odds are you don't. What the company does should be simple enough that you can explain it to a five-year-old. More importantly, the five-year-old should be able to *understand* what you're saying.

This also helps you get to the level of understanding of a company that you need to be successful as an investor over time.

If a kindergartner isn't around, a financially maladroit member of Congress will suffice.

Does the business have a consistent operating history?

Consistency is a great indicator because, well, it's boring. Investors who want excitement will flock to a company like Apple for their latest consumer tech. That's all fine and well, until consumers have enough of their products. Companies like Apple have to constantly innovate.

Don't get me wrong, Apple has been a consistent operator over the past ten years. But, in the 1980s and 1990s, it was a disorganized mess. Remember, when it was still Apple Computers, the company never got more than 5 percent of the computer market and needed a bailout from Microsoft. The key to prevent yourself from weeding out a company like Apple today is to set an operating history that's reflective of the industry it's in. It's fair to look at Apple within the past 5–10 years.

Companies like Kraft, on the other hand, don't rock the boat so much and allow potential investors to look back to decades of consistent operating history. Their products might get some new packaging or a few ingredients might slightly change, but ultimately the company has a long history of operating some of the world's best-selling food products.

Obviously, some changes are inevitable. But often that goes beyond a company's operating history and into changing technology and processes. Newspapers have a consistent operating history dating back centuries, but many just can't compete in the Internet age.

If a company's only constant is change, find a different company to invest in.

Does the business have favorable long-term prospects?

Ultimately, there are two different types of businesses, those that can pass off rising costs onto consumers and those that can't.

In the first category, you'll find companies that own world-renowned brands, like Coca Cola or Unilever. In the second, you'll find companies that produce a commoditized product, like ArcelorMittal.

The first category makes for great long-term prospects (when bought at the right price). The second category makes for great short- to mid-term prospects (again, when bought at the right price).

That's because, ultimately, companies in a commodity-type business might have to sell their product at a loss — or even go out of business. Companies with a strong, branded product, however, can continue to grow their way out of most trouble.

Does management run the company for the benefit of themselves or the shareholders?

A company that generates cash in excess of its needs has three options.

First, it can continue to reinvest at current rates. But, due to diminishing marginal utility, continual reinvestment will eventually lead to lower rates of return. Second, it can make acquisition, effectively buying growth. Last, it can return the money to shareholders in the form of dividends (cash payments) or share buybacks (increased ownership stake).

The most responsible course is to return that money to shareholders for them to use as they see fit. This comes from raising the dividend. Next, buying back shares benefits shareholders as they now own a larger proportion of the company.

Most importantly, high insider ownership is a key to aligned objectives between shareholders and company management. Higher ownership is better than lower ownership.

Unfortunately, sometimes excess cash will be used on lavish executive compensation, stock options, "toys" like a company jet, or even foolish and overpriced acquisitions of other companies in a different industry.

Is the company entrepreneurial or more like the Department of Motor Vehicles (DMV)?

A start-up company is nimble and rapidly changing. If something needs to get done, someone somewhere does it, with little regard for protocol and paperwork. As companies grow, they develop increasing layers of bureaucracy. The roles of workers fall into smaller and smaller niches.

When that happens, we come to an "institutional imperative" whereby the needs of the institution come ahead of doing things that make money (or make sense). It's why a big company will spend money on a first-class stamp to send you a two-cent check for overpaying on your last bill.

I am also suspicious when a company builds a new grandiose headquarters. Was it necessary? Was it pragmatic or simply an ego trip by senior management and the board of directors?

As this type of behavior sets in, the company becomes resistant to change, both internal and external. This ultimately spells the death knell of a company. If you invest in large-cap companies, you may have to tolerate some level of bureaucracy, but the less that the company is focused on the process, the more it's focused on its products.

How does management define success?

Most managers focus on earnings per share (EPS). It's what analysts look for too. But there's a problem with EPS. It focuses on something that can be changed via creative accounting methods.

Rather, management that defines success by reaching more customers, growing a dividend or book value, or other tangible methods may be a better holding for the long haul, as opposed to companies that are focused only on making analysts happy with short-term predictions.

It takes rare courage when a CEO commits to managing for the long term at the expense of quarterly earnings. Look for this courage, and you may be well rewarded.

Is there a high profit margin?

A company with low profit margins might simply be unable to succeed. It might not be able to earn money at a rate that gives investors a chance of making a decent return. It might be susceptible to the higher costs brought about by monetary and government chaos.

Conversely, a company with a high profit margin will likely have prudent debt levels, a branded product, rapid expansion and growth, few or weak competitors, the ability to fight inflation with higher prices passed on to consumers, or the ability to continually find ways to lower costs.

There are structured differences in profit margins of different industries. In such cases, look for the "best of breed."

What is the value of the business? (Also key for when it's time to sell)

Price is established by the stock market, which changes daily (more often second to second). But the value of a business is determined by the net cash flows expected to occur over the life of the business, discounted at an appropriate interest rate, which we learned how to use in Chapter 6.

Can it be purchased at a significant discount to its value?

Using the simple calculation for determining a company's intrinsic, per-share value (Chapter 6), look to see what price offers a significant discount to that value. Use a modest discount for companies with a strong competitive advantage, and a large discount for companies in commoditized industries.

Remember that the discount rate implies your expected return *before* applying your margin of safety.

Are technical indicators bullish or bearish?

While you don't need to know every single style of trading based on chart patterns, knowing which way a stock is likely to move over the short term might give you a slight price edge when buying or selling.

How much capital should I allocate to this trade?

As with all items on the checklist, you will have to make up your own mind as to the specifics that work best for you. But for allocation, I personally try to approximate the following:

- 10 percent for high prospects that won't lose money (deep value)
- 5 percent for moderate prospects (short-term trades, including some options trades)
- 2–3 percent for riskier ventures (well-researched, small-cap companies with huge growth opportunities like niche technology companies or junior gold miners)

That's just a rough rule set that I've found works pretty well. Most investments fall within the 5 percent range, meaning that, at most, I'm dealing with a manageable portfolio of twenty positions. If something looks compelling but also carries a bigger risk, it gets a smaller stake.

For those rare investments that trade at such a huge discount to their true value, however, a 10-percent stake is large enough to move the overall portfolio but not overwhelming.

Consider different rules depending on your risk levels. The specifics of the rules aren't the most important thing. What *is* important is finding a rule set that you can apply consistently and won't abandon at the first sign of trouble.

What criteria will I use to determine if the company is no longer worth owning?

This criteria is determined by the updated prospects of the business and by price. A company bought while substantially undervalued might be sold because it is now correspondingly overvalued. It might have changed its business plan. Management might have embarked on a foolish crusade to expand beyond its core business without any experience. The next chapter is devoted to expanding on this topic.

Through the Rear-View Mirror: Technical Analysis

It will fluctuate. — J.P. Morgan[31]

Looking for a short-term way to profit on the daily fluctuations of the market? Consider using technical analysis to identify trends.

But it's not just for day traders. In fact, if you're looking for a good entry price for a long-term investment, technical analysis can be a useful tool as well.

At the very least, it can prevent investors from losing capital by investing in a company that is on the verge of a technical breakdown and may correct.

Technical analysis is a method of evaluating stocks and currencies by analyzing prior price and volume trends. This is done primarily with the use of charts, where patterns may be revealed that suggest an asset's future price trend.

At its core, technical analysis relies on three assumptions. Let's take a look at them first, before we get into criticisms:

1. **The market reflects all known information.**

   Technical analysis relies on the key assumption that an asset's current price reflects everything that has or could affect the company at any given time.

   That's a form of the efficient market hypothesis that we've already seen and analyzed earlier. However, because enough market participants do believe in the theory, it's still important to know how the other players play the game.

   So, on a technical level, a company's fundamentals don't matter. Neither does the broader economy as a whole. All of these things are already assumed to be "baked in" to the price of a company's stock.

2. **Prices move in trends.**

   In technical analysis, price movements follow certain "trends." This means that after a trend has been established, the future price movement is more likely to be in the same direction as the trend than to be against it. It's best summed up with the trite rhyme "the trend is your friend."

   Nevertheless, this assumption is key for the short-term trading strategies based on technical analysis.

3. **History tends to repeat itself.**

   Another important idea in technical analysis is that history tends to repeat itself, mainly in terms of price movement. In other words, small price cycles in an investment tend to play out over and over again.

This cyclical pattern of price movements is attributed to market psychology. That's because this assumption works on the observation that market participants tend to provide a consistent reaction to similar market stimuli over time. If a company beats earnings estimates, for example, it will rise. But, if a company fails to rise up to analyst expectations on earnings, it will fall.

Because of this cyclical trend, technical analysis requires the use of chart patterns to determine trends and therefore price movements over the short term.

Despite the rapid development of financial markets, many of these charts have been used for more than a hundred years. But, since history repeats itself, chart patterns are still considered useful because they illustrate simply what has happened before and what is playing out now.

Advantages and Disadvantages of Technical Indicators

Clearly, technical analysis has some logical shortcomings: If a technical analyst looks at a company entering an uptrend, and assumes that prices will rise higher, isn't that at odds with the first assumption of fundamental analysis? If all known information about a company is already disseminated into the price, why should it go up (or down) at all?

And, of course, what happens in the event of a sudden change of information about a company? Technical indicators based on past events will no longer apply!

But, like the emotional aspect of the market, it can be useful. Why? Because technical analysts tend to use the same charts and theories to extrapolate future moves. Then they act on them.

So a bullish technical indicator might simply be self-fulfilling, as technical analysts buy in anticipation of higher future prices. This effect can quickly snowball, as technical analysts looking for "confirmation" or using different data points become convinced as well.

So, there's clearly a need to incorporate some level of technical analysis, despite its shortcomings. Combined with the overall evaluation of the market and fundamental analysis, it can provide a final item for your "checklist" before pulling the trigger and investing.

Since technical analysis is based on short-term future movements, it can either provide an opportunity for trades and short-term gains on a long-term position or hold back on establishing a position until better buying opportunities *present themselves.*

WRAP-UP
Checklists Needed, Technical Indicators a Bonus Feature

- A checklist serves many purposes. Mostly, it's to keep emotions in check. Investors need checklists to organize relevant data.
- Checklists should be developed with consideration taken for your risk tolerance, as well as the quantitative and qualitative data you find most useful.
- As investing is more of an art than a science, a checklist need not be as rigid as it would be in industries like health care or aviation. That means that some investment ideas may fail some checklist criteria but will still provide superior returns over time.
- Beyond fundamentals, the case to buy or sell a company also lies on the market price. Relative over- or undervaluation can be gauged by looking at fundamental indicators.
- Technical indicators show repeating short-term patterns in a company's price with no regard for fundamental valuation. It's akin to driving by only looking in the rear-view mirror.
- At best, technical indicators should be the final item to look at after an investment passes through discounted cash flow analysis and through a checklist. The success of technical indicators is the result of a self-fulfilling prophecy. They're still used because other traders and investors use them.

15

Time to Leave
Key Signals That It's Time to Sell Any Asset

"Past managements spent our lush advantage
extravagantly . . . The system and management are
stifling initiative. Leadership and innovation are
impossible . . . Not only are these people of no help,
most of what they do is wrong.**"**

— *John DeLorean, on General Motor's management, 1979*

EVEN THOUGH IT'S BACK on the stock market, General Motors
(GM) is still as bad as it was before the government took it
over. But let's be honest: The company had a good run. When
it began, it was one of *thousands* of American auto companies. While
most were falling by the wayside, GM lasted more than eighty years —
most of those years profitable.

It made it to the final three, even before the early 1980s when Lee
Iacocca managed to convince the federal government that the automakers were essentially too big to fail.

What was the best way to invest in automobiles in the past century? Naturally, Warren Buffett has a folksy way out outlining the
optimal strategy: "Sometimes it's much easier to figure out the losers.
There was, I think, one obvious decision back then. And of course,
the thing you should have been doing was shorting horses . . . There
are always losers."[32]

As stocks continue to rally despite rising commodity prices and rising unemployment, now is the time to weed through your portfolio

and find the losers. Now that they've had a bounce, it's time to give them the boot.

Knowing when to sell a position is one of the hardest questions that an investor has to answer. And it depends on a lot of things. But there are some major red flags that alert you to get out of a long position (and help decide whether or not to go short).

Expensive Conventional Valuation

If you had the foresight to buy a small coffee chain named after an obscure literary character, you rode through some fantastic profits. All through the 1990s and even through the tech bust, it seemed like Starbucks would never cease to open more stores.

Around the time a new Starbucks was opening across the street from another location, though, it was time to get out. Its growth prospects have been hammered. Other coffee chains are after its alluring market share. Even fast food chains have entered the fray.

By the summer of 2011, the balance sheet looked like a train wreck. Let's slow down and rubberneck for a bit: With a trailing price-to-earnings (P/E) ratio of 127, the company failed to pass most analysts' first evaluation of a company's value by a country mile. The profit margin was less than 1 percent, and the operating margin a mere 5 percent. Debt was three times cash. Return on equity (ROE) was only 3.5 percent.

The company still continues to struggle in 2012, although its margins have improved as the company has belatedly worked to improve its standing among its competitors.

Clearly, yesterday's winners can be today's losers — and vice versa.

Technological Changes

Change is the only constant in investing. And technological changes can make an entire company or industry's products obsolete.

That doesn't necessarily mean you should invest in the new technology — you just avoid the obsolete one, or even short it, as it dies off.

Within the auto industry, we've seen technological changes that are partially responsible for the sad state of the American automakers.

Toyota Motors was the first to market with hybrid vehicles — with its flagship Prius. The rest of the industry has been playing catch up since.

Sure, foresight is imperfect, and entrenched interests kept American automakers from fully adapting to this threat.

But the solution wasn't to buy shares of Toyota. It was to stay away from General Motors, Ford, and Chrysler. Add in their uncompetitive cost structures, and it's clear who the losers have been in this industry.

Fuzzy Accounting

How do you know if you're invested in the next Enron or WorldCom? Often times, reading the financial statements will tell you. Or, rather, knowing what financial gimmickry to look for that bad companies try to hide. This also includes business problems that management just isn't managing well.

One of the biggest things I'm looking at in the current investment environment includes companies reporting profits in excess of analyst expectations.

If such gains come from cutting costs, like firing employees, then the numbers being reported aren't going to be sustainable over time. It's the opposite of real sales growth — it's a way of hiding a decline. A lot of service-based companies are guilty on this count in recent quarters, from retailers to restaurateurs.

Think of it as mold that people mistake for green shoots. It's just too toxic to invest in.

The other major accounting areas to look at in this earnings environment are receivables and inventories.

If accounts receivable (AR) is rising, there could be a problem with a customer's ability to pay. Or there's a problem with lax credit to customers to buy products. Either way, it's one of the most obvious red flags you can see without the assistance of a certified public accountant (CPA).

Eventually, toxic AR has to be written off. The illusionary gains become real losses.

Rising inventories are even more problematic. A store offering this year's fashions at 50 percent off may be able to post some good sales numbers. But over time it's a recipe for disaster.

Deeper and prolonged sales shorten the life of the business as lower margins choke off cash flow. Think Circuit City, Linens 'n Things, and a host of other retailers. It's not over in retail by a long shot.

Bankruptcy: A Kodak Moment

Here's a real-world example that hits close to home with me: the rumors of bankruptcy swirling around Eastman Kodak in late 2011.

It should have been no surprise to anyone who had been watching the company's accounting numbers come in quarter after quarter. By late 2009, the company was unable to even breakeven on its core business, photographic film. In a world that had long since gone digital, this was no surprise. The company was a late adapter and at a substantial disadvantage to competitors who got in early.

In the fourth quarter of 2009, the company reported a surprise $430 million in earnings. A full 98 percent of those earnings, or $421 million, came from so-called "nonrecurring revenue." In accounting-speak, that means that there was a one-time event that boosted earnings. Basically, if a company sells a division or some assets and it's not part of its core business, it's reflected in that area.

Kodak's nonrecurring revenues, however, became a recurring event. That falls into what can be called "fuzzy accounting," an area that should raise red flags to you but might not constitute outright fraud. As these nonrecurring events became the driver of earnings, the company's core business continued to decline.

Anyone looking at the numbers could tell something was off. Despite the company's SEC filings, however, there wasn't an explanation into these nonrecurring revenues.

It didn't take a CPA to notice that there was something less than opaque in the company's earnings. Even back in 2009, I did something that most Wall Street analysts won't do: I called the company to ask a few tough questions.

Now, I'm a numbers guy. I know in part that when you call a company as an investor, a public relations employee is likely to paint you a picture of the company that's full of unicorns and rainbows.

With Kodak, I got the public relations (PR) department's voice mail. I'm still waiting for a call back. Sometimes, the most important thing isn't what a company is saying: It's what a company *isn't* saying. That's the event that clinched it. That's how I knew Kodak was in serious trouble.

The few other times I've called companies to ask questions, I've gotten a wealth of information. Here's a hint: the *tone* of someone's voice will tell you if they're genuinely excited about their prospects or if they're trying to mask an uncomfortable truth.

Capital Transactions

Companies worth owning for the long term don't need to issue new debt right now. (Some of the best ones are borrowing smartly, however, due to record low interest rates.)

They certainly don't need to go to the capital markets and issue stock to shore up reserves either. While this clearly applies to all the household-name financials, other companies have quietly been raising capital in the midst of this bear market rally as well.

Any company that has to sell off assets or divisions right now is one worth reevaluating. Even in the absence of the worst credit crunch of all time, it would still be a red flag.

Within this category, I'll also mention insider selling — it's a form of raising equity, only it benefits management, not the company. And certainly not the shareholders.

Combined with other red flags, it's the closest thing to a leading indicator I've seen that a stock is going to fall. Be especially aware of multiple insiders selling *en masse*.

Customer Concentration

There's more than one way to make a profit. In investing, the term "pin action" — stolen from bowling — means that if one industry is on fire, related industries will benefit as well. The same thing applies when it's time to sell. When one industry tumbles, related ones will tumble as well.

Companies that are highly dependent on one major customer face a huge problem when that customer faces a moderate problem.

Not to flog the dead horse of American automakers, but there was more than one way to profit from their demise. A whole host of supplier companies are facing tough times too — and likely to go the way of GM.

Their biggest problem was concentration. Making a product that's only bought by one customer means that when the customer goes out of business, so does their monopoly supplier. The stock of Lear Corp. (NYSE:LEA), a supplier to GM, took the same long decline in the past year.

Now that they're finally defaulting on their bonds — it's already too late to short the stock, which declined over 90 percent between 2008 and 2009, as seen in Figure 15.1.

When Selling Isn't Enough: The Role of Shorting

The stock market isn't a one-way ride. Many individual companies will buck any trend, and many companies simply fail and go out of business. Or, fear sweeps the markets and sends all companies down — the good *and* the bad. That's just a fact.

Markets go up, and markets go down. Why limit yourself to only half of the market's activity? That's where short selling comes into play.

Shorting stocks offers one of the fastest ways to profit in the market. Like a balloon filled with helium, stocks may gently rise for years and years. When the bubble bursts, gravity kicks in.

Short selling is by no means a new concept. For centuries, short sellers have been using this technique to make a killing when markets have crashed . . . The Dutch East India Tea Company was the world's first global conglomerate. And while it didn't become as overpriced as tulips during the Holland mania, the stock was still overpriced and ripe to fall.

Isaac Le Maire, a merchant for the company, as well as board member and major shareholder, is widely regarded as the world's first real short seller.

Taking a position against the company in 1609 by borrowing shares from anyone willing to lend them, he sold them at market and profited immensely when the Dutch Republic's stock exchange crashed in 1610, taking the East India Tea Company down with it.

History doesn't tell us how well he performed when the market crashed (the days before the income tax were a simpler, more elegant age) — but it certainly got someone's attention. Restrictions were placed on the exchange to prevent short selling, and it's all attributed to Le Maire.

It was the first restriction of an exchange in history, thus beginning the disdain against short selling that continues to this day.

But that's hardly contemporary, is it?

So let's consider some more recent profitable short sellers:

- **Jim Chanos**, the fund manager famous for shorting the popular and perpetually rising stock of market-darling Enron back in 2000. Thinking he just got lucky? Not a chance. Not only did Chanos see the fall coming. He didn't just close his position when the first wave of questionable practices came to light either.

  Nope, Chanos *increased* his short position when the first Enron cautionary tales hit the news. He recognized that one bad event can precede another. By the time the dust settled, Chanos and his clients enjoyed a billion-dollar payday.

- **Warren Buffett** has a reputation as a long-term "buy-and-hold" investor. If only that were true. But the fact is, Buffett plays the short side of the market too. In his 2007 annual report, he gloated about his $21 billion short position against the US dollar.

  "In the last five years, the Brazilian currency, in terms of the American currency, has doubled in value," stated Buffett.[33] Sounds more like a swipe at the dollar as opposed to a glowing endorsement of the Brazilian real!

- **George Soros** taught the Bank of England a humbling lesson back in 1992. Soros made over £1 billion by shorting the pound. But most people forget that his investment was £6.5 billion — producing a 15 percent profit.

  Of course, had it gone the other way, today people would be asking themselves, "George who?"

- **John Paulson** is a legendary contemporary investor. He foresaw the crisis in subprime mortgages. Yes, the very one that, according to Wall Street's narrative, "nobody" saw coming. He took a short position using the oft-maligned credit default swaps.

  But Paulson didn't see his short position as dangerous. Quite the opposite: "Risk arbitrage is not about making money, it's about not losing money. If you can minimize the downside, you get to keep all your earnings and that helps performance."[34]

  By structuring his fund to "not lose money," Paulson personally took home a paycheck of over $1 billion in 2007.

Really, that's all shorting is. It's all about not losing money — especially when markets migrate South.

Of course, most investors don't need to hunt for a big target to short. But, in today's age of chaos and government-created uncertainty, it will pay well to have a few short positions to profit from extremely volatile markets.

The Long and the Short of Short Selling

Shorting a stock is a pretty simple concept. Here's an example of how it works: You borrow 100 shares of, say, Amalgamated Conglomerates at $80. You then sell those shares to obtain $8,000 ($80 × 100). That money stays in your "margin" account. Then Amalgamated Conglomerates falls to $60. At that point, you must return the shares you borrowed. To do that, you would "buy to cover," paying $6,000 ($60 × 100). Then you keep the difference, in this case $2,000.

Shorting stock has some problems. Not every stock is available to borrow easily. And, if you short a dividend-paying stock, you're the one who gets to make that payment to the shareholder you borrowed from.

Add in periodic government restrictions on short selling (like Europe did with financial companies in the fall of 2011) and lack of leverage, and it seems as though shorting stocks isn't all it's cracked up to be.

In fact, borrowing shares to short may cut it for hedge fund managers, but for investors today who need to stay safe against periodic and sharp market corrections, there's a better way that ties up less capital and doesn't force investors to deal with margin calls: *put options.*

By buying put options (or selling calls), not only can you take a short position, but you can leverage a bet ultraspecific to an individual stock.

Buying put options doesn't require a margin account (so you can actually protect your retirement accounts and thrive in times of market downturns). Best of all, the most you stand to lose is the premium you pay for their option. So, for a few hundred dollars per year, you could buy puts on one of the S&P500 ETFs to hedge against a substantial market decline.

If they're wrong, the only cost is a few hundred dollars. If there is a substantial decline, you can cash out the options position several thousand dollars in the black.

Again, this type of overall hedging strategy will allow average investors to avoid losses during periods of intense market volatility. For specific companies facing potential bankruptcy, an upstart competitor, or a sudden change in management, the use of options to short specific companies can also play out well.

If you find companies that fail many of the key steps on you check-list for going long, you may want to employ this strategy. Of course, it's not for everyone. But with prudent risk management, you need to stay nimble enough to profit from any market condition.

WRAP-UP
How to Sell (and Sell Short)

- One of the hardest questions facing investors once they own a position is when to sell. A company that trades at a substantial premium to its peers, the stock market in general, or other port-folio positions may be good candidates to sell.
- A company in a rapidly changing industry may not be able to keep up with the latest changes in technology, causing the com-pany to be at a disadvantage, as its products are now out of date or too expensive to make to compete properly.
- Repeated questionable acts of accounting may indicate a com-pany is trying to hide some unpleasant truths from investors.
- In addition to selling, you may wish to consider selling short an extremely overvalued company. Since markets fluctuate both up and down, it's sensible to play both sides rather than limit your-self. Most professional investors have implemented short trades to take advantage of pricing errors.
- For most investors, put options are the optimal way to short. There's no worry about having to borrow shares, face a margin call, or pay for margin. The downside is limited to the price paid for the put options, and shorting stocks is sometimes banned (typically when it's an optimal time to short), but there has yet to be a ban on the use of options.

CHAPTER 16

A Model Portfolio to Grow Your Wealth over the Next Three to Five Years

***

"Investors should always keep in mind that the most important metric is not the returns achieved but the returns weighed against the risks incurred. Ultimately, nothing should be more important to investors than the ability to sleep soundly at night.**"**

— *Seth Klarman, founder of value investment firm Baupost Group*

OST PEOPLE DON'T have the time, effort, or energy to responsibly position their investments every time things change. I get it. People like the idea of being able to "set and forget." I can understand the appeal.

Laziness can be great — and when done right, most investing is simply that. It truly is an exercise in patience. You *can* be a lazy investor. But it means waiting for the price of an asset to come down into an acceptable purchase price or waiting for an investment to appreciate in price enough to justify selling.

By foregoing buying and selling, you can focus on a few key assets that you know and understand well. You'll also avoid brokerage fees and short-term tax considerations. Whether you're the kind of person who wants to make ten trades before grabbing your morning coffee or whether ten trades per decade is more your style, laziness *can* pay off.

Indeed, the bulk of an investment portfolio should, over time, favor assets that can be held indefinitely. This saves on brokerage fees and taxes, simplifies estate planning, and makes it easier to keep tabs on your portfolio, even when your time is best spent elsewhere.

That's where this sample portfolio comes in. I've based it loosely off of the annual portfolio review that I perform with my family around the holidays. The goal is simple: construct a portfolio that can benefit from the most likely trends to occur over the next several years, while still keeping an eye on downside risk.

In other words, grow wealth without getting blown up by the markets if there's another big crash.

The Passive Investor Portfolio at a Glance

Fair warning: The portfolio I'm about to outline can't predict any seismic changes in the economy that may occur. Substantial changes may be necessary as new economic information presents itself. This portfolio also can't take into consideration for current or future investment needs, nor your tolerance for risk.

This breakdown is based on how I would invest for someone today with the caveat that investors shouldn't cash out for at least three years. It's based on the view that there is a low risk of a major bout of deflation over the next few years and that inflation will likely be moderate at best.

Again, for passive investors, this portfolio allocation should emphasize the trends most likely to occur over the next few years, while also being positioned to avoid market dangers that may lurk along the way.

Specific investment ideas for each category have already been discussed in their respective chapters earlier in this book. Even lazy investors will still have to do some homework in finding investments that can perform well over the long term and fit your risk parameters — so you can profit and sleep well at night. Here's an example of a diversified portfolio that is good for a passive investor:

25 Percent: Dividend Growth Stocks

This component of the passive investor's portfolio should include a basket of ten to fifteen stocks that have a history of continually increasing their dividends over the last twenty years. This significantly weeds out most stocks that are highly susceptible to economic cycles and instead focuses on companies with strong brands or consumer goods.

Such stocks may include companies like Proctor & Gamble (NYSE:PG), Johnson & Johnson (NYSE:JNJ), Campbell Soup (NYSE:CPB), Kraft Food Group (NASDAQ GS:KRFT), Intel (NASDAQ:INTC), Microsoft (NASDAQ:MSFT), and the like.

Dividend growth stocks may, over the short term, fluctuate a bit. Over longer time periods, increasing dividends should keep stock prices going up as well. You also have the opportunity to reinvest a growing cash dividend if your focus is on long-term growth as opposed to an immediate cash payout.

15 Percent: Commodities

On the other end of the spectrum from dividend growth stocks are highly cyclical investments in commodities. This should include some physical gold and silver as a potential insurance against unexpected and extreme market events.

Beyond that, funds and individual stocks can offer a way to invest in base metals, precious metals, and agriculture while offering better liquidity and lower volatility than commodity options and futures.

While commodities have done particularly well as an asset class in the past decade, this trend can easily reverse and suffer setbacks. So it's important that passive investors stick with commodity investments that have little leverage. There is another place in this portfolio for leverage, in the area of high-yielding investments.

If you feel strongly about the prospects of a small, exploratory commodity company, such as an early stage gold mining concern, you would include such a high-risk venture in this category.

10 Percent: High-Yielding Investments

The forecast for the passive investor calls for interest rates near zero for a few more years, followed by only modest increases in interest rates.

Rather than try to earn an income from savings or bonds, it will be necessary to invest in a few high-yielding investments to provide for a moderate level of dividends in the average investment portfolio.

With the expectation that interest rates will remain low, a 15 percent stake in some high-yielding investments such as leveraged funds, foreign bond funds, or mortgage REITs should provide current income for those who need it. If you want to stay fully invested, high-yielding plays will allow you to rapidly generate cash for new investments.

15 Percent: Energy and Infrastructure

The coming years may see the need for more government stimulus and efforts to create more jobs for those thrown out of work. Some of this will include spending on infrastructure, which in the United States is rapidly aging. This also includes energy infrastructure, such as new oil pipelines and wells.

Globally, the need for new energy and infrastructure is surging in emerging market economies, offering global companies the chance to increase their revenue in coming years.

Ideally, you should invest in this area with income from pipeline master limited partnerships (MLP) investments and large, established firms. But this category should also include growth opportunities as well, particularly in small-cap "wildcatter" energy companies — akin to the junior gold miners in the commodity section.

15 Percent: Real Estate

For some investors, an allocation toward real estate should include an actual rental property outside a primary residence.

As outlined in the chapter in real estate, the real returns of a property purchased with 20 percent cash down can produce effective returns of over 15–20 percent in markets that have been hit the hardest and are in the process of bottoming.

Being long leveraged in real estate (i.e., having a mortgage) is also an effective way to diversify *away* from the dollar.

If there is a serious pickup in inflation, fixed mortgage payments will decline in real terms over time, while rents can be raised. Of course, if inflation picks up, so will taxes, fees, and repair costs over time.

One major caveat with this investment: A second property will require some work on the part of the owner. For those with the skill and acumen to make small repairs and the like, however, it can still be a good deal. The worse the property, however, the more likely those expensive repairs will be a regular feature.

Given the backlog of foreclosures, it shouldn't be too difficult to find a property in great condition trading at a price that throws off great cash flow each month in bombed-out property markets.

If you're looking for truly lazy and passive returns, you would be wise to invest in real estate investment trusts (REITs) with cash yields of over 5 percent. Some major REITs have rallied so much since the bottom of the financial crisis that they can no longer even clear this dividend yield threshold.

Relative to individual property ownership, REITs offer diversification across several properties, and management. The only thing a lazy investor needs to do is sit back and collect cash payments every ninety days.

10 Percent: Cash and Cash Equivalents

Cash offers a cushion against the unknown. Outside of precious metals, it serves as an insurance policy against a catastrophic market correction that sends other asset classes falling. It also offers you the "dry powder" necessary to take advantage of extreme opportunities that may take place from time to time over the coming years.

In the area of cash, the US dollar tends to rally when other assets are selling off. However, the overall trend of the dollar is to decline in value. Thus, cash positions should include foreign currencies and perhaps even foreign bills and bonds that offer a higher interest rate as well.

Foreign currencies can be held through a variety of exchange-traded funds (ETFs), which offer greater convenience and lower fees than driving to an airport to exchange currencies.

10 percent High-Growth Companies and Speculative Opportunities

Here's where you get to have some fun. This part of the portfolio is where you can gamble, speculate, or do just about anything else. That's why the allocation is so small. Any investor can stomach a loss of 10 percent of their portfolio. If you want to truly "play" the markets, this section is where most of your focus should lie.

Want to buy call options on a hot biotech company? It goes here. Do you want to invest in some sector seeing rapid growth? It goes here. Forex trades? Yep, here.

A friend or family member has a business idea and needs some starting capital? It goes here too.

Passive investors who are more interested in sleeping well at night can instead use this part of the portfolio to "hedge" against the other positions.

This would include selling covered calls against open positions, using long-dated options to profit from a potential market decline, or using inverse funds to profit from an overvalued area of the market that is likely to correct soon.

Speculative opportunities may also include options to go "short" the market. Whether this is done by selling short shares of an individual security or by using put options against a stock or index, a small short position can hedge the overall portfolio from an unexpected pullback.

This is where you can make some mistakes. It won't affect the overall portfolio too much. Any big successes can, however, have a tremendous effect on your overall wealth.

This is also the category that can include high-flying growth names, such as Apple Inc. (NASDAQ:AAPL) or VMware (NYSE:VMW). Because this portfolio is designed to navigate choppy investment waters over the next few years only, growth stocks may experience exceptional turbulence. That's why their allocation in this model portfolio is more limited.

The Big Picture: What the Passive Investor Portfolio Should Resemble

Taken together, the passive investor portfolio looks as follows in Figure 16.1.

Hopefully by now, the overall advantages of this hypothetical portfolio should be clear: it should perform well with assets being propped up by low interest rates and periodic interventions in the years ahead.

Dividend growth stocks should be relatively insulated from short-term economic gyrations. Commodity investments should capture the next bull move and hedge against potential inflation.

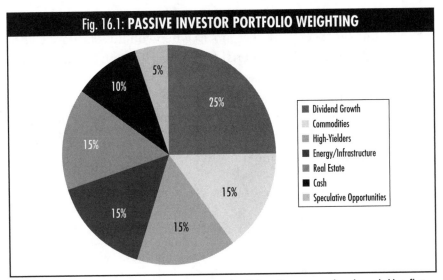

Fig. 16.1: PASSIVE INVESTOR PORTFOLIO WEIGHTING

- Dividend Growth
- Commodities
- High-Yielders
- Energy/Infrastructure
- Real Estate
- Cash
- Speculative Opportunities

For passive investors, a broad mix of investment sectors should do well to accommodate the probable inflationary environment that will develop over the next few years but should also thrive if there's modest deflation.

You have the opportunity to invest in assets that are both loved and hated right now. Over time, the assets that are loved will become hated — and vice versa.

But the passive investor will own a little bit of everything to capture the best possibility of outperforming the market with the risk spread around, *and with having to make as few trades as possible.*

If you don't want to be *completely* lazy, you should also use these hypothetical allocations as a guideline. Over time, the fluctuation of asset values will cause these areas to change significantly in value.

You may want to sell areas that appreciate the most, to reinvest in areas that have underperformed. The passive investor portfolio as-is is simply designed to start at this allocation level and see how the markets play out.

There are some disadvantages that I'd be remiss if I didn't mention. This portfolio may not protect against extreme events. Individual components may have unforeseeable business risk. A bout of extreme deflation may adversely affect the portfolio, which is designed in part to assume low inflation and interest rates for the next few years.

And, of course, there's nothing wrong with preaching caution for caution's sake.

If you're interested in building such a portfolio, you should take into account short-term market moves when you invest. A good idea is to break down a few investment ideas in each category. You can then add positions on a regular basis, say, every month over the course of a few months, rather than invest all at once.

For most investors looking to follow this portfolio, only a few changes will be needed. Others may have to start from scratch. Either way, it can be done easily and quickly.

EPILOGUE

BEING AN INVESTOR is a journey, not a destination. The path that that journey will take will largely stem from you. This journey isn't to a fixed place, marked on a map. It's ever-changing, reflecting the dynamic of the market process, and the inevitable economic chaos of today's hypermanaged economy.

Like everyone else, I'm still learning. We all are. There will be more successes and more failures along the way. And we'll see situations along the way that we could have never foreseen.

Fortunately, there are some ideas and principles that, when applied, can throw the returns of the average investor far ahead of the curve. In short, they're the things that prepare you for those unpredictable opportunities that present themselves.

You've already seen how a commitment to responsible investment analysis can help grow your wealth and prepare against the chaotic world we live in. Put those principles to work in your portfolio.

Perhaps the most important thing that's needed today is a cool head amidst the chaos of today's market. It's especially critical to stay nimble and to be ready to move when governments change their whims without a moment's notice.

Stay safe, stay nimble, stay rational, and stay solvent.

APPENDIX A

Case Studies
A Tale of Six Trades

I have never let my schooling interfere with my education.

— *Mark Twain*

L ET'S FACE FACTS: There's no "one-size-fits-all" solution to investing, even when markets aren't as turbulent as they are today. You must balance fundamentals, psychology (not only of yourself but of other market participants), technical indicators, and time frames.

Investing properly isn't difficult. You don't need a PhD or an advanced degree in mathematics. But you do need discipline. That's truly the hard part.

Honesty is another critical element. Anyone can talk about the markets and enjoy it on an academic level but hardly ever participate in it. That takes *doers*, those willing to undertake the risks and reap the rewards.

I started undertaking those risks during the tech boom. I managed to grow my wealth during America's lost decade for stocks.

In the case studies below, I'll show you how I did it, what I looked for, and how it's tied in with everything else I've shared with you in this book.

The bottom line is simple though: You must invest. Your capital faces too much of a risk from the destruction of the dollar if you don't. You have much to lose by simply putting all your money under a mattress.

But there's much more to gain with a sound investment strategy confidently applied throughout any market.

Lessons in Investing during America's First Lost Decade

Investing isn't for the layman. At least, that's what fund managers, Wall Street bankers, and talking heads on CNBC all try to convey to the average investor on a regular basis.

If the small investor *does* want to make a decision independent of the crowd, he or she may have to fight his broker, his family, and his friends, or face ridicule.

And, in a sense, they're right. While it's comfortable to be with the crowd, you certainly don't want to be there when the crowd starts emulating lemmings and jumping off cliffs.

In other words, the average investor just isn't equipped to outperform their peers.

But, still, it can be done.

The principles of investing are timeless. But the application of these principles must always be considered within the context of contemporary market conditions.

In this section, I'll share with you how the investment philosophy I've outlined throughout this book has worked in practice as I've honed it. While I won't detail every small trade I've ever made, I will be sharing with you some of my biggest successes *and* worst failures, as well as the lessons from each.

Why here, at the end? For one, this is largely a story, namely, my story. It can be read independently of the main text. But it's written to build on what I've shared with you in this book.

I'd rather share this with you outside the core book so that you can be familiar with who I am as an investor without being distracted by the core principles I've outlined here.

The Love of Investing Is the Root of All Superior Returns: My Journey as an Investor

I've always been interested in money . . . not for the sake of money itself, but for the fact that it can be used to buy things. Or, instead of buy things now, it can be accumulated to buy even bigger things later.

Growing up, that manifested itself in many ways. Around the age of six or seven, I was looking for ways to boost my allowance. I tried some of the normal things, washing cars, pulling in some extra yard work at home, the usual kid stuff.

But at the same time I was also starting to develop an interest in collecting coins.

So I guess you could say it all started with pocket change. At most supermarkets today, you'll find Coinstar machines. These convert change into dollar bills. But even in the late 1980s and early 1990s, no such thing existed. If you wanted to convert dimes into dollars, you had to do it the old-fashioned way: sort by hand and haul off rolls of coins to the bank.

So that's just what I did. I would take neighbors' loose change and put it in rolls and take it to the bank to convert into bills. Our agreement was I could do whatever I wanted with the coins. And, I'd get a 10 percent fee (a nickel for every roll of pennies I made).

It worked well for my "clients." But it worked even better for me.

One neighbor in particular was my best client. An elderly lady, who lived off the dividends from a portfolio of dividend-growing companies, managed to accumulate a few large jugs full of coins.

Have you ever seen $800 in spare change? It's quite the pile. But I went at it with gusto.

While rooting through this huge pile of change, something interesting caught my eye — specifically dimes and quarters from before 1964. They were heavier and felt different than the other change.

They were 90 percent silver.

So, at age eight, I had made my first investment, and in a physical commodity to boot! (I still love silver as an investment — more on that later.)

I didn't realize it at the time, but I got to pay face value for something now worth sixteen times more. It's a great bargain to acquire silver for a face value that's considerably less than the value of the silver.

And, of course, I got paid to do so.

But perhaps best of all was seeing the look on the teller's faces when I wheeled in a suitcase that had about sixty pounds worth of change in it.

At the age of thirteen, after several years discussing the basics of such things as compound interest, my parents helped me set up an investment account.

And, walking that fine line between being overprotective or not, they set me up with a mutual fund. To be fair, it was the hot asset class of the time, offering diversification and the ability to invest small sums of money — a good starting ground.

Of course, the explosion of mutual funds in the 1990s led to all sorts of funds with unusual strategies and sectors. But I ended up in one of the dozen or so funds that were designated as a "youth investment fund" — essentially investing in big-cap names that would appeal to kids.

McDonald's, Nike, Disney, and the like were all there and all overweighted. But it could have been worse: after all, it wasn't tech, which was rapidly overtaking these well-known but "boring" brick-and-mortar companies!

As the fund doubled, then was halved following the tech bust, I had cut back on my entrepreneurial activities. But it wouldn't be enough to keep me away from my desire to earn more money or my love of finance.

There were still some opportunities, and one came from taking advantage of a monopoly. Our school had an exclusive right to sell one less-than-popular brand of soda in the cafeteria and various vending machines.

More often than not, I'd always be able to find a buyer or two to sell a more popular brand for some spare change. It wasn't a lot, but it added up. Another friend focused reselling the world's most popular brand of soda and became known, rather humorously, as the campus Coke dealer.

Fortunately, that didn't lead to any misunderstanding.

By my senior year of high school, I was juggling a part-time job for a hair over minimum wage (and start funding my Roth IRA). It was an unusual time. Tech had finally blown up and markets were crashing. Stocks felt listless. I was mostly letting cash pile up, waiting for the falling to stop.

You're supposed to learn a lot from your first job, and mine was no exception. I saw the hardest working people get the least compensation. I learned from one coworker how to "milk that minute." That was his term for waiting for the last possible second to clock in or out so that you would get paid for a minute's worth of work even though you were only clocked in for a few seconds of it.

I learned that basic skill of workplace productivity: if you can get away with doing the least amount of work possible, you will.

But I tried to avoid such things. Consequently, I got promoted the day after I turned eighteen, the first day that I was eligible. I spent another year, working full time (and sometimes beyond), while still finding in time for a full academic load.

At this point, I had been funding my Roth IRA to the fullest, and was adding to my somewhat depleted account, where I finally had control at eighteen and sold off the mutual fund.

That's when I went off the deep end.

I started buying individual stocks. By then I knew how to research, how to look up SEC filings on the Internet, and a whole host of other ways to look at markets that were still somewhat new to amateur traders.

I haven't looked back since.

The rest of the market had been dragged down by tech stocks. Bargains abounded. A feeling of fatigue was in the air when newscasters talked about the stock market. It was a golden time. And I was able to keep throwing cash in.

When I decided to go halfway across the country to finish college, I made another decision about my investments that might shy away most investors. I decided that I would only trade when home on vacation, so that I could focus on college. I knew that if I didn't do that, I'd just end up in my dorm room most of the time glued to the latest markets and trends.

It was one of the best decisions I could have ever possibly made. Although today I might feel remiss if I don't constantly check the markets in a work-related capacity, I don't mind going a week or month without checking all my positions . . . or even waiting for my monthly brokerage statements.

So, while home on breaks, I would sit down and drill down on new investment ideas that met my rough checklist, and I'd reposition my portfolio accordingly. This strategy kept me blissfully unaware of many minor market bumps.

It's also the secret to the success of some of my best trades ever.

After college came the great job hunt. But the economy was buzzing along, and I had managed to intern before graduating at a mezzanine lender. There were opportunities for me in real estate and private equity before turning to financial writing. All of these offered me the opportunity to hone my analytical skills, come up with new investment ideas, and better determine risk.

I continued to invest nearly every dollar I could scrounge together until about late 2007. By then, however, a series of events increasingly drew me to cash.

First, some small-cap companies that I owned were subject to a buyout offer. It's always been my policy to take cash in the event of a buyout offer. (You'll almost always lose money down the line if you choose to take the shares of an acquiring company.)

Secondly, I started selling investments that had surged in value tremendously. My rule of thumb at the time was to sell any stock that had doubled in less than a year. While it's a bit simplistic, I've found that there are always opportunities, so closing out something that's gotten overvalued to buy something undervalued is a great strategy over time.

I was caught up in the market crash like everyone else. But I had plenty of cash on hand. Given the dollar's rally in 2008 as a result of this fear, I ended up only slightly down.

At what was the bottom of the stock market in 2009, though, I started putting my cash back to work in the tremendous bargains that emerged. I also turned to financial writing, bringing together two of my greatest pastimes. I haven't looked back since.

Six trades in particular have taught me the most about investing. Five are winners. One is a loser. All have offered valuable lessons.

Trade #1: BRT Realty Trust (NYSE:BRT)

On October 17, 2002, I bought shares of BRT Realty Trust for $12.60. This investment appealed to me on numerous levels.

Real estate was relatively undervalued at the time, the company was trading at compelling levels relative to other REITs, particularly book value, and the yield on this investment was a mouth-watering 8.1 percent.

With a market cap of less than $200 million, it stood to reason that there was little analyst coverage to report on this company's growing portfolio of profitable mezzanine loans.

Sure enough, shares advanced more rapidly than expected as the real estate boom began in earnest. While the dividend was raised along the way, the company's price advanced at a rapid rate.

Within fourteen months, shares had more than doubled to over $28, advancing well ahead of the company's financial metrics. More importantly, there were better opportunities for investments elsewhere.

Fig. A1: **BRT REALTY TRUST PERFORMANCE, OCTOBER 2002–DECEMBER 2003**

Yahoo! Inc. © 2011

Selling at this price proved prescient. Following that price spike in 2003, shares declined, then hit a new high above $30 in 2007. As with other investments in the finance industry, the credit crunch hit hard.

Armed with a mezzanine portfolio of loans (the commercial real estate equivalent of a second mortgage), BRT Realty Trust wasn't in the best place to cash in on its collateral when it needed to. Shares crashed to below $5 in 2007–2008, and since then haven't been able to break through $10. Compared to other lender REITs, BRT is fortunate to still remain in business.

Trade #2: Chesapeake Energy (NYSE:CHK)

On July 1, 2003, I bought shares of Chesapeake Energy for $9.57. The company was trading at a relatively cheap level and sported a dividend yield of 2.4 percent. As a producer and explorer for natural gas, the company was in the midst of a global commodity boom. Chesapeake was also staking out some of the best natural gas resources yet found in the United States.

Shares advanced at a respectable pace, but by August 2005 the overall valuation had once again failed to keep up with the company's share price. I sold at $27.15.

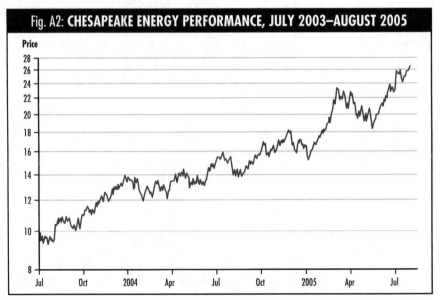

Fig. A2: **CHESAPEAKE ENERGY PERFORMANCE, JULY 2003–AUGUST 2005**

Yahoo! Inc. © 2011

Although the company was rapidly expanding its reserves, so was the rest of the country. According to the Energy Information Administration (EIA), total natural gas reserves surged over 60 percent between 2000 and 2009.

In short, the success of Chesapeake and its competitors in finding new natural gas reserves had such a dramatic impact on supply that the boom in natural gas began to look unsustainable. On a fundamental level, that made me uneasy.

Being in a commodity industry, Chesapeake had no real control over the spot price for all these new reserves they were finding. Aside from that concern, the company was executing a competent plan to rapidly grow in a growing industry, even relative to its peers.

In retrospect, I could argue that I sold too early, as shares continued to advance. As natural gas prices collapsed by 75 percent when commodities went bust in the summer of 2008, subsequent gains in Chesapeake Energy since the time I sold were quickly wiped out.

Shares trade at a respectable level compared to other energy companies today; however, the market is flooded with natural gas. While it may make an excellent substitute for other sources of energy, there isn't the infrastructure yet in place to take full advantage of this commodity.

Trade #3: Peruvian Copper/Southern Copper (NYSE:SCCO)

On December 9, 2004, I purchased shares of Peruvian Copper (eventually renamed Southern Copper) for $46.19. I was impressed by the company's copper reserves, the world's largest.

Although a commodity company, shares offered a high dividend yield of 9.4 percent, supported in part by a low stock price due to labor strikes that were soon resolved.

Copper made for a simple, effective way to play off the big-picture trend of rising commodity prices (and economic growth in general).

Unlike gold and silver, however, copper is a purely industrial metal and requires large veins of relatively pure concentrations to be economically viable. Why? Because copper is incredibly expensive to refine into a pure product.

Fig. A3: **SOUTHERN COPPER PERFORMANCE, DECEMBER 2004–FEBRUARY 2006**

Yahoo! Inc. © 2011

Shares, predictably, had a substantial run-up, as well as a stock split along the way.

I sold on February 7, 2006, at $87.90 as copper appeared over-priced, as did shares of the company. Furthermore, other investment opportunities were more appealing for the potential risks and rewards, and it was time to rotate out of this trade and into one with more value.

In retrospect, this was another situation where I could have made more money had I continued to remain in shares.

However, given other opportunities available, as well as the lack of downside protection for falling copper prices, locking in this company profit was more important to me than trying to time the absolute peak in the stock market cycle.

This is one of the few companies with a higher share price today than when I sold. That's partly as a result of the execution of the company, the importance of copper as an investment, and the rapid growth of the stock before selling off with the commodities complex in mid-2008. I still use options to make short-term profits from Southern Copper.

Trade #4: Diana Shipping (NYSE:DSX)

By 2006, the boom in commodity prices left few high-reward, low-risk opportunities. However, the shipping sector was an exception. Although new ships were expected to become operational within a few years, surging global trade had led to rising shipping prices.

That's why I bought shares of Diana Shipping at $10.37 on July 13, 2006.

The deficit in shipping was allowing existing companies to finance new projects and pay fat dividends to shareholders. Diana had a yield of 9.2 percent when I bought shares. That wasn't as high as some competitors, but it was still a very handsome reward, at least until the supply of shipping vastly increased a few years down the line. I also liked DSX because it had the lowest debt in its industry.

Shares moved up rapidly. In fact, they started rising so far, so fast, that I sold only a year later, on October 9, 2007, at $30.00. It didn't help that the fundamentals of the shipping sector were already beginning to change and shipping prices were already starting to falter.

Shares of Diana Shipping surged even more over the next few months. The price eventually popped up to $70 amidst an orgy of

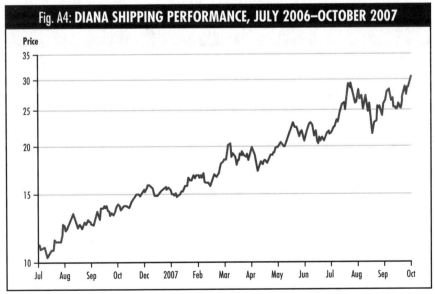

Fig. A4: **DIANA SHIPPING PERFORMANCE, JULY 2006–OCTOBER 2007**

speculation in 2008 and on the recommendation of a few talking heads in the financial media.

With the collapse of just about everything else in 2008, shippers got slammed hard. Diana, one of the more conservatively financed companies, has managed to survive, although shares are back below $10 today. Along the way, the dividend was eliminated.

If shipping recovers, Diana may be a worthwhile investment — but not yet.

Trade #5: Thornburg Mortgage (OTC Pink:THMRQ), a Losing Trade

I don't regret taking a substantial loss in Thornburg Mortgage.

Thornburg operated on a business model similar to other mortgage REITs but with one twist. The mortgages were on "jumbo" loans, that is, for mortgages in excess of $417,000. These loans had a lower historical rate of default than other sizes of loans. They were typically backed by homes worth in excess of $1 million and individuals with high income and/or a high net worth.

But, Thornburg's mortgages were missing one critical thing: government support. Traditional mortgages were underwritten

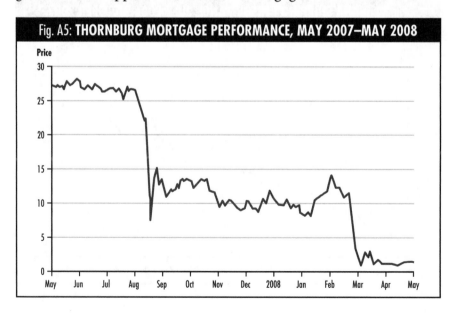

Fig. A5: **THORNBURG MORTGAGE PERFORMANCE, MAY 2007–MAY 2008**

through government-sponsored agencies (GSAs) like Fannie Mae and Freddie Mac. While most of the mortgage industry got a bailout via funding for Fannie and Freddie, jumbo loans were left out on a limb.

Add in the leverage Thornburg was using to make a substantial return on its profits, and it didn't take much of a decline in housing prices for share prices to drop like a rock. After the initial decline in late 2007 from the high $20s to the low teens, shares looked like a potential bargain.

That, of course, was assuming that the government would come to the rescue in this sector. It didn't. Thornburg filed for bankruptcy in early 2009.

Today, the company trades on the pink sheets for about a penny per share. The lesson here is to avoid excessive debt, which I now do with discipline. Also, it's important to trailing stop losses to ensure that gains are protected.

Trade #6: Eastman Kodak (US:EK) Short

On December 2, 2009, I went short on Eastman Kodak (US:EK). I did this due to declining fundamentals in the company's core business and suspicious recurring "nonrecurring" events (see earlier section in book on potential accounting trouble).

At the time, the share price was $4.19, and it continued to rise in spite of the economic reality of its failing business model. I reiterated the short in April 2010 as shares hit $8, close to last high for the company before falling to under a buck in late 2011.

Besides the declining fundamentals, nobody at the company expressed any interest in talking to me about the nature of their nonrecurring revenue, nor returning my calls. This only hardened my resolve to wait for the inevitable decline that would lead me to profits.

While this trade was an eventual victory, there were some painful lessons along the way.

Successful short-side trades can take time, and you must be prepared for markets to move against you. If the facts had changed, I would have been fine closing out at a loss.

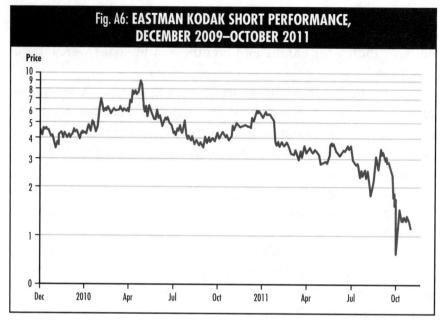

Fig. A6: **EASTMAN KODAK SHORT PERFORMANCE, DECEMBER 2009–OCTOBER 2011**

Yahoo! Inc. © 2011

But the facts got worse, so I interpreted that as one of those situations where the market was simply in denial. As with a value investor who goes long a stock only to see shares fall by half before advancing ten-fold, so this trade started out feeling like defeat, only to blossom into victory.

That's also a reason why shorting is difficult. You can have all the facts lined up in a row, but the markets may still move against you. That's why shorting isn't for most investors. It takes a careful eye and knowledge of the fundamentals, the resolve to see things through. But it also takes the willingness to get out of that trade the instant the facts change and it looks like the wrong place to be.

If you're an advanced investor, you may look into strategic positions to short overvalued companies where technical indicators show an imminent downturn. If you're not an advanced investor, you would do well to place a small amount of you portfolio in index puts to hedge against a general market decline.

Core Investment Themes
Fifteen Principles to Invest in Times of Turbulence and Chaos

1. Government's nature is to expand; this expansion will lead to chaos (and opportunities).

- It is the nature of all individuals and groups to acquire as many resources as possible at the lowest cost in terms of energy.
- Central banks have been created to allow governments to spend beyond their means and promise things they otherwise couldn't. This breeds inflation.
- Government is always "behind the curve" when it comes to new technologies, so before the chaos of bad legislation, there will be the opportunity of other investments.

Takeaway for investors:
Invest in various countries to "diversify" from your own government's actions. Invest across asset classes to avoid the pain of a stock market shutdown, gold confiscation, and so on.

2. "Crisis" always creates calls for more government action, but most actions are done to merely keep the status quo (or as close as possible) and to "kick the can down the road."

- Crisis means opportunity, too. At this point of what Sir John Templeton called the "point of maximum pessimism," you can reap the largest rewards.

Takeaway for investors:
Successful investing is largely a function of getting into the right asset at the right time, namely, while it's the most unloved. Identifying potential crises and the likely policy responses by government are also good for long-term investing.

3. You must pay attention to long-term and short-term effects. Wall Street and politicians focus on the short term, leading to poor long-term decisions.

- Most investors focus on the short term, following the idea of John Maynard Keynes that "in the long run we're all dead." These investors focus on short-term capital gains, which lead to larger risk and larger volatility.
- Frederic Bastiat's 1850 essay, "That Which Is Seen, and That Which Is Not Seen" is a great elucidation of this phenomenon.
- While the government can create problems in the short term that lead to good investment ideas, you should also invest with the long term in mind.
- The long-term effects of short-term decisions and actions are "unintended consequences."

Takeaway for investors:
You can look at the short-term effects of a government policy or Wall Street darling stock and see a problem developing. This prevents you from joining investment bubbles and also allows you to step in after the chaos ensues to pick up assets for pennies on the dollar.

4. Gold is the optimal store of value in chaotic and turbulent times.

- Gold is the closest thing to a stable currency that mankind has discovered. It can't be artificially created (counterfeited), and no one has figured out how to transmute any more abundant element into gold (manufactured).
- Its value will fluctuate with the supply coming onto the market and demand from the market, just as any currency's value will fluctuate based on supply and demand. But such changes are less than what can be changed by government in the short term.
- While gold prices can be manipulated by central banks, physical bullion is still the antifiat currency play.
- As a baseline, 10 percent of one's wealth should be in hard gold bullion, irrespective of where everything else goes.
- Silver has a lot of the same characteristics with less government influence but is also susceptible to industrial demand.

Takeaway for investors:
In the age of economic chaos, gold reigns supreme. Like any asset, it won't go up or down in a straight line. It's also important to note that as the concerns that send investors flocking to gold fade, it will decline.

5. Fiat currencies are subject to political pressure for an "easy way out."

- A fiat currency is a sophisticated method of theft used by politicians and central bankers to steal from their citizens via inflationary policies.
- Not all fiat currencies move the same way at the same time. Wealth can be preserved — possibly enhanced — if there is a constant rotation from overvalued to undervalued fiat currencies.
- You can profit through international currency differentials, but you must always remember that all currencies are money-by-fiat with no true underlying value.

Takeaway for investors:

You must rely on more than just cash to preserve and grow your wealth. This includes international investments in stocks, bonds, and Forex trading when extreme opportunities present themselves.

6. The US government's current policy is destructive: destroy the dollar in the hope of growing the economy.

- Any "rescue," whether of banks, consumers, or certain industries, is merely an acceleration of the long, slow destruction of the dollar. The trillions of dollars in stimulus since 2008 have failed to grow the economy, and unemployment remains stubbornly high. Interest rates are near zero, and policymakers are at a loss for better solutions.

Takeaway for investors:

You can predict the inflationary and easy-money policies of central bankers. Now more than ever, American investors must diversify into countries capable of competently growing their economies without resorting to extreme measures to do so.

7. This time is *not* different: be a student of history.

- When someone says "This time it's different," run the other way.
- History is rife with examples of those who profited immensely from following counter-trends and doing the opposite of the herd.
- This is a core investment principle for any market, at any time. Always have a set exit strategy in place and stick to it.

Takeaway for investors:

The markets have seen it all already. You should always have a strategy in place to get out of investments that take a turn for the worse.

8. Three-sigma events happen more frequently than Wall Street wants you to know about (e.g., 1987 market crash, tech bubble crash, housing crash).

- Recognize that, no matter how well an investment is thought out and analyzed, there is always the possibility of an exogenous event that can cause an investment to tank.
- Investment or asset protection methods that don't take a potential "worst case scenario" into account — no matter how rare it seems — can ultimately fall apart.
- Investments often divert substantially in value from reality. If you stay grounded in reality, you should do well over the long run.

Takeaway for investors:
Stay away from "the next big thing." Whether it's tech stocks or real estate, the next big thing tends to become the next big crash. (The only exception is if *you* know it's "the next big thing" and *nobody* else does.)

9. Markets are irrational.

- "Mr. Market" is a pendulum, always swinging from fear to greed, and is therefore never fully rational. If the market does appear rationally priced, that's because it either is moving from extreme fear to extreme greed, or vice versa.
- The market is made up of individuals. Most individuals aren't rational either. Run, don't walk, from an investment advisor who tells you an investment is a "sure thing."

Takeaway for investors:
Sometimes, it's best to just sit tight and wait for the market to display the next extreme.

10. Wall Street is a rigged game. Brokers are fundamentally salesmen, not analysts. And they usually have "inventory" their bosses tell them to sell.

- The efficient market hypothesis (EMH) is the basis for most traders and the bulk of the money on Wall Street. It is inherently flawed and riddled with false presumptions, all in the name of creating a "rational" market.

- All of us have conflicts of interest, and every person makes his choices based on rigging the transaction in his own favor.
- The wise person looks ahead to the longer term and realizes that it's in one's own self-interest to make every exchange a win-win exchange by telling the truth, keeping your word, and delivering on promises.
- Crooked money managers are also part of the "rigged" game. Diversify your money managers. Most individuals, armed with the right advice, can use a low-cost brokerage and manage most of their wealth themselves.

Takeaway for investors:
Stay skeptical with your investments — and the people running them.

11. Everyone has an agenda.

- Caveat emptor: trust but verify.
- Consider the source of an idea and follow the money. The largest lobbying group in the world is the National Association of Realtors. No wonder lending standards during the housing boom were ignored by congressional overseers!
- This includes members of Congress as well. One of the biggest cheerleaders for the leverage at Fannie Mae was Barney Frank. He was also one of the biggest recipients of campaign funds from the now-bankrupt firm.
- Many in the media who offer financial advice tell you to follow the herd.

Takeaway for investors:
It's better to lead the herd than follow the herd. It's even better to avoid getting trampled by doing the opposite of the herd.

12. Despite the harm caused by governments, they also give you some of the best tax benefits around. Take full advantage of them.

- You can utilize 401(k) plans and various IRA programs to invest in nearly every investment asset.
- Investments grow faster when their compounding isn't interrupted every year by the tax man.
- You can invest in various assets like real estate investment trusts (REITs) and master limited partnerships (MLPs) to substantially boost your dividend income in a low-yield world.
- Current long-term capital gains tax rates and dividend tax rates make it better to be an investor than an employee.

Takeaway for investors:
Take full advantage of any plan the government offers you (but pursuant to other concepts listed above, be sure to diversify into other areas as well).

13. A poorly regulated market is better than one rampant with corruption.

- The SEC was repeatedly warned about the Ponzi scheme run by Bernard Madoff. They ignored those warnings. Similar regulatory agencies have also ignored similar warnings in their area of expertise.
- "Regulatory capture" creates perverse incentives for regulators to be lax in exchange for jobs at the industry they were supposed to be regulating. Changes must be made.
- The government's core role is to provide law and order: that means it must enforce contracts, weed out con artists, and do so in a way that impedes as little as possible on the freedom of individuals to decide what's best for them.

Takeaway for investors:
You should vote with their money to a diversified group of countries and exchanges that follow the rule of law and create a level playing field.

14. Remember Sturgeon's law: 90 percent of everything is crud.

- Most of what the market generates is short-term noise. Learn to filter it out. Remember, all investors at some time or another will fall prey to their emotions. A hefty dose of skepticism provides an optimal lens for making decisions.
- Don't accept what others say at face value: "Trust but verify."
- People hold crud because they expect someone else to come along with a higher price to bid it away. Bubbles start when the quality goes downhill and the quantity ramps up.

Takeaway for investors:
Identify holes in the analysis of others, determine where bubbles may be forming and find pockets of unloved values. Find safer, alternative ways to profit. Avoid leverage on assets loved by the crowd.

15. There's no such thing as a free lunch.

- Government can't simply create wealth or jobs through taxation or debt-financed government spending or tariffs. Any such thing comes at the expense of whatever would have been created by the private sector, if left alone and unmolested.
- Markets that are outperforming cannot do so indefinitely.

Takeaway for investors:
Keep a close eye on the markets. Be aware of where there may be an opportunity to buy and where it may be time to take profits or even go short.

In conclusion, be willing to pay up for quality investments. High-quality companies command high premiums for their franchises compared to lower-quality companies. But, in the age of chaos, sell-offs may allow you to pick up phenomenal qualities at a decent price.

APPENDIX C

Sample Checklist

- ☐ What is the company's moat? How strong is it?
- ☐ What are the risks — market, industry, company, competitive, valuation?
- ☐ What are the historical and projected growth rates of the company?
- ☐ Does the company have a clear and understandable business model?
- ☐ Has the business' earnings been consistent throughout a relevant time period?
- ☐ Does the company meet my financial metric criteria for its industry?
- ☐ Does the company meet my balance sheet criteria for its industry?
- ☐ Does the company have sufficient cash flow to continue operation without outside funding?
- ☐ Is management focused on long-term success or short-term success?
- ☐ Does management have some meaningful stake in the company?
- ☐ What is my estimated per-share value for this company?
- ☐ What price is a sufficient discount to that price to provide a sufficient margin of safety?
- ☐ Does this investment fit in with my overall portfolio goals? If overlapping, what will I sell?
- ☐ What criteria will I use to determine that the investment is no longer buying?

NOTES

1   Dorothy M. Nichols, "Modern Money Mechanics," (Chicago: Federal Reserve Bank of Chicago, 1961) 2.

2   Nichols, "Modern Money Mechanics," 2.

3   "Federal Reserve Act." Last modified August 13, 2008. http://www.federalreserve.gov/aboutthefed/section2a.htm

4   Warren E. Buffett. "How Inflation Swindles the Equity Investor." *Fortune*, May 1977

5   Two points bear mentioning about Keynes. First, he was one of the greatest investors of his era. He deftly determined the value of a business and bought its stock well below the perceived value for both his own funds and for the endowment of King's College. Secondly, I seriously doubt that he would approve of what is today called Keyn esian economics, as his theory called for governments to be responsible and run budgetary surpluses when the economy was doing well.

6   Ludwig von Mises. *Human Action.* (Auburn: Ludwig von Mises Institute, 2006) 249.

7   Mises, *Human Action*, 249.

8   Alan J. Ziobrowski, PhD, Ping Cheng, PhD, James W. Boyd, PhD, and Briggitte J. Ziobrowski, PhD, "Abnormal Returns from the Common Stock Investments of the U.S. Senate," *Journal of Financial and Quantitative Analysis,* Dec. 2004.

9   Nineteenth-century laissez-faire French economist, best known today for the "broken window" fallacy. Under such a fallacy, the wanton destruction of a shopkeeper's window is viewed positively because it will employ a glazier. What this overlooks is that the shopkeeper is no longer able to purchase a new suit. He must now do without the suit and pay to replace the window, making him *worse* off than before.

10   Daniel Kahneman. *Judgment under uncertainty: Heuristics and biases.* (Cambridge: Cambridge University Press, 1972).

11   Bernie DeGroat, "Roadway Deaths Up After 9/11 Due Largely to Local Driving." *The University Record Online*, Nov. 24th, 2004.

12 R.P. Feynman. "Appendix F — Personal Observations on the Reliability of the Shuttle." (Washington: US Government Printing Office, 1986), 1.

13 "Statistics." http://www.planecrashinfo.com/cause.htm

14 Feynman. "Appendix F."

15 "Greenspan: Housing Market Worst May Be Over." Reuters, Oct 9, 2006.

16 *CNBC*. Bernanke Interview, July 1 2005.

17 Two years before imposing wage and price controls.

18 Paul Davidson. "Feds Cut Off Phone Tax After 108 Years." *USA Today* May 26, 2006.

19 Ian Urbina. "U.S. Said to Allow Drilling Without Needed Permits." *New York Times* May 13, 2010.

20 Hiroko Tabuchi, Norimitsu Onishi and Ken Belson, *"Japan Extended Reactor's Life, Despite Warning" The New York Times* March 21, 2011.

21 "Median Age." https://www.cia.gov/library/publications/the-world-factbook/fields/2177.html

22 David Lieberman "Harry Potter Inc: Warner Bros' $21B Empire." July 13,2011. http://www.deadline.com/tag/harry-potter-net-profit-statement/

23 Eugene Fama, Kenneth French. "The Cross-Section of Expected Stock Returns". *Journal of Finance* 47 1992.

24 Meena Krishnamsetty. "Insider Trading Returns Calculated by Josef Lakonishok and Inmoo Lee." Oct 26, 2010. *http://www.insidermonkey.com/blog/insider-trading-returns-calculated-by-josef-lakonishok-and-inmoo-lee-546/*

25 Rothbard, Murray N. "Stocks, Bonds, and Rule by Fools," in *Making Economic Sense*. (Auburn, AL: Mises Institute, 1995)

26 Jeremy Siegel. *The Future For Investors*. Crown Business, 2005.

27 Bet you didn't know that one!

28 Jefferson died in 1826 with $107,000 in outstanding debts — more than $1.5 million in today's dollars.

29 *CNBC*. Bernanke Interview. July 12, 2005.

30 John Schamel. "How the Pilot's Checklist Came About." Last updated 9/10/12. http://www.atchistory.org/History/checklst.htm

31 When testifying on the nature of the stock market before Congress.

32 Warren Buffett. Sun Valley, Idaho speech. July 1999.

33 "Warren Buffett Says Has Been Buying Brazilian Real." Reuters. Oct 18, 2007.

34 Christine Williamson. "Excellent Timing: Face to Face with John Paulson." *Pensions and Investments Online*, July 9. 2007.